T0358416

ROUTLEDGE LIBRARY EDITIONS:
FINANCIAL MARKETS

Volume 10

# FINANCIAL MARKET LIBERALIZATION IN CHILE, 1973–1982

# FINANCIAL MARKET LIBERALIZATION IN CHILE, 1973–1982

ALEJANDRA MIZALA SALCES

Routledge
Taylor & Francis Group

LONDON AND NEW YORK

First published in 1991 by Garland Publishing, Inc.

This edition first published in 2018
by Routledge
2 Park Square, Milton Park, Abingdon, Oxon OX14 4RN

and by Routledge
711 Third Avenue, New York, NY 10017

*Routledge is an imprint of the Taylor & Francis Group, an informa business*

*British Library Cataloguing in Publication Data*
A catalogue record for this book is available from the British Library

ISBN: 978-1-138-56537-1 (Set)
ISBN: 978-0-203-70248-2 (Set) (ebk)
ISBN: 978-1-138-56519-7 (Volume 10) (hbk)
ISBN: 978-1-315-12288-5 (Volume 10) (ebk)

**Publisher's Note**
The publisher has gone to great lengths to ensure the quality of this reprint but points out that some imperfections in the original copies may be apparent.

**Disclaimer**
The publisher has made every effort to trace copyright holders and would welcome correspondence from those they have been unable to trace.

# Financial Market Liberalization in Chile, 1973–1982

Alejandra Mizala Salces

GARLAND PUBLISHING, INC.
NEW YORK & LONDON
1991

LIBRARY OF CONGRESS CATALOGING-IN-PUBLICATION DATA

Mizala, Alejandra
Financial market liberalization in Chile, 1973–1982 / Alejandra Mizala
Salces.
p. cm. — (Developing economies of the Third World)
Includes bibliographical references.
ISBN 0-8153-0633-4 (alk. paper)
1. Monetary policy—Chile. 2. Finance—Chile. 3. Chile—Economic
policy. 4. Chile—Economic conditions—1973–    I. Title. II. Series.
HG845.M59 1991
338.983'009'047—dc20
91-28343

Designed by Lisa Broderick

Printed on acid-free, 250-year-life paper.
MANUFACTURED IN THE UNITED STATES OF AMERICA

*To Jaime, Camila, and Damián*

# TABLE OF CONTENTS

# PREFACE

The research for this book was done in 1983-84; the object of the study was to analyze the effects on the Chilean economy of the liberalization of the financial market which took place during the 1973-82 monetarist experiment. The book ends, therefore, with the 1982 crisis which is considered to have been the second most important crisis in Chile's economic history.

Today, almost a decade after the 1982 crisis, the Chilean economy has undergone both external and internal adjustment, and it is in better relative condition than most other Latin American economies as it enters the 1990's.

In this preface I would like to take a retrospective look at the post-crisis adjustment process in order to provide the reader with a more complete view of the Chilean economic experience during the past decades.

The 1982 crisis can be explained by the serious macroeconomic imbalances which existed because economic policy was concentrated on reducing inflation and neglected external balance. In pursuit of the control of inflation, the real exchange rate lost one third of its purchasing power, foreign debt duplicated in a period of three years, the rise in exports halted and even receded in 1981-82, and the external gap rose to disproportionately high levels.

These imbalances were induced by excessive internal expenditures in the private sector stimulated largely by financial liberalization policies. The foreign debt crisis demonstrated the extreme vulnerability of the economy to external shocks that was created by monetarist policies and the passive attitude of the state.

In response to the 1982 crisis, modifications to the economic reforms and changes in the rules of economic policy were made during 1983-89. In the early years of the period (1983-84) the state had to abandon neutral economic policies in order to help out the bankrupt business sector. The next period (1985-89) was characterized by the imposition of a new orthodox strategy, with emphasis on long-term reforms, but with a greater degree of economic regulation and pragmatism than had been evident in the 1973-82 period. During this second period the economy began to experience a sustained recovery, especially as of 1986.

The strategy adopted to meet the crisis was based on the following elements: a policy of aggregate demand consistent with external restriction and a sustained policy of devaluations in the exchange rate; a strategy of negotiation rather than confrontation with foreign creditors; new banking legislation that corrected previous errors in financial regulation and a support program from the Central Bank to benefit the overly indebted private sector.

The debt crisis made it imperative to generate a surplus in the trade balance to pay part of the interest on the foreign debt. The improvement in the foreign trade situation was accomplished through expenditure-switching policies (increase in exports and substitution of imports) as well as expenditure-reducing policies; output had to exceed expenditure which necessarily implied high adjustment costs (Meller, 1990).

The devaluation of the exchange rate was one of the most important instruments of post-crisis economic policy. Real devaluation of the exchange rate led to a change in relative prices between non-tradable goods and tradable goods, reassigning resources to the latter sector. The policy of nominal devaluations took place at the same time wages stagnated; these paralyzed wages became the most important factor in maintaining real devaluation.

The duplication of the real exchange rate between 1982 and 1988 was successful in expanding exports; they represented 26.4% of GDP in 1981 and 37% of GDP in 1989. This boom in exports has been considered one of the most positive results of the Chilean adjustment process.

In regard to foreign debt the government defined a non-confrontational policy on one hand. This policy implied that the state provided its guarantee for the Chilean private financial sector's unguaranteed foreign debt (the amount of non-recoverable loans in the private banking sector corresponding to foreign credit has been estimated at US$ 3,500 million by the World Bank); the Chilean government also paid all interest on the foreign debt punctually. In exchange they received a very important, methodical reprogramming of most of the capital. On the other hand, the Chilean government sustained that the application of coherent macroeconomic policies and a serious effort at adjustment would attract foreign credit and make it possible for the country to gain access to the international voluntary credit market. Nevertheless, until 1989 the investment in reputation had an effect only on multilateral organizations which granted loans to Chile for five consecutive years for an amount equal to 3% to 4% of GDP.

However, the country not only faced the foreign debt problem; the liquidity and solvency crisis in the productive and financial sector turned internal debt into one of the most urgent problems as of 1983. The Central Bank played a crucial role in this regard as the "lender of last resort", providing a continuous flow of liquidity to avoid the collapse of the financial and productive system.

There were three kinds of economic agents that benefited from Central Bank subsidies: debtors in foreign currency, debtors in local currency and the private banking sector.

Debtors in foreign currency received two kinds of subsidies. First they had access to a subsidized exchange rate or "preferential dollar"; this dual exchange rate system implied high subsidies of US$ 3,000 million in the 1982-87 period. Second, a de-dollarization process was put into effect, i.e., the conversion of dollar debts into peso debts, just before a sudden new devaluation in September 1984. The subsidy provided by the Central Bank in this de-dollarization process reached US$ 232 million.

The government tried originally (1982) to apply the market solution to peso debtors; they tried to solve the problem through bankruptcies and auctions of the guarantees associated with unpaid credits, thereby distributing losses between debtors and creditors. However this solution, besides being politically unfeasible, implied a generalized loss in the financial system and a process of indefinition of property that would have multiplied the recessive effects of the 1982 crisis. Therefore, the Central Bank financed the reprogramming of debts between commercial banks and their debtors. This program was put into effect in 1984-85, and its beneficiaries were the debtors in the productive sector, as well as mortgage and consumer loan debtors. The program made it possible for debtors to exchange short-term debt at market interest rates for long-term debt at subsidized interest rates.

On the other hand, to avoid total financial collapse major private banks received complete support from the Central Bank, while the rest of the private banks received important emergency loans. The Central Bank took two different measures to re-establish a solvent financial system. They were the following (Meller, 1990): (i) a commercial bank could sell its risky, poor quality portfolio to the Central Bank for the equivalent of twice the bank's capital, with the obligation of buying it back; sales of private banks' poor quality portfolios represented 18% of GDP in 1985. (ii) the second mechanism used to help the commercial banking sector was related to the subsidized interest rate paid by the Central Bank through swap operations. A commercial bank could make a deposit in foreign currency in the Central Bank for Libor plus 4% (a spread that declined over time) and receive at the same time a loan in pesos whose interest rate was the same as the rate paid for deposits. In a swap operation the Central Bank guaranteed the sale of foreign currency and also absorbed the risks and losses associated with a possible devaluation.

Estimates (Eyzaguirre and Larrañaga, 1990) indicate that rescue and support operations cost the Central Bank US$ 9,000 million. The financing for these operations came basically from the issue of Central Bank bonds and seigniorage. The cost of the program was thus distributed over time. The Chilean treasury in turn had to provide resources (government bonds) to the Central Bank to avoid its bankruptcy.

In spite of the size of the resources involved, it is important to remember that the Central Bank, in its role as lender of last resort, avoided the financial collapse of the most important part of the country's productive and financial system. The cost of the program was focused on those who had to pay more taxes or received fewer social benefits because the public sector had to allocate 2% of GDP every year to cover the deficit generated by these operations.

Regarding the 1986 reform of the financial system, the most important changes in the regulatory and supervisory systems governing financial institutions consisted of the introduction of a variety of mechanisms to control solvency and a substantial withdrawal of the state guarantee on deposits (Held, 1990).

In summary, the post-crisis macroeconomic policy can be characterized first by a sustained increase in the real exchange rate and a policy of aggregate demand consistent with external restriction. Second, the debt problem was faced by the distribution of its cost over time, by renegotiation abroad, and internally by a Central Bank support program which benefited the financial sector and private debtors. At the same time reforms in the financial system were implemented which made stricter regulation of the system possible. This strategy was developed in an environment of more favorable external conditions, with decreases in the international interest rate and improvements in the terms of trade. The support of multilateral institutions (IMF, World Bank and IDB) can be added to the above list. Finally, it should be pointed out that the structural reforms that Chile had implemented during the 1970's were most helpful in the economy's recovery process. The public sector had a surplus, and there was a low level of public debt which provided the necessary space to finance aid to the private sector. Major reallocation of resources in favor of the export sector and a redistribution of the overindebtedness of the private sector to the public sector took place during the post-crisis recovery process.

The Chilean economy reached the end of the 1980's with a higher economic growth rate and lower unemployment than before the 1982 crisis. Inflation on the other hand, although higher than in 1989, was low for Latin American standards. Nevertheless, it is important to point out that during the adjustment process there has been differential treatment of economic agents, providing substantial subsidies to agents with higher incomes and reduced subsidies or none to an important percentage of the unemployed. Consequently, a deterioration in the distribution of income has taken place (Torche, 1988).

The labor market was the main adjustment valve for the policies followed in the 1983-89 period; reduction of the real wage was the main factor in obtaining real devaluation. The average real wage was reduced almost 20% between 1981 and 1987, and minimum income was reduced 40%. On the other hand, effective unemployment was over 24% during the 1982-85 period, reaching a maximum of 31.3% in 1983.

The persistence of high levels of unemployment for long periods of time, the abrupt decrease and slow recovery of real wages, and the less active role played by the state in the social area led to a deterioration of the workers' standard of living. Consumption deteriorated severely after the 1982 crisis; the deterioration was such that even in 1989 consumption remained four points below the 1981 level. This situation poses a serious challenge to the economic leadership of the democratic government that came into power in March 1991.

Finally, one may ask what the Chilean experience of almost two decades of economic policies with profound structural reforms has left as its legacy. I believe that the most important aspect has been the emergence of a greater degree of consensus between different sectors and social agents in regard to the economic system. There is agreement on the following subjects: the necessity of maintaining and improving outward-oriented policies, the role of private enterprise as the engine in the development process, the crucial importance of macroeconomic balance in the success of any development strategy, and the necessity for an adequate regulatory framework in a market economy.

The past experience has also left important challenges for the Chilean economy in the future. They are the necessity of increasing investment in order to achieve a path of stable growth in accordance with price stability and external restrictions, and the imperative necessity of improving the living conditions of the majority of the population.

Alejandra Mizala
July 1991

# ACKNOWLEDGMENTS

I would like to give special thanks to my professors at Berkeley Jeffrey Frankel and Albert Fishlow for their invaluable help and encouragement. I would also like to extend my appreciation to David Collier, Lovell Jarvis, Sherman Robinson and Laura Tyson for helpful discussion.

This study benefited from a year and a half of research at CIEPLAN, Santiago, Chile, which offered me unlimited hospitality and help. I am deeply indebted to all its researchers for their valuable comments and suggestions, especially to Ricardo Ffrench-Davis, Manuel Marfán and José Pablo Arellano.

I also wish to express my thanks to the World Bank project on liberalization and stabilization policies in the Southern Cone countries and to Vittorio Corbo for providing access to their information. Valuable information was also provided by the Superintendencia de Valores y Seguros.

A special word of appreciation goes to my husband, Jaime, for his constant support, his reading of earlier versions of this book and his valuable suggestions.

A word of gratitude goes also to Caroline Simian for her help in editing the book and to Gladys Cavallone and Regina Mateluna for typing the final version.

Finally, I would like to thank the Social Science Research Council, the American Council of Learned Societies and the Inter-American Foundation which granted me a doctoral fellowship which made this research possible.

# 1. INTRODUCTION

During the 1970's important changes in policies occurred in Chile which are of interest to economists studying the development process of Latin American countries. The liberalization and stabilization policies that took place during the period 1973-82 implied drastic changes in the trade regime and the role of markets.[1] In fact, the case of Chile has been considered the purest example of comprehensive economic liberalization in the Third World.

Financial aspects have played a crucial role in the transformation process of the Chilean economy. The financial reform initiated in 1974 resulted in important economic transformations. The most significant change was the freeing of bank interest rates which moved from real levels that were historically negative to levels that were not only positive, but also above international levels. The real interest rate averaged more than 30% during the period 1975-82.

The purpose of this research is to analyze the Chilean experience from the time liberalization and stabilization policies were put into effect in 1973 until 1982. The objective is to estimate empirically the response of the economy to extensive financial policy changes. The study investigates the impact of changing financial and economic conditions on industrial manufacturing firms.

A number of economists, e.g., McKinnon (1973), Shaw (1973), Galvis (1977), Mathieson (1979) and (1980), Kapur (1980) and others, have argued that domestic financial liberalization is necessary both to attain long-run development in LDC's as well as to stabilize these economies in the short-run.

Even though this approach is more concerned with long-term growth than with short-term macroeconomic policies, as Roe (1982) has pointed out, a bridge has been built between the developmental and stabilization arguments. The International Monetary Fund and the World Bank are now strong advocates of the liberalization of domestic financial markets as part of their stabilization plans for LDC's.

The central argument of this view is that financial repression, i.e., distortions of financial prices including interest rates and foreign exchange rates, reduces the real rate of growth and the real size of the financial sector relative to non-financial sectors. Foreign exchange controls, interest rate ceilings, and high reserve requirements are the main characteristics of a financially repressed economy. The results are non-price rationing, a segmented credit market, and a strong tendency to finance investments which yield returns barely above the ceiling interest rate.

The policy prescription is to raise institutional interest rates and/or to reduce the rate of inflation. Abolishing institutionally fixed interest rates would increase financial savings, maximize investment and increase investment's average efficiency.

The reasoning goes as follows: Financial repression involves rationing in the financial market, brought on by the existence of interest rates below the market equilibrium level, which causes the savings level to fall below the desired investment level. Hence, the need to ration credit. It is contended that financial repression would lead to segmented markets since the maintenance of interest rates below the equilibrium would require credit allocation mechanisms outside the market. This would commonly result in credit access for large enterprises with political and financial connections whereas new, small, unknown enterprises would find credit severely restricted. Improvement of the financial intermediation process through an increase in the deposit real interest rate would bring about an increase in the savings-flow, as well as in the quantity and quality of investment. Quality of investment would improve because the interest rate would be the main rationing mechanism, and would furthermore discriminate against inefficient investments.

The McKinnon and Shaw view challenges the traditional monetary theory approach that money and capital are substitutes in the portfolios of private wealthholders and in the aggregate economy. In rejecting the traditional view, the two authors propose and defend the thesis that money and capital are likely to be complements in less developed, fragmented economies where the financial sector has been severely repressed. Potential investors must accumulate money balances prior to their investments; therefore, conditions that make financial assets attractive to hold (i.e. a higher real interest rate on deposits) enhance rather than inhibit private incentives to accumulate physical capital. That is, in the underdeveloped economy the "conduit effect" of financial assets is likely to prevail over the "competing-asset effect" stressed by the traditional portfolio approach.

McKinnon (1973) and (1981) also argues that repression of the financial sector is paralleled by the use of tariffs and quotas in an effort to promote development by manipulating the foreign trade sector. He claims that if existing protective tariffs and quota restrictions on imports were eliminated, an enormous implicit burden on export activities would be lifted and, therefore, the need to give them preferred access to low cost credit would be avoided. At the same time more neutral resource allocation would result. Hence, a more effective strategy for economic growth would proceed from a thorough liberalization of financial markets and the lifting of restraints on foreign trade.

Moreover, McKinnon (1973) and (1982) points out that the order of economic liberalization is crucial to attain successful results. The main question is which market should be liberalized first. He argues that trade liberalization and the liberalization of domestic finances should proceed simultaneously. However, liberalization of the current account of the balance of payments should precede the elimination of exchange controls on the capital account.

The argument is the following. Once the domestic financial market has been liberalized, the opening of the capital account may result in large inflows of foreign capital, triggered by substantial interest rate differentials. If such capital inflows are absorbed in real terms, this could force a trade deficit and real exchange rate appreciation on the economy. Since financial markets adjust much faster than goods markets, this real appreciation would be quite abrupt, and imply severe anti-protection in the production of tradable goods.

In this study we will contrast the objectives raised and the assumptions of the "repressionist paradigm" with the response its application elicited from the Chilean economy. The type of questions posed and the short length of the period studied make it necessary to work with microeconomic data rather than with standard aggregate data. Since financial markets are more highly developed for corporations than for households, a study of the effects the financial liberalization had on the industrial manufacturing corporation will be more fruitful empirically. The most important source of information used in this research consists of microeconomic financial data from a large representative sample of publicly held corporations in the Chilean manufacturing industry.

To anticipate the conclusions of this research three main results are important to note. The first principal finding is that the financial liberalization reform, as implemented in the Chilean economy, made for decapitalization and speculation instead of real investment. Chilean gross fixed investment declined from an average of 20.2% of GDP during the period 1960-70, to 15.5% of GDP during the period 1974-82, while investment in financial assets experienced an important increase from 2.7% of GDP in 1970 to 5.3% of GDP during the period 1977-82. Market signalling, mainly the high real interest rates, led productive firms to decrease their investment in physical capital and to increase financial intermediation. Chapter 4 of this study shows that industrial manufacturing enterprises which survived the period 1977-82 changed their asset composition. The share of financial assets in their total assets increased, and the share of fixed assets in their total assets decreased during the period. This phenomenon not only represents capitalization of interest rates accrued by the financial assets, but also reflects a drop of fixed asset investment in absolute terms. In the financially liberalized Chilean economy the "competing-asset effect" dominated the "conduit effect". The greater attractiveness of financial assets due to the increase in the real interest rate inhibited accumulation of physical capital. Moreover, when comparing the behavior of productive firms that survived the period of the reforms with firms that went bankrupt, one can see that the latter did not invest in financial assets as a response to the new situation in the internal financial market. It may be that these firms were incapable of adjusting by recomposing their assets as the rest of the manufacturing enterprises did, because they faced important economic difficulties. The impossibility to adjust kept these enterprises from taking advantage of profitable speculative opportunities offered by the market which might eventually have reduced their losses. In other words, contrary to what advocates of financial liberalization in LDC's postulate, the domestic financial reform brought about a perverse financial deepening in the Chilean case.

As mentioned earlier, theories promoting financial liberalization in LDC's argue that segmentation is one of the characteristics of "repressed" financial markets. The second finding of this study is that the Chilean liberalization process did not eliminate the financial market segmentation characteristic of financially repressed economies. Chapter 5 shows that when the differential between internal and foreign real interest rates surpassed an annual 30%, foreign currency credit became concentrated in a few economic sectors. These include the industrial sector up to 1977, and thereafter the financial sector.

It can be argued that there is nothing wrong with the fact that most of the external credit became concentrated in the financial sector, since its role is precisely to allocate these resources. However, as Dahse (1979) has shown, since the financial reform of 1975 the Chilean capital market was characterized by the existence of economic conglomerates; that is, a group of firms organized around one or more domestic banks. Under these conditions financial intermediaries pursued the objectives of the economic group to which they belonged rather than the objectives of the depositors. The present research confirms this hypothesis: Chapter 5 also shows that large enterprises with connections to the economic groups had privileged access to cheaper foreign credit. This differential access to credit led small firms without connections to borrow in domestic currency in the recently liberalized internal financial market, and to pay the persistently high real interest rates being charged in this market. Therefore, the completely deregulated domestic loan market played a similar role to the one performed by informal credit markets in financially repressed economies. In contrast with a repressed-economy formal financial market, where firms willing to pay high interest rates do not necessarily obtain loans, in the Chilean peso-loan market firms willing to pay the high interest rates had ample access to loans. Two facts explain this behavior: On the one hand there was "portfolio liberalization", i.e., the elimination of regulations ruling credit allocation brought about by the financial liberalization; on the other hand, from 1977 on there was strong competition for market shares in the banking industry. One of the elements which explains this fact was the expansion of the existing banking system as well as the entry of new banks. These new banks were responsible for around 45% of the credit expansion during the period 1977-82. The increased competition, however, did not manifest itself in price competition; banks did not increase deposit interest rate and decrease lending rates in order to maintain or increase their market shares. On the contrary, increased competition manifested itself in a relaxation of the criteria used to select debtors, and a lowering of the standards and quality of collateral required. The result was a great increase in the risk of banks' portfolios. This perverse behavior of the domestic credit market revealed a very weak financial structure that could go bankrupt any time. In fact a serious problem was the collapse of the liberalized banking and financial sector that occurred in 1982. This collapse was the consequence of a very large proportion of bad loans held by the banks.[2]

The third main finding of this research is that during the 1974-82 period many firms borrowed in order to overcome what they foresaw as only transitory difficulties. Specifically, an important part of bank loans were used to cover current operating losses incurred by firms hard hit by increased foreign competition. [3] In Chapter 6 a cross section time-series microeconomic financial data set of Chilean manufacturing firms is examined. The results show that bank borrowing of import-competing firms went to finance not only investment but also operating losses. In the case of export firms and firms producing nontradable goods, losses were not a statistically significant determinant of bank debt. Import-competing firms borrowed in the recently liberalized financial market in order to remain in operation, and were able to do so because their losses were believed to be temporary.

Moreover, during a period when an outward looking development strategy was being implemented firms producing tradable goods, which theoretically should have been the dynamic engine of the new economic model, suffered an important decline in profitability. Chapter 6 also shows that firms producing nontradables enjoyed very positive conditions during the period. These firms showed the best results in terms of profitability; they had easier and more fluid access to cheaper foreign credit, and they registered an important increase in fixed-asset investment. In contrast, export firms ended up the period with a level of fixed assets similar to their 1977 level, and import-competing firms suffered a significant decline in fixed assets in absolute terms. Therefore, in the Chilean case the interaction of domestic financial liberalization with foreign trade and external financial liberalization resulted in a perverse resource allocation,

The financial liberalization reform, as implemented in Chile, induced a substitution between real and financial investment. This substitution was encouraged by the enormous differences existing between the returns on real capital and interest rates in the financial market. This fact implied unbalanced economic growth between the real and financial sectors. The performance of the liberalized domestic financial market, together with service-oriented economic growth, led to increasing indebtedness in the real sector that gave rise to the deep financial crisis which began in 1981.

Moreover, during the period the tradable goods sector experienced a decrease in profitability vis-a-vis the nontradable goods sector. Also, investment loan demand had to compete with loan demand from losses in the import-competing sector. The problem for economic growth engendered under these conditions is that changes in relative prices do not increase the demand for products generated. The contrary occurs if investment is oriented toward export industries.

Finally, it is important to point out that it is not the aim of this research to question the structural changes the Chilean economy needed at the beginning of the seventies. These changes include the development of an efficient capital market designed to improve resource generation and allocation and a greater openness of the domestic economy to foreign trade, with specialization in those productive sectors with higher growth possibilities. What is being questioned is the way these changes were implemented in the context of the monetarist model in use during the 1974-82 period. On the one hand, a fast opening-up of the economy proceeded at the expense of domestic industrial growth, instead of accompanying a domestic industrialization process. Successful trade liberalization requires greater, more rapid growth in the tradable goods sector. This implies a reallocation of resources toward this sector throughout the years and, therefore, a relatively higher return in the tradable sector than in the nontradable sector. A successful opening-up to foreign trade requires a change in the productive structure. Tariff cuts are only a tool which needs to be complemented with active development policies. Trade liberalization requires an increasing allocation of investment in infrastructure (transport and communications), research and development, and human capital. Moreover, the exchange rate policy should ensure a stable real exchange rate in order to make the traded goods sector permanently profitable and competitive.

On the other hand, there was a financial reform which relied completely on the ability of the market to allocate funds efficiently. The application of "neutral" rules produced non-neutral results in an environment where unequal market power and unequal initial distribution of wealth prevailed. Economic reform wherein market forces are left free to guide most of the economy's decisions can not produce neutral results in a context where there is an oligopolistic structure. In this sense rules were only seemingly neutral in the Chilean case. For instance, the government was unwilling to regulate the behavior of economic conglomerates and their financial institutions in order to ensure sound practices on the part of financial intermediaries. Moreover, the persistent disequilibrium between the interest rate and the rate of return on real capital encouraged financial investment, speculation, and consumption of luxury goods instead of real investment. Active financial and monetary policies should be used in a financial development strategy. This program should be aimed at encouraging and complementing capital accumulation and discouraging short-run speculation.

This study is organized in the following manner: Chapter 2 discusses the main issues related to the theory of financial liberalization in LDC's. Chapter 3 presents a description of the policies implemented in the Chilean economy during the period under study: 1973-82. The objective is to provide background information concerning the effects of the policies on the performance of the financial sector. Chapter 4 studies the effects of the financial reform on the Chilean manufacturing industry. It analyzes the behavior of the firms which adjusted and survived the period of the reforms as well as the behavior of the firms which went bankrupt during this period. Chapter 5 investigates the extent to which financial reform eliminated segmentation of the financial market characteristic of financially repressed economies, i.e., whether large firms and firms connected with financial institutions maintained differentiated access to cheap credit. Domestic financial market liberalization was only one of the structural changes which enterprises had to adjust to during the period under study. Trade reform and the liberalization of the capital account of the balance of payments also influenced the behavior of manufacturing firms. Chapter 6 investigates the effect of the interaction of these reforms on the behavior of industrial firms. It also attempts to answer the question of the extent to which import-competing firms chose to contract debt at high existing interest rates in the domestic financial market in order to adjust and survive in the face of increasing foreign competition. Chapter 7 is a case study of a sample of manufacturing firms. The aim of this chapter is to illustrate the problems faced by firms during the period analyzed as well as the decisions taken to confront them. The idea is to present a more qualitative view of the firms' behavior during the period. Chapter 8 analyzes the industrial corporations' financial behavior during the period, in particular their debt and investment policies from a formal point of view. Finally, in Chapter 9 some policy implications of the Chilean financial liberalization are discussed.

**Notes**

1. During recent years an important amount of research has been done on the Chilean experience. See among others: Ffrench-Davis (1983a), Foxley (1981) and (1982), McKinnon (1982), Corbo (1982), (1983) and (1985), Corbo and De Melo (1987), Zahler (1980) and (1983), Cortázar, Foxley and Tokman (1984), Balassa (1985), Edwards (1985b), Edwards and Cox-Edwards (1987) Morandé and Schmidt-Hebbel (1988), and Morán (1989).

2. These bad loans were made not only to the manufacturing sector, but also to the nontradable non-manufacturing sectors. Specifically, a significant amount of bad loans were allocated to the construction sector when a construction boom developed during 1979-81 in the country.

3. As has been pointed out, the financial liberalization reform was implemented together with a monetarist stabilization program, and with a liberalization of domestic commodity markets and foreign trade.

# 2. THE THEORY OF FINANCIAL LIBERALIZATION IN LESS DEVELOPED COUNTRIES. A REVIEW OF THE LITERATURE

## 2.1. Introduction

A number of economists, e.g., McKinnon (1973), Shaw (1973), Galvis (1977), Fry (1978) and (1980), Kapur (1979) and others have attempted to establish the hypothesis that improvements in the financial intermediation process are a precondition for economic growth. Their main concern is the development of financial savings at an appropriate pace. Such a change calls for positive real interest rate policies as opposed to negative real interest rates to stimulate investment.

According to this view the emphasis in the theory of development in the context of LDC's has switched from a lack of basic investment opportunities to removal of financial constraints (Galvis, 1977).

The influence of the McKinnon and Shaw view has reached far beyond the academic ambit. Even though this approach is more concerned with long-term growth and not with short-term macroeconomic policies, as Roe (1982) has pointed out, a bridge has been built between the developmental and stabilization arguments. The International Monetary Fund and the World Bank are now strong advocates of domestic financial market liberalization as part of their stabilization plans for LDC's.[1]

This chapter is organized in the following way: The second section characterizes the financially repressed economy. The third section presents the main policy prescriptions derived from the so called repressionist view. The fourth section analyses the explicit and implicit assumptions contained in this view. The fifth section describes specific experiences in some countries with financial reforms, the last section includes some final remarks.

## 2.2. The Financially Repressed Economy

The financially repressed economy is characterized by a lack of organized bank lending to the rural economy and to small-scale urban industry. Large firms, which receive protection from foreign competition, are often the recipients of officially designated bank credits at negative real interest rates (once domestic price inflation or anticipated exchange rate depreciation are taken into account) which provide them with heavy subsidies.

The historically poor performance of organized bank lending is related to regulated interest rate ceiling and collateral requirements. Private borrowing and lending at equilibrium interest rates does not take place. Usury restrictions on interest rates allow the regulatory authority to give credit subsidies to preferred claimants (Leff and Sato, 1980).

Interest rate ceilings result in a gap between the demand and the supply of funds and the development of an unofficial non-institutionalized financial market, all of which is a symbol of a segmented, repressed economy. Under these conditions unknown, small-scale productive units suffer disadvantages in financial markets because of imperfect information, risk, and absence of economies of scale. Moreover, if the excess demand is large these firms may be squeezed out of access to formal markets and forced into a more expensive informal credit market.

The investors' attempts are frustrated by the reduced availability of funds. Changes in the volume of real credit affect real investment, because LDC firms are generally very dependent on credit to increase their capital stock. The results are a lower level of investment, and a strong tendency to finance investments some of which yield returns barely above the ceiling interest rate, thus stopping or gravely retarding the development process (Shaw, 1973; Fry, 1982).

Foreign trade is rather broadly repressed by quantitative restrictions (or high tariffs) on both imports and exports. The prices of most goods produced and consumed are determined mainly by domestic demand and supply considerations, and in the short-run they are rather insulated from exchange rate fluctuations (McKinnon, 1973).

The domestic financial system is insulated by exchange controls on the capital account of the Balance of Payments.

The monetary system in LDC's has a relatively more important role as an intermediary between savers and investors. Because private financial savings in developing countries are largely in currency and deposits, the monetary authority controls the flow of loanable funds through the issue of currency, acquiring a critical importance in the developmental process. Therefore, what is a purely supervisory and monetary control activity in industrial financially liberalized economies, becomes a highly activist credit-allocation role in LDC's.

The explanation of this difference is found in the low level of development of capital markets in repressed economies, due to the fact that the government can not sell public debt. Therefore, forced sales of government debt to the banking sector through a system of high reserve requirements gives the government access to bank loanable funds (see Aghevli and Khan, 1978).

## 2.3. Policy Prescriptions

There are a number of policy implications derived from the repressionist view (McKinnon, 1973).

(i) For the underdeveloped economy the demand for financial assets and the demand for physical assets are likely to be complementary in the portfolios of private wealthholders and in the aggregate economy. Potential investors must accumulate money balances prior to their investments; therefore, the more attractive the process of accumulating money[2] (i.e., the higher the real interest rate on deposits) the greater the incentive to invest. This is called the complementarity hypothesis.

The basic thesis of complementarity between money and capital challenges the traditional portfolio approach, which treats money and physical capital as substitutable forms of wealth-holding. In rejecting the traditional approach, McKinnon and Shaw argue that in less developed, fragmented economies financial assets are viewed as a conduit through which accumulation takes place rather than as competing assets. In economies where the financial sector has been severely repressed the "conduit effect" of financial assets is likely to prevail over the "competing-asset effect" stressed by the portfolio approach.

Nevertheless, a sufficient rise in the return on holding money eventually makes the competing-asset effect dominant. According to the repressionist view, the competing-asset effect acts favorably to constrain social waste if the return on money is kept positive, because individuals will not hold non-monetary assets whose return is less than the return on highly liquid cash balances.

(ii) The quality of the capital stock (average rate of return) is directly and positively related to the real rate of return on holding money. That is, the demand for money rises pari passu with the productivity of physical capital. The argument is as follows: An increase in the real rate of return on holding money encourages financial savings. As money becomes a more attractive vehicle for maintaining value, non-productive forms of fixed or working capital –previously used to maintain value or as an inflation hedge– will be allocated to more efficient uses. Moreover, a given quantity of savings mobilized through the financial system is more productive than the same quantity mobilized through informal channels. This fact is based on the ability of the financial system to allocate funds to those investors most capable of producing the highest rates of return.

(iii) Private savings are quite sensitive to the real return on holding money and its stability.

(iv) There is a determinate optimal real rate of return on money that is likely to be significantly greater than zero, and a presumption that inflation is a poor way of dealing with the scarcity of real capital.

(v) Indivisibilities are such that investment can be increased using appropriate financial techniques, without diminishing returns. The intramarginal or discontinuous characteristic of investment opportunities available to each firm in LDC's suggests the need for high returns to the holders of money. A high real rate earned on accumulating owned cash balances allows the firm to plan for quantum investments in technology. Otherwise, the firm is confined to small annual marginal investments, with only minor improvements in the old technology.

Therefore, the policy prescription is to raise institutional real interest rates. This implies increasing nominal interest rates and avoiding high and unstable inflation. When inflation is very unstable, it is hard for the banks to offset it appropriately by adjusting nominal interest rates, and thus nominal interest may look too high for borrowers and too low for depositors.

To sum up, abolishing interest rate ceilings and controlling inflation would produce the optimal result of increasing financial savings, maximizing investment and raising investments' average efficiency (Fry, 1982).

Along with the liberalization of domestic finances, liberalization of foreign trade is necessary, because repression of both foreign trade and domestic finances has a certain mutual consistency. Therefore, it is difficult to liberalize one without the other.

On the one hand, successful liberalization of the domestic capital market permits a radical restructuring of tariff, quota and licensing restraints on foreign trade. Users of manufactured goods no longer need to be taxed by tariffs in order to subsidize new domestic producers. Instead, new firms with good prospects will be able to borrow more easily. Similarly, exclusive licenses to import capital goods no longer serve any useful economic purpose in making it easier for their holders to attract financial capital. The case for free trade is clear when the domestic capital market is working freely (Mckinnon, 1973 and 1982).

On the other hand, if existing protective tariffs and quota restrictions on import were eliminated, an enormous implicit burden on exporting activities would be lifted and therefore, the need to give them preferred access to low cost credit would be avoided. At the same time more neutral resource allocation would result (see McKinnon, 1973 and 1981). Moreover, liberalization of foreign trade is necessary to attain effective commodity arbitrage with the outside world, such arbitrage being a necessary ingredient in securing control over the domestic price level. Likewise, a correct policy toward the foreign exchange rate is necessary to secure control of the money supply. Control of both the price level and the money supply are critically important for successful domestic financial liberalization.

McKinnon (1972) and (1982) points out that the order in which markets are liberalized is crucial to attain successful results. He argues that trade liberalization should proceed simultaneously with the liberalization of domestic finances. However, international capital movements should be tightly controlled during the transition period after trade has been liberalized. The main concern is that large inflows of international capital, triggered by interest rate differentials, could force a trade deficit and real exchange rate appreciation on the economy, thereby implying severe antiprotection in the production of tradable goods.[3]

Finally, it is extremely relevant to avoid weak fiscal policy in a financially liberalized economy, since inadequate fiscal policy would force the government to borrow from the Central Bank relying on the inflation tax to cover its fiscal deficit.

## 2.4. Assumptions of the Repressionist Paradigm

It is interesting to discuss the main assumptions of the McKinnon and Shaw view.

One of the most important assumptions of their analysis is the savings effect of higher interest rates, specifically the elasticity of private savings with respect to the interest rate. This is a crucial point because if total savings are to increase, private savings must be very sensitive to the real interest rate. The reason for this is that in the repressed economy the increase in private savings has to more than counterbalance the decrease in the volume of savings previously collected by the government through the inflation tax.[4] Theoretically, the effect of higher interest rates on savings is not clear because there are substitution and income effects which work in opposite directions. Empirical studies related to the effect of higher interest rates on savings are not conclusive. There are studies which find a positive effect of interest rates on savings (see Boskin, 1979 and Fry, 1980), whereas Howrey and Hymans (1978) and Giovanini (1983) do not find any significant effect.

Another crucial assumption considered by financial liberalization advocates is the likely complementarity between money and physical capital in less developed, fragmented economies. In other words, the absorptive capacity constraint inherent in LDC's is loosened by the increase in financial intermediation. This assumption rests on the neoclassical view, as opposed to the Keynesian view, that the investment level is determined by the saving level. That is, a higher saving level precedes a higher investment level.[5] According to the repressionist view, the sole existence of a liberalized financial market which will expand the volume of financial savings implies a higher level of real investment.

However, it is not clear what the mechanism inducing entrepreneurs to invest is, given the fact that the expected return of investment projects does not change when the marginal propensity to save increases. Moreover, it is unlikely that the increase in financial intermediation would solve all the obstacles that exist for capital formation in LDC's. For instance, even if entrepreneurs had the option to borrow easily from the liberalized financial market they might not want to undertake investment projects if their expectations regarding the future were not favorable. In this case they might want to hold their own savings in highly liquid financial assets. Furthermore, nobody guarantees that investors will make use of additional savings that are newly available but at high historical cost. That is, it is not clear that the extra savings generated by financial liberalization will translate automatically into higher investment. Finally, the allocation of increased financial resources is very important. In capital markets which continue to be fragmented even after liberalization, increased private savings are as likely to go into imported goods, services and housing as well as more socially useful investment (Taylor, 1974).

A third assumption of this repressionist paradigm which is not set forth explicitly in the analysis is related to the structure of asset markets in LDC's. McKinnon, Shaw and Kapur among others assume that the portfolio shift into financial savings is coming out of unproductive assets like gold, cash, commodity stocks, etc. Van Wijnbergen (1983a) and Taylor (1983) show that whether an increase in time deposits is expansionary or contractionary depends on whether time deposits are close substitutes for unproductive assets, providing no pass through into capital, or for productive assets like loans extended in the unofficial credit market (curb market). Van Wijnbergen (1983a) analyzes the case where time deposits are close substitutes for loans made in curb markets, in which case an increase in time deposits rate is contractionary and will also accelerate inflation. The argument is as follows: People shifting out of curb markets leads to tight credit conditions because the curb market provides more intermediation than the banking system[6]. The resulting high real cost of credit leads to an acceleration of inflation in the short-run due to the link between credit and the supply side of the economy via the financing of working capital[7]. This initial increase in the rate of interest will lead to a lower profit rate and therefore lower investment and medium-run growth rate. The net effect on growth depends on the response of the savings rate: If financial asset accumulation slows down, less growth is inevitable; if financial deepening results, the net effect on growth is ambiguous. Van Wijnbergen (1983b) demonstrates the relevance of these problems with some simulation results for a quarterly econometric model of the Korean economy where an important curb market exists.

## 2.5. Empirical Cases of Financial Liberalization

Two country-cases are always mentioned among the successful stories of domestic financial liberalization: Taiwan and South Korea. Both countries operated with nominal deposit rates well in excess of 20%, i.e, real rates that at times reached 15%, during their periods of economic transformation in the fifties and sixties.[8]

Taiwan implemented an active interest rate policy in 1949. One of the main goals of this policy was to control the inflation rate.

Initially the policy comprised a combination of very high interest rates on very short-term maturities. Due to the high inflation rate it was unrealistic to expect the public to buy bonds of medium or long term maturities. The authorities, however, ensured that the rise in deposit rates was not communicated to loan rates, since this would have affected the working capital requirements of trade and industry. Accordingly, a strategy was adopted to ensure a ceiling on loan rates as well as floor for deposit rates.[9] To protect the commercial banks against losses on preferential deposits a "redeposit facility" was created. Banks were given the option of placing excess deposits in the Bank of Taiwan at rates equal to or above those paid by commercial banks.

During those years total deposits rose and there was a restoration of public confidence. Then, the authorities attempted to increase the maturity of deposits.

In 1959 the high interest rate strategy was extended to government borrowing. The years 1958-59 marked the completion of the stabilization phase that created an environment where the interest rate could be viewed as a normal policy instrument.

Although there is no data covering the whole period, there is reason to believe that the share of unorganized finance in Taiwan has gradually declined as a result of the policy of realistic rates in the organized market.

The efficacy of high interest rates in stimulating total private savings in Taiwan is difficult to evaluate. Even though the ratio of monetary private savings to GNP improved from about 3% in 1953 to 10-13% in the sixties, there is not a consistent trend in aggregate private savings in relation to GNP.

Undoubtedly, to understand the success of interest rate policies in Taiwan in mobilizing voluntary private savings we need to consider the general economic situation, notably the availability of significant amounts of U.S. foreign aid and economic assistance, and also the gradual elimination of the foreign exchange gap through export growth.

The Korean financial reform was part of a broader program which consisted, among other things, of a 100% devaluation of the won in 1964, a number of export incentives, and a substantial tax reform. Part of the program was to raise interest rate ceilings and to dismantle the extensive system of direct quantitative credit controls.[10]

The main objective of the financial reform was to increase capital formation. The other objective of the reform was to increase financial intermediation in the organized financial sector, i.e., to attract funds from the unorganized sector (curb market) into the banking system, thereby extending and strengthening the monetary authorities' area of effectiveness.

Since the interest rate reform of September 1965 there have been diverse adjustments in the Korean interest rate structure. These adjustments attempted among other things to simplify the existing structure of interest rates; to eliminate the inverse differential that existed between some deposit rates and bank lending rates; to reduce the level of deposits and loan rates to more normal levels, i.e., to realign interest rates with the prevailing rate of return on investment; and to decrease costs of bank financing for domestic enterprises.

As a product of the high interest rate structure there was a spectacular rise in monetary savings: 123% in 1966, 84% in 1967 and 94% in 1968. The flow of private savings increased from virtually nothing to about 8% of GNP. Time deposits increased at a higher rate than other types of savings because of the more favorable rate associated with them. However, this increase in private sector savings, and particularly the large rise in time deposits, can not be explained only through the rise in the interest rate. A large portion of what has been recorded as an increase in savings might have been a portfolio switch from assets held in the unregulated market

(Van Wijnbergen, 1983b).[11] In fact, despite the very rapid growth in the real size of the domestic financial sector, in the early 1970's Korea remained heavily dependent on foreign savings which amounted to about 11% of GNP (see McKinnon, 1976).

On the whole, it may be conceded that the policy of realistic interest rates has improved the efficacy of the price mechanism in the organized money market in Korea.

While the interest rate policy in Korea has been successful in achieving its objectives, some of the concomitant factors which contributed to the results cannot be overlooked.

Absorptive capacity limitations, a typical feature of LDC's, which according to the repressionist view would be loosened by increased financial intermediation, were absent in Korea (as well as in Taiwan). The country enjoyed many years of U.S. foreign aid at very favorable rates and also direct contact with North American know-how before it "took off".[12]

Moreover, government or semi-government institutions account for a substantial part of commercial banking, which made implementation of the reform much easier than in the case of a private banking sector.

Finally, the interest rate policy, although important, was only one element in the overall stabilization program which comprised appropriate budgeting credit and exchange rate policies.

More recently, during the seventies, the Southern Cone Latin American countries; Argentina, Chile and Uruguay carried out a liberalization reform of their domestic financial markets. Financial liberalization was pursued as part of a broader reform package which included foreign trade liberalization, opening up of the capital account of the balance of payments, deregulation of domestic commodity markets and short-run stabilization policies.[13]

The reforms started around 1974 in Uruguay, 1974-75 in Chile and 1976-77 in Argentina. As pointed out above, financial market liberalization was a common feature of the reforms in the three countries. The deregulation of domestic financial markets adopted diverse forms: (i) interest rate ceilings were eliminated; (ii) selective and quantitative restrictions on credit were eliminated; (iii) there was an important reduction in the barriers to entry (mainly in Chile and Argentina) into the financial market. New banks and financial institutions could easily be established, and foreign banks were free to set up branches in these countries; (iv) there was a progressive decrease in legal reserve requirements. In summary, the restrictions and regulations of financial intermediaries were substantially reduced.

However, these experiences can not be considered successful stories of financial liberalization. These attempts at reforms resulted by 1983 in domestic financial sectors characterized by widespread bankruptcies, massive government interventions and low domestic savings and investment. See Gaba (1981), Arellano (1983), Díaz-Alejandro (1984a), Ramos (1986), and Corbo and De Melo (1987).

In general, domestic financial deregulation encouraged many kinds of financial savings. Nevertheless, total domestic savings did not increase in the Southern Cone experiments. In Chile gross domestic saving fell from an average of 17% of GDP during the period 1964-73 to 12% during the period 1974-82. In Argentina the proportion of gross domestic savings in the GDP remained the same. During the period 1966-75 domestic savings represented 19.9% of GDP; this figure reached 20.5% of GDP during the period 1976-82. Only Uruguay showed a positive evolution with, gross domestic savings increasing from 10.4% of GDP during the period 1965-74 to 13.4% of GDP during the period 1975-82.

Furthermore, the external debt of these countries increased dramatically, mainly during the period 1980-81. In those years external savings reached an average of 6%, 13% and 7% of GDP in Argentina, Chile and Uruguay respectively.

Moreover, the performance of aggregate investment as a whole was unfavorable. Chilean gross fixed investment, for instance, declined from an average of 20.2% of GDP during the period 1974-82. Investment performance in Argentina and Uruguay was better than in Chile, because public sector capital investment did not decrease in those countries as it did in Chile. Argentinian gross investment was 20.0% of GDP during the period 1966-75 and 21.5% during the period 1976-82. In the case of Uruguay, gross investment as a percentage of GDP grew from 10.2% during the period 1965-74 to 16.4% during the period 1975-82.

The liberalization of interest rates and the relaxation of restrictions and regulations of financial intermediaries resulted in extremely high short-term real interest rates despite massive international capital inflows, and in the intermediation of very short-term maturities.

The results of financial deregulation included a deeply indebted productive sector in the cases of Argentina and Chile. Many firms had financial leverage ratios wherein total debts more than doubled the firms' net worth.

In sum, domestic financial market liberalization is one important element in explaining the poor performance of these countries during the 1970's. In Chile, during the period 1950-73 GDP per capita grew at an annual average rate of 1.5% while the accumulated annual growth rate during the period 1974-82 was -0.2%. Moreover, in 1982 Chilean real per capita GDP declined 15.5%. The figures are similar for Argentina where real per capita GDP grew at an annual average rate of 1.7% during the period 1950-75 while the accumulated annual growth rate during the period 1976-82 was -1.8%. Between 1981 and 1982 real per capita GDP decreased 7.3%. Uruguay improved the growth rate of per capita GDP from 0.6% during the period 1950-74 to 1.8% during the period 1975-82; however, between 1981 and 1982 real per capita GDP declined 5.1%. It can not be argued that these results are only a product of the external conditions faced by these countries. During the period 1975-82 the real per capita GDP of Latin American countries, excluding the Southern Cone countries, grew at an annual average rate of 1.8%, while it declined by 1.1% between 1981 and 1982.

## 2.6. Summary and Final Remarks

McKinnon and Shaw's central argument is that financial repression, i.e., distortions of financial prices including interest rates and foreign exchange rates, reduces the real rate of growth and the real size of the financial sector in relation to non-financial sectors. Foreign exchange controls, interest rate ceilings, and high reserve requirements are the main characteristics of a financially repressed economy. The results are non-price rationing, a segmented credit market, and a strong tendency to finance investments some of which yield returns barely above the ceiling interest rate.

The policy prescription is to raise institutional interest rates and/or to reduce the rate of inflation. Abolishing institutionally fixed interest rates would maximize investment and increase the average efficiency of investment.

The repressionist view rest on some crucial assumptions. For instance, positive interest rate savings elasticity, the assumption that money and physical capital are likely to be complements in less developed, fragmented economies, and the assumption that the increased financial savings brought about by domestic financial liberalization come from non-productive assets which are transformed into productive assets. The validity of these assumptions for LDC's is an empirical fact, and they must be evaluated in every specific country. The empirical work that has been done is not conclusive.

The lesson we can draw from the empirical cases of financial reform is that in order to attain successful financial liberalization it is necessary to take into account the existent financial structure of the country. It is important to understand the way financial markets behave before liberalizing them. There are no simplistic rules such as "raise the interest rates" that will work for any less developed economy.

Furthermore, it is not at all clear that the increase in financial inter-mediation would solve all the obstacles to capital formation faced by less developed financially repressed economies. The successful cases always mentioned by the advocates of liberalized financial markets, implemented interest rate reforms as part of an overall stabilization program. Apart from interest rate reforms these programs include more significant contributory factors, such as exchange reforms, monetary and fiscal policies and important amounts of foreign aid. Moreover, the interest rate reforms in these countries did not take the form of a once-for-all high interest rate strategy and complete financial deregulation, but were a transitional phase wherein the authorities steadily intended to normalize the interest rate level and structure.

Although financial repression is an obstacle to development in many countries, the experiences of financial reforms suggest that flexible rather than rigid policies are needed. There are not universally valid criteria to define interest rate policies, since these have to be determined in terms of an overall savings and development strategy.

## Notes

1. In fact, Kapur (1976) argues that the increased availability of funds for working capital purposes, made possible by financial liberalization, increases output and so reduces inflationary pressures given aggregate demand in the short-run. This is called the "intermediation-led" model of price stabilization.

2. Here money is defined broadly to include savings and time deposits as well as currency in circulation and demand deposits.

3. Chapter 6 discusses this issue in more detail.

4. Assuming the government has been spending its money efficiently.

5. According to the Keynesian approach savings and investment are not equal ex-ante, inasmuch as it is the level of income which moves in order to obtain ex-post the equality between savings and investment. The income level is determined by the aggregate demand which in turn is determined, among other things, by the investment level. Moreover, since savings are a function of the income level, a shift in the latter via changes in aggregate demand and investment implies a variation in the level of savings. Therefore, a higher level of investment today brings about a higher level of savings in the future.

6. This fact is explained because reserve requirements and credit ceilings in the official banking system are bound to be stricter than those in the unofficial market.

7. Assuming that the effect of high interest rates on aggregate supply is stronger than the effect on aggregate demand. See Bruno (1979) and Cavallo (1979) for an analysis of the link between credit and the supply side of the economy via the financing of working capital, a transmission channel shown to be of importance in LDC's.

8. The description of Taiwan's and South Korea's financial policies is based on the paper by Chandavarkar (1971).

9. The rationale of the interest rate policy which primarily accentuates deposit rates rather than loan rates comes from the need, in a inflationary context, to increase savings by diverting funds from consumption rather that by merely restraining investment.

10. In September 1965 the ceiling on time deposit interest rates at commercial banks doubled from 15% to 30%. Similarly, the rate on installment savings went form 10% to 30%, and lending rates were increased as well.

11. This statement is also supported by the relatively low observed interest rate savings elasticity over longer periods of time.

12. Nearly 6% of total Korean imports were financed by the U.S. in the decade 1953-63. Likewise, counterpart funds generated by foreign aid accounted for nearly 41% of the government's total budgetary receipts during 1957-63.

13. The next chapter presents a more detailed description of the main policies implemented in the Chilean economy during the period being studied: 1973-82.

# 3. CHILEAN ECONOMIC REFORMS
# AND THEIR IMPACT ON THE FINANCIAL SECTOR
# 1973-1982.

The period can be divided into four phases.[1]

## 3.1. Market Deregulation and Shock Treatment.
## September 1973-June 1976.[2]

The pre-1973 economy was characterized by high levels of inflation and great imbalance in the main economic variables. The first objective of economic policies in this phase was the restoration of equilibrium values for prices, the exchange rate, and interest rates; however, the evolution of wages was basically determined by government authorities. In October 1973 most prices were freed. Between September and October 1973 the exchange rate was devalued by 230%, and the interest rates charged by banks were raised sharply and afterwards freed in 1975.

The second objective of economic policies in this period was to reduce the public sector deficit and the relative size of the government by contracting government expenditures and increasing taxes.[3] The fiscal deficit decreased from 22.7% of GDP in 1973 to 2.9% of the GDP in 1975,[4] contributing to the drop in output observed in this phase.

The third objective was to prepare the economy for long-run structural changes. Some of the most important structural changes took place in the financial sector.

Prior to the financial reforms initiated in 1974 Chile's financial sector consisted of a Central Bank, a number of private commercial banks, a state commercial bank (Banco del Estado), and a savings and loan system (SINAP).[5] The SINAP system captured a significant portion of private financial savings due to its ability to issue indexed liabilities that were more liquid than the ones issued by other financial institutions.

The Chilean financial reform which started in May 1974 ended SINAP's monopoly of the issuance of attractive financial assets. As interest rate restrictions were lifted, considerable freedom was given for indexation in operations of over 90 days; moreover, quantitative credit controls on domestic currency were eliminated.

At the same time authorization was given for the creation of financial institutions (financieras) which were able to lend and borrow at flexible interest rates. The minimum capital these financial institutions were required to have was lower than in the case of banks and in the beginning they were not subject to reserve requirements.[6] This led to the establishment of a large number of financieras whose operations focused on very short-term assets and liabilities.

These regulatory changes, along with a modification of the indexing procedure on SINAP's liabilities, created serious difficulties for the SINAP system. By August 1974 a rapid transfer of funds from SINAP to the financieras had begun. These transfers accelerated during the first half of 1975 and in June 1975 the authorities began to limit withdrawals from SINAP. While the Central Bank eventually allowed SINAP depositors to convert their SINAP claims into Central Bank readjustable savings certificates, this process effectively eliminated the SINAP system as a viable financial intermediary.

The banks however, continued to be subject to a maximum legal monthly lending rate of 9.6%. In April 1975 when all interest rates were freed, the annual real interest rate jumped from negative values in 1974 and the first half of 1975 to more than 100% in the second half of 1975 and around 60% in 1976 (see table 1). The most striking characteristic of the behavior of the financial market during this period was the extremely high level of the real domestic interest rate and the large spread between the lending and deposit rates. Short-term operations predominated, with 30 days being the most common unit of time.

The first step toward international capital mobility was taken at the beginning of 1974 when article 14 of the Foreign Exchange Law was changed to allow individuals and firms to bring capital in freely and guarantee them access to the foreign exchange market for debt service under the same regulations in existence at the time of the inflow. The freedom to bring in these loans was, however, limited as regards minimum duration periods and the amounts involved. In addition to these general rules, several regulations affecting financial intermediaries were in effect. The banks, in particular, were subject to ceilings on the amount of their foreign borrowing.

At the end of 1973 most commercial banks were in state hands; during the last quarter of 1975 most of them were sold to the private sector. In the beginning the government intended to control the concentration of bank property. In pursuing this goal the authorities established a maximum amount of shares a person could buy.[7] Nevertheless, this regulation was violated and after some time abolished. The banks were sold to their former owners and to the new economic conglomerates. Moreover, in December 1974 the restrictions which prohibited foreign bank operations in Chile were eliminated. Furthermore, during those years the government returned private property that had been nationalized during the Allende administration to former owners and began the privatization of public enterprises.

The process of opening up the Chilean economy to foreign trade started in 1974. The first measures to be enacted consisted of the elimination of non-tariff restrictions then in effect and the reduction of all tariffs exceeding 200%. All quantitative restrictions were lifted, import prohibitions were eliminated, and excessive advance import deposits were abolished. Moreover, in March 1974 it was announced that through periodic reductions no tariff was to be higher than 60%. This measure would be fully effective in 1977. However, in 1975 a range of tariffs between 10% and 35% was established according to the type of manufactured goods. This range was to reach full effect in the first semester of 1978.

The exchange rate policy consisted of mini-devaluations. The exchange rate was changed between one and four times a month to reflect the medium term equilibrium of the foreign sector. The government announced that these mini-devaluations would be used to adjust the real exchange rate to compensate for the lifting of tariffs which began in 1974 and for fluctuations in world copper prices. The latter was important because in late 1974-early 1975 there was a substantial drop in the price of copper, which is the traditional exportable commodity that accounts for about half of total Chilean exports.[8]

The reduction in aggregate demand due to contractionary fiscal and monetary policies and the increased financial cost faced by domestic firms due to freed interest rates led to a severe recession in 1975. Real per capita gross domestic product decreased 14.4% in 1975; the unemployment rate rose from 4.8% in 1973 to 16.5% in 1975 and to 20.2% in 1976. Meanwhile, the inflation rate decreased from 605.9% in 1973 to 34.3% in 1975.

To summarize, the most important measures affecting the financial sector in this phase consisted of lifting interest rate controls. Given the conditions existent in the Chilean economy, this implies notably high rates. Capital mobility was gradually increased with many mechanisms being used as a brake on inflows and outflows in an attempt to control the money supply. Quantitative restrictions predominated and mostly affected the ability of domestic financial institutions to borrow abroad.

Table 1. MACROECONOMIC VARIABLES

| Year | Net inflow of cap. a/ (Article 14) | Total net cap.inflow | Surplus comm. acc. b/ | Surplus of current account | Changes in reserves c/ | Changes in monetary base d/ | Changes in money supply d/ $M_1$ | $M_2$ | Real Interest rate Peso loans | Dollar loans | Real exchange rate e/ | Growth rate of CPI |
|---|---|---|---|---|---|---|---|---|---|---|---|---|
| | (1) | (2) | (3) | (4) | (5) | (6) | (7) | (8) | (9) | (10) | (11) | (12) |
| | ( m i l l i o n   d o l l a r s ) | | | | ( 1 9 7 7 ) | % | % | % | % | % | % | % |
| 1975 | 63.0 | 262 | 76 | - 534 | - 262 | -12.6 | -21.3 | -10.1 | 121.0 f/ | - - | 32.1 | 343.3 |
| 1976 | 256.7 | 215 | 693 | 160 | 269 | 25.9 | - 0.9 | 25.8 | 51.2 | -21.1 | 25.9 | 197.9 |
| 1977 | 240.2 | 572 | 34 | - 551 | 157 | 3.7 | 17.8 | 42.8 | 39.4 | - 0.8 | 21.5 | 84.2 |
| 1978 | 599.0 | 1718 | - 376 | - 965 | 658 | 17.3 | 26.4 | 58.6 | 35.1 | 2.7 | 23.8 | 37.2 |
| 1979 | 717.2 | 1748 | - 276 | - 933 | 856 | 6.9 | 14.9 | 25.6 | 16.9 | - 0.1 | 23.2 | 38.9 |
| 1980 | 1249.6 | 2186 | - 528 | -1382 | 1079 | 4.6 | 21.5 | 17.3 | 12.2 | - 8.6 | 20.1 | 31.2 |
| 1981 | 1986.3 | 3190 | -1818 | -3348 | - 195 | -15.0 | - 0.5 | 40.4 | 38.8 | 11.6 | 16.9 | 9.5 |
| 1982 | 596.7 | 844 | 44 | -1693 | - 777 | -41.4 | -24.7 | -13.8 | 35.2 | 46.9 g/ | 19.6 | 20.7 |

Notes:

a/ This channel of capital inflows, known as article 14 of the Foreign Exchange Law has been the one most used by the private sector.

b/ FOB values.

c/ Absolute change with respect to December.

d/ Real rates of change from December to December.

e/ Nominal exchange rate times the relevant external price index for Chile deflated by the corrected-CPI (Ffrench-Davis, 1984 and Cortázar and Marshall, 1980).

f/ The real peso interest rate corresponds only to the second semester of 1975. Bank interest rates were controlled until April 1975.

g/ The real interest rate on dollar loans was estimated using the preferential exchange rate established by the government after June 1982.

Sources:

Col. (1), (2) and (5), Central Bank of Chile. Monthly Bulletin.

Col. (3) and (4), Central Bank of Chile. Balance of Payments.

Col. (6), (7) and (8), Estadísticas Trimestrales de Producto y Dinero para la Economía Chilena 1960-81. Universidad de Chile, 1980-84; Central Bank of Chile.

Col. (9) and (10), Arellano (1983).

Col. (12), Cortázar and Marshall (1980) and INE (Institute of National Statistics).

## 3.2. Curbing Cost-Push Factors and Expectations.
## June 1976-June 1979

This phase can be generally characterized by the de-indexation of some key prices to reduce cost pressures and brake inflationary expectations.

In spite of the "shock treatment" implemented in the previous phase, the rate of inflation accelerates during the first half of 1976. With no fiscal deficit and a lower rate of monetary growth, the economic authorities decided that the key variable to be used to reduce these expectations would be the exchange rate. In June of 1976 and March of 1977 the exchange rate was revalued 10% each time. The two revaluations helped to bring down the rate of inflation, but also brought about a reduction in the real exchange rate. That is, the price level did not fall as quickly as the exchange rate.

With the exception of these two revaluations the exchange rate policy consisted of what McKinnon (1981,1982) calls a "passively downward crawling peg". That is, every month the government devalued in a series of very small randomized steps by an amount equal to the difference between domestic and foreign inflation in the previous month.

The aim of bringing down inflation was also behind the tables of daily exchange rate adjustments for 1978 and 1979. This is what McKinnon (1982) calls "active downward crawl" a pre-announced calendar of ever decreasing rates of devaluation, i.e., the government pre-announces the crawl at a rate lower than current domestic inflation. Hence, the economic authorities abandoned the exchange rate policy aimed at compensating producers of import-competing goods for the effects of the drop in tariffs. Thereafter, the exchange rate was used as an anti-inflationary tool.

This new approach was complemented by more drastic tariff reductions. The announced range of tariffs between 10% and 35%, according to the type of manufactured goods, which was to be fully in effect in the first semester of 1978 was moved up. In August of 1977 it was already in effect. Three months later, in December of 1977, another modification of the tariff policy was introduced. The government announced a uniform tariff of 10% to be completely in effect by mid-1979, the only exception being cars (see table 2).

The tariff policy during the period 1974-79 was announced by phases evolving more and more towards free trade.

Important structural changes occurred during this period in the financial sector. In late 1976 a number of financieras went bankrupt, and as a result, a large shift of funds from the financieras to banks took place. The crisis was explained by the extremely high level of domestic interest rates and the reduced diversification of the financial institutions' loan portfolios. There was a close relationship between the debtors of these financial institutions and their owners. Faced with these facts the authorities argued that these were only isolated problems and that a stronger control of the financial market was not necessary. They opted for an increase in the minimum amount of capital required for a financiera, a requirement that was raised ten times; however, the new minimum was equivalent only to 75% of the minimum capital required for a commercial bank. At the same time the state offered official deposit insurance up to 2740 dollars of 1977 per depositor.

As noted before, one feature of the financial market in the first phase was the large spread between lending and deposit rates. It was argued that the size of the spread was due to the cost of holding reserves.[9] The authorities influenced this cost during 1977 and 1978 through interest paid by the Central Bank on reserves and through reductions in the reserve requirement ratio from 47% in January 1977 to 20% in December 1978. As a result the net spread tended to decline. During the period July 1979-July 1980 it averaged 0.5% per month (see table 2).

A major change in the openness of the capital account occurred in September 1977. Commercial banks were authorized to utilize article 14 of the Foreign Exchange Law for their capital inflows. Until 1977 the non-financial private sector borrowed abroad directly because of the restrictions domestic banks faced with respect to these operations. In 1978 the domestic financial sector began to acquire a larger role as a direct financial intermediary in private foreign borrowing. Loans brought in by the banks under article 14 were transferred at their external cost plus a spread to domestic firms. These loans were denominated in foreign currency, so that banks did not have to face the exchange risk.[10]

Moreover, the authorities started to relax capital controls with the objective of integrating domestic and international capital markets. Chilean capital controls consisted of: (i) Minimum maturity requirements on foreign borrowing. (ii) Limitations of the total amount of foreign borrowing. In general these limitations were expressed as a maximum ratio between foreign liabilities and the banks' capital and reserve accounts. (iii) Limitations on the amount of foreign funds that could be utilized each month or quarter.[11] The relaxation of capital controls took the form of raising the allowable ratio of foreign liabilities to the banks' capital and increments in the rates of utilization of foreign funds.

Table 2. TARIFFS LIBERALIZATION: 1973-79

(rates on CIF imports value)

| Dates | Maximum tariff | | Tariff mode | | Average | Total |
|---|---|---|---|---|---|---|
| | Rate | Percentage of all items | Rate | Percentage of all items | tariff | of items |
| | (1) | (2) | (3) | (4) | (5) | (6) |
| 12.31.73 | 220% | 8.0 | 90% | 12.4 | 94.0% | 5125 |
| 03.01.74 | 200% | 8.2 | 80% | 12.4 | 90.0% | 5125 |
| 03.27.74 | 160% | 17.1 | 70% | 13.0 | 80.0% | 5125 |
| 06.05.74 | 140% | 14.4 | 60% | 13.0 | 67.0% | 5125 |
| 01.16.75 | 120% | 8.2 | 55% | 13.0 | 52.0% | 5125 |
| 08.13.75 | 90% | 1.6 | 40% | 20.3 | 44.0% | 4958 |
| 02.09.76 | 80% | 0.5 | 35% | 24.0 | 38.0% | 4952 |
| 06.07.76 | 65% | 0.5 | 30% | 21.2 | 33.0% | 4956 |
| 12.23.76 | 65% | 0.5 | 20% | 26.2 | 27.0% | 4959 |
| 01.08.77 | 55% | 0.5 | 20% | 24.7 | 24.0% | 4981 |
| 05.02.77 | 45% | 0.6 | 20% | 25.8 | 22.4% | 4984 |
| 08.29.77 | 35% | 1.6 | 20% | 26.3 | 19.8% | 4985 |
| 12.03.77 | 25% | 22.9 | 15% | 37.0 | 15.7% | 4993 |
| 06.78 | 20% | 21.6 | 10% | 51.6 | 13.9% | 4301 |
| 06.79 | 10% | 99.5 | 10% | 99.5 | 10.1% | 4301 |

Source:    Ffrench-Davis (1980).

The result of these measures was a sustained capital inflow in 1978 and the first semester of 1979. The desire to control the money supply and thus inflation led the Central Bank to practice a great deal of fine tuning with respect to regulations of capital inflows. External inflows of capital facilitated the accumulation of reserves. The high level of reserves by mid-1979 made the transition to phase 3 possible.

### 3.3. Global Monetarism. June 1979-June 1982.[12]

It was argued that with free trade, domestic prices should follow international ones plus any devaluation. This reasoning led, after the government reduced the average nominal tariff from 94% in 1973 to a flat 10%, to the freezing of the nominal exchange rate at 39 pesos per dollar in June 1979. The approach which emphasized fiscal discipline and the right real exchange rate and which had prevailed in the previous years was replaced by the law of one price.[13]

Thus, the system used and the criterion on which adjustments in the exchange rate were based have been the result of a series of changing aims.[14] Originally, the aim was to establish rates which would reflect the medium term equilibrium of the foreign sector. Later, the exchange rate was used as a means of influencing inflationary expectations and, finally came the attempt to use the nominal exchange rate as a parameter determining the domestic price level. The effect of exchange rate variations on flows of capital was virtually excluded from the objectives on which exchange rate policy was based. In fact, the use of the exchange rate as a stabilization tool resulted in lower inflation. However, the pace at which this process occurred was insufficient to halt the decline of the economy's competitive position. As a result of the domestic inflation rate's being higher than external inflation up to the second half of 1981, and due to the appreciation of the dollar during that period, there was a rapid appreciation of the real exchange rate and therefore a deterioration of international competitiveness (see table 3).[15]

In April 1980 all quantitative restrictions on external borrowing under article 14 were eliminated. The only remaining restrictions were the limits on total borrowing which was 20 times capital plus reserves, and the minimum maturity requirement of two years.

During this phase (June 1977-81) the economy recovered from the 1975 recession. Per capita GDP was 15% higher in 1981 than in 1970, and the unemployment rate decreased slowly, reaching 15.6% in 1981.

Table 3. REAL EXCHANGE RATES [*]
1979.II = 1.0

|      |      | PM/PNI (1) | PX/PNI (2) | PT/PNI (3) | PM/PN12 (4) | PX/PN12 (5) | PT/PN12 (6) | PT/W (7) | PX/PM (8) |
|------|------|-----------|-----------|-----------|------------|------------|------------|----------|----------|
| 1975 | I    | 1.639 | 1.664 | 1.650 | 1.541 | 1.565 | 1.553 | 2.165 | 1.014 |
|      | II   | 1.662 | 1.689 | 1.675 | 1.545 | 1.571 | 1.559 | 2.487 | 1.015 |
|      | III  | 1.702 | 1.707 | 1.703 | 1.579 | 1.585 | 1.582 | 2.201 | 1.003 |
|      | IV   | 1.751 | 1.779 | 1.762 | 1.629 | 1.654 | 1.641 | 2.203 | 1.015 |
| 1976 | I    | 1.731 | 1.775 | 1.751 | 1.595 | 1.637 | 1.616 | 2.214 | 1.025 |
|      | II   | 1.528 | 1.524 | 1.525 | 1.407 | 1.404 | 1.405 | 1.922 | 0.996 |
|      | III  | 1.339 | 1.371 | 1.355 | 1.280 | 1.311 | 1.297 | 1.628 | 1.022 |
|      | IV   | 1.177 | 1.278 | 1.226 | 1.173 | 1.272 | 1.222 | 1.422 | 1.084 |
| 1977 | I    | 1.095 | 1.151 | 1.122 | 1.103 | 1.161 | 1.132 | 1.249 | 1.051 |
|      | II   | 0.903 | 0.992 | 0.946 | 0.940 | 1.031 | 0.984 | 1.117 | 1.095 |
|      | III  | 0.910 | 0.940 | 0.924 | 0.961 | 0.994 | 0.977 | 1.048 | 1.032 |
|      | IV   | 0.952 | 0.968 | 0.960 | 1.014 | 1.030 | 1.022 | 1.169 | 1.015 |
| 1978 | I    | 1.016 | 0.967 | 0.990 | 1.057 | 1.008 | 1.033 | 1.104 | 0.951 |
|      | II   | 1.015 | 0.907 | 0.959 | 1.048 | 0.937 | 0.991 | 1.076 | 0.892 |
|      | III  | 0.998 | 0.875 | 0.934 | 1.042 | 0.914 | 0.975 | 1.045 | 0.876 |
|      | IV   | 0.998 | 0.899 | 0.946 | 1.032 | 0.930 | 0.980 | 1.063 | 0.899 |
| 1979 | I    | 0.987 | 0.925 | 0.954 | 1.012 | 0.950 | 0.981 | 1.002 | 0.937 |
|      | II   | 1.000 | 1.000 | 1.000 | 1.000 | 1.000 | 1.000 | 1.000 | 1.000 |
|      | III  | 1.082 | 1.186 | 1.132 | 1.025 | 1.124 | 1.073 | 1.050 | 1.095 |
|      | IV   | 0.984 | 1.103 | 1.041 | 0.946 | 1.063 | 1.003 | 1.030 | 1.121 |
| 1980 | I    | 0.939 | 1.118 | 1.025 | 0.897 | 1.070 | 0.980 | 0.920 | 1.191 |
|      | II   | 0.925 | 1.092 | 1.003 | 0.880 | 1.039 | 0.957 | 0.864 | 1.178 |
|      | III  | 0.916 | 1.018 | 0.965 | 0.872 | 0.969 | 0.919 | 0.831 | 1.110 |
|      | IV   | 0.874 | 0.917 | 0.894 | 0.831 | 0.873 | 0.851 | 0.736 | 1.049 |
| 1981 | I    | 0.846 | 0.844 | 0.843 | 0.812 | 0.812 | 0.812 | 0.686 | 0.998 |
|      | II   | 0.784 | 0.775 | 0.779 | 0.767 | 0.761 | 0.764 | 0.630 | 0.989 |
|      | III  | 0.725 | 0.709 | 0.716 | 0.724 | 0.709 | 0.716 | 0.571 | 0.978 |
|      | IV   | 0.703 | 0.679 | 0.691 | 0.716 | 0.693 | 0.705 | 0.561 | 0.966 |

[*] The nominal exchange rate is defined as the number of units of domestic currency required to purchase one unit of foreign exchange rates.

Notes: PNI = Price index for nontradables obtained from the Cortázar-Marshall CPI based on the equation estimated in Corbo (1982).

PN12 = Aggregate of PM and price of differentiated tradables (Corbo, 1982).

PX = Export price index in pesos, measured as a Divisia Index of the major Chilean exports.

PM = Import price index in pesos, obtained as Divisia Index of the exchange rate adjusted industrial components of the wholesale price index for Argentina, Brazil, United States, Japan and Germany, using the structure of imports from each of those countries as a weighting base. The index is also adjusted for average custom duties.

W = Nominal Manufacturing Wage Rate.

PT = Geometric average of PX and PM with weights of 0.50 for each.

Source: V. Corbo (1982), PX excludes copper.

Two aspects of the Chilean financial reform need to be pointed out: the high real interest rate which averaged more than 30% between 1975 and 1981; and the large spread between ex-post peso real interest rate of dollar-denominated loans and the ex-post peso real interest rate of peso-denominated loans, despite relaxation of international capital controls (see table 1).

### 3.4. 1982 Crisis

Toward the end of 1981 it was clear that the key prices in the economy were out of equilibrium, especially the exchange rate and the interest rate. A fixed nominal exchange rate, during a period when domestic inflation was consistently above world inflation and the dollar was appreciating strongly, resulted in a large appreciation of the real exchange rate. The deterioration of international competitiveness generated large trade and current account deficits that were equivalent to 10.7% and 15.1% of GDP. Moreover, debt service over exports of goods and services was 57% in 1981, and the outstanding debt was approaching 50% of GDP. As a result capital inflows decreased, and a deficit in the overall balance of payments was generated. Faced with these facts the authorities decided to leave the correction of these disequilibria to the automatic adjustment mechanism implicit in the monetary approach to the balance of payments. According to this approach, any disequilibrium between income and expenditures is automatically corrected via changes in money, interest rates and prices.[16]

The automatic mechanism began to work. Reserves flowed out, the money supply fell, the interest rate rose and aggregate demand fell. However, the next step of the predicted adjustment, i.e., the fall in domestic prices was never sufficient to permit a devaluation of the real exchange rate. Therefore, the loss in competitiveness continued, and the economy entered into the second-worst recession of the century. The economic authorities insisted on the automatic mechanism, maintaining a fixed exchange rate system, as the way out of the recession.[17] The adjustment process was helped by a wage law reform necessary for the deflationary effects of the automatic adjustment mechanism to be realized. It was argued that the increase in real wages, which led to a wage-price spiral, contributed to real exchange rate revaluation during the period (Corbo, 1983). In fact, domestic prices did not respond and the revaluation of the real exchange rate continued.

An alternative policy could have included a change in financial policy, since it was likely that financial costs were much more important than labor costs in the production cost structure due to the rise in debt and in the interest rate.

The recession intensified to the point where the financial sector seriously deteriorated, many firms were not able to repay their debts due to high interest rates. In the second half of 1981 a financial crisis developed which resulted in eight financial institutions having to be rescued by the Central Bank and intervened by the Superintendencia de Bancos e Instituciones Financieras (Superintendency of Banks and Financial Institutions). These institutions held 8.4% of the financial system's total deposits in national currency.

The level of unpaid loans was so high in early 1982 that the government decided to "buy" them from the banking sector to avoid a major banking collapse. Later, in January 1983 the government took over a group of banks and financial institutions due to the existence of "serious deficiencies in the administration of these institutions".[19] The origin of such problems stemmed mainly from the volume of owner-related portfolios consisting of credits of uncertain recoverability which endangered the solvency and liquidity of such institutions (see table 4).[20] Five banks were intervened, three banks were liquidated, and two others were placed under the direct supervision of the Superintendencia de Bancos e Instituciones Financieras. These ten financial institutions accounted for 45% of the financial system's total capital and reserves. The banks of the two most important economic conglomerates were among the banks that were intervened. The situation created doubts and uncertainties with respect to the financial sector as a whole.

In June 1982 the exchange rate was devalued; however, the events that followed confirmed the fact that the devaluation was "too little too late". The loss of confidence produced a run on the peso which was followed by a sharp reduction of reserves and hence of the money supply which worsened the recession. In August 1982 the government shifted to a floating exchange rate, but in September they fixed it again, this time to a set of different currencies using a "crawling peg" system.[21]

To summarize, this phase is characterized by a loss of competitiveness, deficits in the balance of payments and extremely high interest rates, all of which produced a sharp fall in employment and industrial production by 1982 with a record number of bankruptcies and plant closings.[22] An important financial crisis developed, and the government had to intervene among the major financial institutions and commercial banks to avoid the break-down of the entire financial sector.

Table 4.  OWNER-RELATED LOANS IN FINANCIAL INSTITUTIONS

| Economic group | Financial   Institution | Owner-related loans as a % of the total loans of the institution | | Loans of the institut. as a % of total loans |
| --- | --- | --- | --- | --- |
| | | Jun. 82 | Dec. 82 | Dec. 82 |
| | **Banks:** | | | |
| BHC | Banco de Chile | 16.1 | 18.6 | 20.0 |
| | Banco BHC | 17.1 | 18.5 | 3.3 |
| | Banco Morgan Finansa | 7.2 | 7.0 | 1.6 |
| Cruzat-Larraín | Banco de Santiago | 44.1 | 42.3 | 11.8 |
| | Banco Hipotecario de Fomento Nacional | 28.2 | 27.4 | 3.3 |
| | Banco Colocadora Nacional de Valores | 23.4 | 23.8 | 2.0 |
| Edwards | Banco de A. Edwards | 15.9 | 14.9 | 3.1 |
| Errázuriz | Banco Nacional | 29.1 | 25.7 | 1.9 |
| Matte | Banco Industrial y de Comercio Exterior | 4.0 | 4.0 | 1.2 |
| Yarur | Banco de Crédito e Inversiones | 8.6 | 11.9 | 5.1 |
| Luksic and others | Banco Sudamericano | 13.0 | 14.8 | 4.6 |
| | Banco O'Higgins | 8.0 | 9.1 | |
| Gómez-Gallo | Banco Internacional | 20.1 | 22.8 | 1.1 |
| Concepción | Banco Concepción | 17.0 | 12.2 | 4.1 |
| Others | Banco del Trabajo | 5.1 | 1.6 | 2.9 |
| | Banco Unido de Fomento | 5.1 | 7.6 | 2.1 |
| | Banco del Pacífico | 10.6 | 10.0 | 0.5 |
| | Banco Osorno | 3.4 | 5.6 | 2.1 |
| | **Financieras:** | | | |
| Marín | Ciga S.A. | 26.3 | 24.1 | 0.2 |
| Others | Corfinsa S.A. | 19.3 | 20.8 | 0.1 |
| | Fusa S.A. | 21.0 | 22.5 | 0.4 |
| | Fintesa | 14.9 | 15.4 | 0.1 |
| | Condell | 11.5 | 6.8 | 0.2 |
| | Davens S.A. | 9.1 | 0.2 | 0.1 |
| | Comercial | 5.8 | 1.5 | 0.2 |
| | Mediterráneo | 0.2 | 0.1 | 0.1 |

Sources:   Economía y Negocios.  El Mercurio 03.15.83.  Información Financiera.
Superintendencia de Bancos e Instituciones Financieras.  December 1982.

## Notes

1. Foxley (1982).

2. Demand restrictions were so severe that the stabilization package which was implemented became known as the "shock treatment".

3. According to the evaluation of economic authorities the fiscal deficit and the size of the public sector were the principal causes of high inflation rates observed.

4. Foxley (1979).

5. The National Savings and Loan System was created in the sixties mainly for financing housing.

6. In 1975 the financieras were made subject to an 8% reserve requirement.

7. A private individual could not hold more than 1.5% of a bank's shares. An institution could not hold more that 3% of a bank's shares.

8. The below "normal" copper price during the period could justify some increase in foreign borrowing. The "normal" copper price has been estimated by Ffrench-Davis at $ .80 per pound in 1977 dollars.

9. See McKinnon (1981) and Sjaastad and Cortés (1978).

10. The authorization given to banks to act as intermediaries for foreign loans brought in under article 14 of the Foreign Exchange Law was known as "agreement 1196".

11. For a detailed analysis of the financial opening of the Chilean economy see Ffrench-Davis and Arellano (1983); also see Hoffmann (1979).

12. This concept is used in the same sense as it is used by Whitman (1975).

13. That is, on the stabilization side the old approach which emphasized fiscal discipline and the right real exchange rate was replaced by the new approach which gives prominence to purchasing power parity and the monetary approach. The old approach regards the money supply as the main determinant of the domestic price level and uses the exchange rate as a tool to meet balance of payment targets. In contrast,

the new approach favors manipulation of domestic credit expansion as the key to achieving balance of payment targets, and maintains that the exchange rate determines the price level. See Dornbusch (1982) for an analysis of these issues.

14. See Ffrench-Davis (1979).

15. The decrease in the real exchange rate produced the same effect on domestic activities as a further reduction in tariffs.

16. See Whitman (1975).

17. The authorities believed that a devaluation of the nominal exchange rate would not modify relative prices.

18. Past due loans as a percentage of banks' capital and reserves increased from 10.5% at the end of 1980, to 22.4% at the end of 1981 and to 47% in November 1983, reaching 113% in May 1983.

19. Carlos Cáceres, former president of the Central Bank of Chile and former Finance Minister.

20. Banks which belong to economic conglomerates or economic groups allocated loans of uncertain recoverability to firms owned by the same conglomerates.

21. The Chilean recession of 1982 has produced interesting economic literature. See, among others, Corbo (1983), Flaño (1982), Edwards (1985a), Arellano and Cortázar (1982), Muñoz (1982), Harberger (1985) and Morandé and Schmidt-Hebbel (1988).

22. During 1982 real per capita GDP fell 15.5%, the rate of unemployment increased to 27%, and the rate of inflation accelerated to 20.7%.

# 4. FINANCIAL REFORM AND THE MANUFACTURING INDUSTRY: 1977-82

## 4.1. Introduction

During the 1975-82 period Chile set an example of an economy which implemented financial reform as part of a more general program. The reform package included foreign trade liberalization, openness of the capital account of the balance of payments, deregulation of domestic commodity markets and short-run stabilization policies. As regards the financial market, the program included the liberalization of the interest rate, elimination of credit controls, a reduction in the rates of reserve requirements for savings and checking accounts, a significant slowing down of money issuance by the Central Bank, and opening up the financial system to inflows of foreign capital (see chapter 3).

The financial reform introduced important changes in the Chilean economy. Freeign bank interest rates led to extraordinarily high real interest rates, despite massive international capital inflows. The average real interest rate was higher than 30% during the 1975-82 period. Another important change was brought about by the paying out of interest on 30 day deposits, thus encouraging the intermediation of very short-term maturities. Finally, what has been called "portfolio liberalization", i.e., the elimination of regulations on credit allocation, was also brought about (see chapter 3).

Financial market liberalization along with the rest of the economic reforms undertaken produced important resource allocation effects. In this chapter we will contrast some of the objectives and the assumptions of the "repressionist paradigm" (see chapter 2) with the response its application elicited from the Chilean industrial manufacturing sector. It is interesting to analyze what happened to capital accumulation as regards productive enterprises, i.e., to what extent financial intermediation increased and contributed to financing investments in fixed capital by industrial firms. In other words, one of the aims of this chapter is to investigate to what degree the "conduit effect" of financial assets prevailed over the "competing-asset effect" in the financially liberalized Chilean economy.

It is likewise interesting to study how the financial structure of firms has been affected by the financial reform. What changes did the asset and liability structure and the cost and profit composition undergo during the internal financial market liberalization? In particular, it is interesting to investigate how the firms' liability composition between commercial credit (which is directly related to the enterprise turnover) and bank credit was influenced by the increase in financial intermediation. Financial market reform can be expected to have brought with it the increasing importance of bank credit compared to suppliers' credit.

It is also the aim of this chapter to investigate why so many manufacturing firms went bankrupt during the period. In fact, if the National Manufacture Census of 1967 is compared with the National Manufacture Questionnaire of 1982, it can be observed that the total number of industrial establishments decreased 13% between 1967 and 1981 (see Cortázar, Foxley and Tokman, 1984). Specifically, it is important to study to what extent high financial cost were at the root of bankruptcies and if they were, why enterprises contracted debts at real interest rates higher than an annual 30%, when these were real interest rates that productive firms were not able to pay. In order to find an answer it is important to consider the effect the internal recession which affected the Chilean economy in 1975 may have had on these enterprises, as well as the impact of the opening up to foreign trade. In other words, it is necessary to study the relationship between the depressed demand facing firms in 1975 and growing foreign competition as it affected their decision to go into debt.

Moreover, one should consider the incidence the loss of foreign market competitiveness may have had on the bankruptcy of these firms - a loss of competitiveness brought about by the fixed nominal exchange rate policy maintained between mid 1979 and mid 1982. Finally, one should also consider the impact the decrease in aggregate demand, as a product of the internal recession that came at the end of 1981, may have had on manufacturing firms.

The type of questions posed and the briefness of the period studied make it necessary to work with microeconomic data rather than with standard aggregate data. The source of information used consists of a sample of 233 publicly held corporations in the Chilean manufacturing industry during the period 1977-82. These corporations annually present their financial statements to the Superintendencia de Valores y Seguros (Superintendency of Holdings and Securities). This information was provided by the World Bank project on liberalization and stabilization policies in the Southern Cone countries (see Gálvez and Tybout, 1985).[1]

The sample corresponds to two groups of publicly held corporations, those who survived the 1977-82 period (190 corporations), and those who went out of business (43 corporations).

The chapter is organized in the following way: The second section describes the global evolution of the industrial sector during the period 1975-82. The objective of the third section is to give a general idea of the direction of the changes that occurred in the financial structure of the industrial firms post financial reform. The fourth section presents an analysis of the sample of manufacturing firms that survived the 1977-82 period. In the fifth section the results of the manufacturing firms who went bankrupt during the 1977-82 period are discussed. These results are compared with those of the non-bankrupt firms. Finally, the sixth section summarizes the main conclusions. Two appendices are attached, the first one presenting a summary of balance sheets and income statements of the firms. In the second appendix some concepts employed throughout the chapter are explained.

## 4.2. The Evolution of the Industrial Sector During the Period 1975-82[2]

The manufacturing industry was one of the sectors most affected by economic reforms during the 1975-82 period. The industry lost importance during this period in absolute and relative terms.

The share of industrial employment in total non-agricultural employment decreased from 24% in 1970-71 to 19% in 1981. A similar situation can be observed in relation to the share of industrial production in the total product. Here the share decreased from 25% in 1970-71 to 20.2% in 1982, measured in constant prices.

The industrial employment and production indexes also show a decline in the absolute role of industry throughout the 1975-82 period. The employment index of the Sociedad de Fomento Fabril (SOFOFA, a private industrial entrepreneurs' organization), the base of which is 1970-71=100, decreased from 101.2 in 1970 and 109 in 1974 to 72.4 in 1982. Moreover, the industrial production index of the National Bureau of Statistics (INE) the base of which is 1968=100, declined from 99.8 in 1970 and 108.3 in 1974 to 83.9 in 1982.

It can be argued that external conditions faced by the country during this period explain the poor performance of the industrial sector. However, the evolution of industrial employment and production in other Latin American countries points in another direction, indicating that the main factors responsible for events in the industrial sector may have been internal to the Chilean economy.[3]

Table 1.  SANTIAGO:  NUMBER OF INDUSTRIAL ESTABLISHMENTS.
(1967=100)

| | Type  of  industry   (SIIC  code) | 1981 |
|---|---|---|
| 31 | Food manufacturing, beverages and tobacco | 110 |
| 32 | Textiles, clothing and footwear | 64 |
| 33 | Wood, wood products, furniture and fixtures | 84 a/ |
| 34 | Paper and paper products | 103 |
| 35 | Chemicals and rubber products | 110 |
| 36 | Non-metallic mineral products | 74 |
| 37 | Base metals and metal products | 78 |
| 38 | Electrical and non-electrical machinery, appliances and equipment | 81 |
| 39 | Other manufacturing industries | 79 |
| | Total manufacturing industry | 87 |

Source:      Cortázar, Foxley and Tokman  (1984).

Notes:

a/           Although the 1975 internal recession did affect the wood and wood products industry, the important decline in the number of establishments in this industry is due to the fact that many establishments that were classified as industrial in the 1967 census were left out in the industrial questionnaire of 1982.

Table 2.   TOTAL NUMBER OF BANKRUPTCIES:  1973-82.
(Number of establishments)

| Year | |
|---|---|
| 1973 | 23 |
| 1974 | 75 |
| 1975 | 81 |
| 1976 | 131 |
| 1977 | 224 |
| 1978 | 312 |
| 1979 | 344 |
| 1980 | 415 |
| 1981 | 431 |
| 1982 | 810 |
| Total 1975-82 | 2748 |

Source:      Sindicatura Nacional de Quiebras.

As a result of the different shocks suffered by the industrial sector during the 1975-82 period many firms went bankrupt. In fact, if the National Manufacture Census of 1967 is compared with the National Manufacture Questionnaire of 1982 it can be observed that the total number of industrial establishments decreased 13% between 1967 and 1981. The industrial sectors most affected were: textiles, clothing and footwear industries (31, SIIC code) where the number of establishments decreased 36%; electrical and non-electrical machinery, appliances and equipment industries (38, SIIC code) where the number of establishments declined 19%; non-metallic mineral products industry (36, SIIC code) where the number of establishments diminished 26%; and the base metals and metal products industries (37, SIIC code) where the number of establishments decreased 22% (see table 1).[4]

There is a point that needs to be stressed: although bankruptcies occurred during the whole 1974-82 period, they were heavily concentrated in the last years of the period, mainly in 1982. The existent data about the total number of bankruptcies (industrial and non-industrial) confirms this fact (see table 2).

Unfortunately, similar information for the industrial sector is not available. However, there is some evidence which supports the hypothesis that most industrial bankruptcies were also concentrated in the very last years of the period mentioned. Comparing the Fourth National Manufacture Census of 1967 with the Fifth National Manufacture Census of 1979, the total number of establishments which employed 10 or more persons increased from 3461 to 3566, i.e., 4.2% between 1967 and 1979 (see PREALC, 1984; table 11). Nevertheless as has been pointed out before, they declined 13% between 1967 and 1981. Therefore, despite the negative effects of the economic shocks a relatively small number of firms went bankrupt during the first years of the period when the shocks took effect. It was not until 1982 that bankruptcies increased sharply.

To summarize, during the 1975-82 period a significant number of industrial firms went bankrupt, and the industrial sector suffered a significant decrease in its absolute and relative role in the national economy, both in terms of employment and production.

## 4.3. Financial Behavior of Manufacturing Firms Pre and Post-Financial Liberalization

The objective of this section is to give a very general idea of the direction of the changes domestic financial market liberalization elicited in the financial structure of manufacturing firms.

Unfortunately it has been impossible to find adequate information to carry out an exhaustive comparison of the enterprises' financial behavior, pre and post-financial liberalization.

Reference will be made below to two previous studies of the financial structure of manufacturing companies: One carried out by Insora (1962), and a financial analysis of a sample of manufacturing firms for the 1974-76 period (Trivelli, 1978).

In 1962 Insora did a study of the financing of Chilean industry wherein an analysis was made of the sources and uses of funds for a sample of national manufacturing industries. Even though results of the study do not yield the most fitting reference standard, as the last year studied was 1960 and also because of differences which might exist between that sample and the one used in current research, both results are compared. The uses to which the new resources obtained annually were assigned, as well as the sources from which they were derived, both in nominal terms, are contrasted (see table 3).[5]

As to the uses of funds, what seems most noteworthy is the increase observed in 1981 in the item 'other assets'; this item is basically made up of financial assets. The increase in other assets is compensated by a decrease in resources assigned to working capital.

Table 3. MANUFACTURING INDUSTRY. SOURCES AND USES OF FUNDS
(percentages)

|  | 1955-60<br>(1) | 1978<br>(2) | 1981<br>(3) |
|---|---|---|---|
| **Uses of Funds** | | | |
| Fixed capital | 22.7 | 31.3 | 37.4 |
| Working capital | 73.8 | 57.1 | 21.6 |
| Other assets | 3.0 | 9.5 | 32.2 |
| Decrease in liabilities | 0.5 | 2.1 | 8.8 |
| Total | 100.0 | 100.0 | 100.0 |
| **Sources of Funds** | | | |
| Short-term debt | 39.9 | 31.4 | 51.4 |
| Long-term debt | 1.4 | 24.5 | 44.1 |
| Net worth | 57.3 | 44.1 | 12.4 |
| Decrease in assets | 1.4 | 0.0 | 15.9 |
| Total | 100.0 | 100.0 | 100.0 |

Sources:

Col. (1):   Insora (1962).
Col. (2)(3): elaborated on the basis of data in this study.

In regard to sources of funds, historically speaking, companies worked with relatively high levels of short-term debt. Due to the existence of low or negative real interest rates this kind of credit had almost no cost for enterprises. On the other hand, the share of long-term debt in the total sources of funds was very insignificant. During the financial liberalization period new fund sources obtained underwent important changes; the share of long-term as well as short-term debt increased whereas net worth decreased notably in importance as a source of funds.[6]

The tax reform implemented in 1975 might have been a cause for the decrease of net worth share as a source of funds. This reform unifying income tax with additional tax, prevented shareholders in stock corporations from paying twice on the same profits. A taxation credit equivalent to 40% of perceived dividends was therefore established. This being so, the reform discouraged retention and profit reinvestment in the same enterprise while encouraging profit distribution; in this way, fund flow accrued in the financial market and the latter then took it upon itself to take care of allocation.

A more recent study of the financial behavior of manufacturing companies is Trivelli's (1978) for the 1974-76 period.

This author worked on the balances and profit and loss accounts of a sample of 274 stock corporations. Unfortunately, it is not possible to directly contrast the results obtained by Trivelli with those obtained in this study, because he employed the median as the population center whereas this study utilizes the weighted average. A brief review of the results obtained by Trivelli will, however, convey an idea of the manufacturing companies' financial situation in the period immediately prior to the period covered in this study.

During the 1974-76 period increased liquidity in the companies can be observed. The explanation for this lies in a short-term debt decrease due to a slump in the economic activity of companies during those years, and to an increase in monetary assets encouraged by high rates of interest offered in the short-term capital market.[7]

As regards contracting debt Trivelli (1978) points out that during 1974 and 1975 fewer than 50% of the enterprises had long-term debt whereas in 1976 this percentage did not exceed 30%. Throughout those three years large enterprises (measured according to sales and total-asset levels) increased their long-term debt due to their access to credit in foreign currency. However, small enterprises operated preferably without long-term debt because they had difficult access to this type of financing. Trivelli deduces that there is a close relationship between debt-contraction and size (measured according to total assets and sales levels). Small firms functioned with lower levels of debt-contracting than the large ones.

The analysis of the firms' profitability implies that in 1974 only 16.7% of the companies did not show a profit; this result contrasts with the values obtained for later years; 52.2% in 1975 and 57.2% in 1976. The strong profit decrease was principally due to the slump in sales as a result of the 1975 internal recession. Profit indexes calculated for companies grouped according to size, indicate that small companies obtained larger profits even if profits decreased during the three years studied. On the other hand, the large enterprises presented the lowest profit levels.

### 4.4. Financial Behavior of a Sample of Manufacturing Firms that Survived the 1977-82 Period

In order to analyse the evolution of the financial behavior of companies during the financial liberalization period microeconomic financial data is required.

The source of information used in this section consists of the financial balances and income statements of 190 publicly held corporations in the Chilean manufacturing sector. The sample corresponds to those firms that survived the 1977-82 period. Up to 1981 the sample includes closed and open stock corporations.[8] Unfortunately, it was not possible to obtain the 1982 balances for closed stock corporations because they were no longer public.[9]

This is why the size of the sample of surviving firms was reduced to 85 companies in 1982. In spite of this, results obtained from the group of manufacturing companies for which a 1982 balance was available are included.

The sample represents 56% of the total assets of establishments with 50 or more employees, based on the 1979 Manufacturing Industry Census.

The financial balance statement was completed with information on the companies that contracted debt in foreign currency. Debt in foreign currency with the national financial system is being included on the one hand; information on this has been available only since 1980.[10] On the other hand, direct debt of enterprises in the international financial market is included, this debt was contracted through article 14 of the Foreign Exchange Law.[11,12]

The company sample is quite representative as regards the industrial sector contracting debt in foreign currency. The percentage of debt with the financial system corresponding to indebtedness in foreign currency was

56.4% for the whole industrial sector, and 69.3% for the 1980 company sample. The figures were 62.6% and 69% in 1981 for the industrial sector and the company sample respectively.

Finally, it is important to explain that the aggregation of individual balances was carried out by adding these balances. Therefore, the largest companies have greater weight in the aggregate results.

We will now analyze results of the total balances of the sample of manufacturing firms which survived the 1977-82 period. Table 4 presents these results.[13]

As regards assets, an important increase can be observed for financial assets as a proportion of total assets, especially for investment in related companies.[14] Financial assets as a fraction of total assets increased from 17.8% in 1977 to 26.3% in 1981, and 34.6% in 1982 (col. 3, table 4).[15] The share of assets in related companies in total assets increased from 9.2% in 1977 to 23.7% in 1981, and to 28.1% in 1982 (col. 4).

One can also note a decrease in the relative importance of trade-stock (col. 6). This is an expected outcome in view of the high opportunity cost involved in keeping inventories in the context of extremely high real interest rates.[16]

Fixed assets (land, constructions, facilities, machinery and equipment) decrease their share in total assets. Nevertheless, long-term assets increased their share in total assets; the explanation arises from an accrual of long-term investments in related companies. This turn out to be a very important phenomenon during the 1977-82 period. Manufacturing firms, as a way of adjusting to the new economic conditions governing the financial market, increased their financial assets, the latter being more profitable owing to the circumstances, whereas investment in physical assets decreased. It can be argued that the noticeable increase in financial asset share was due to capitalization of the high returns obtained on those assets and not necessarily to an increase of investment in financial assets and a decline of investment in physical assets. Nevertheless, the results indicate a decrease of the fixed asset absolute level throughout the period. These diminished from a level equivalent to 100 in 1977 to 91.5 in 1981 (col. 2).

It could also be argued that this phenomenon does not only respond to the existence of better opportunities for investment detached from the main turnover of productive enterprises, but rather to an adjustment made by the firms to minimize the financial problems they encountered. Bernanke (1981) argues that companies normally react by reducing their investment in capital when faced with liquidity problems. However, the period analyzed in this study is a period of financial expansion during which firms did not face serious liquidity problems (liquidity problems started to appear at the end of this period, in 1981). Moreover, those companies with the worst liquidity problems were the very ones which went out of business during that period, and among these firms investment reduction in physical assets is not apparent with the same degree of intensity.[17]

Therefore, in the financially liberalized Chilean economy the "competing-asset effect" dominated over the "conduit effect" of financial assets stressed by the theories promoting domestic financial liberalization in LDC's (see chapter 2). The greater attractiveness of financial assets due to the increase in the real interest rate inhibited accumulation of physical capital in the manufacturing industry.[18]

Now, if we observe what happened with the companies' liabilities we notice an increase in credit from banks and financial institutions. The interpretation of this phenomenon is not quite clear, as it might be the product of an increase in financial intermediation brought about by financial reform, or it could reflect a process of interest accumulation. Bank debt as a proportion of total debt increased from 27.8% in 1977 to 46.7% in 1981, and to 53.9% in 1982 (col. 7).

Net worth remains stable during the period with a decrease in 1981 and 1982. This decline is the consequence of net profit reduction during those years (see appendix 1, table A1).

The profit and loss statement shows stability in gross margin behavior, with the exception of 1981 when a decrease may be noticed. The gross margin reflects changes in the relative prices of the product and non-financial inputs, and is therefore a dimension where movements in the exchange rate and labor cost may be influencing a firm's profitability (table A1).

Due to the high interest rates facing companies during the period, financial expenditures represent an important percentage of sales. Financial expenditures more than make up for the income generated outside the main turnover of the firm, and they are the main cause of non-operational negative results obtained each year.

Until 1981 the behavior of financial expenditures is the consequence of the decrease, from very high levels, of the domestic real interest rate and of the massive inflows of international capital into the country during those years.[19]

Companies with access to foreign credit changed the composition of their debt from domestic to foreign credit, as a way of reducing the average cost of that credit.[20] The indebtedness in foreign currency subscribed by companies through article 14 reached 4.1% of total debt in 1977, rising to 10.1% in 1981 (col. 8). On the other hand, the volume of debt in foreign currency with the internal financial system represented 31.3% and 32.2% of the firms' total debt in the years 1980 and 1981 respectively (col. 9).

A more fitting indicator of average conditions for credit access, is the financial cost. Financial cost is defined as the ratio between financial expenditure and average debt accruing interest; this indicator considers access to credit at different rates, terms, periods of remission and other conditions. Column 10 presents the financial cost for the sample of companies; they varied between 27.9% in 1977 and 14.9% in 1980, the latter having been the year when it reached its lowest level. An estimate for the average cost of credit for the whole economy during the period is also presented.[21,22]

In order to get an idea of the importance financial costs acquired during the period, we should remember that in 1970 the real average cost of bank credit was 4.9%, and the real maximum cost of bank credit was 6.7% (see Ffrench-Davis, 1973).

Until 1980 firms earned profits. In 1981 losses represented 8.4% of sales. This fact is due, principally, to financial expenditure and, on a smaller scale, to an increase in operational and administrative as well as sales costs. The net result obtained by firms in 1982 deserves extra comment. As may be seen in table A1 of appendix 1, negative non-operational results reach a figure equivalent to 28.6% of income for sales, implying a net loss equivalent to 20.8% of sales. Explanation of this result would seem to lie in the real devaluation of the peso that took place between June and December of 1982 which seriously affected firms with high leverage in foreign currency. In terms of the income statement, the effect of that devaluation is reflected in the financial expenditure and monetary correction accounts; hence, both accounts show a substantial increase in 1982 compared to 1981.[23]

The peso devaluation was, therefore, the main factor accounting for the poor results that 1982 balance sheets were projecting; just as the non-devaluation was the main factor responsible for results not having been worse in the previous years.

## 4.5. Financial Behavior of a Sample of Manufacturing Firms that went Bankrupt during the 1977-82 Period

The objective of this section is to investigate why manufacturing firms went out of business during the period under study. Specifically, the aim is to determine the role played by the liberalization of the domestic financial market in the behavior and bankruptcy of these firms. To this end the financial balances of a sample of 43 industrial manufacturing corporations that went bankrupt during the 1977-82 period are analyzed.

Table 4.   TOTAL SAMPLE OF INDUSTRIAL COMPANIES THAT SURVIVED THE PERIOD 1977-82.

| | Assets (1977=100) a/ | | as a % of total assets | | | | as a % of total debt | | | Financial costs b/ | Average cost of credit | Total debt / Net worth |
|---|---|---|---|---|---|---|---|---|---|---|---|---|
| | Total | Fixed | Financial assets | Assets in related firms | Total debt | Inventories | Debt with banks | Foreign currency debt (art.14) | Foreign currency debt with dom. fin. system | | | |
| | (1) | (2) | (3) | (4) | (5) | (6) | (7) | (8) | (9) | (10) | (11) | (12) |
| 1977 | 100.0 | 100.0 | 17.8 | 9.2 | 45.3 | 18.7 | 27.8 | 4.1 | n.a. | 27.9 | 17 | 0.8 |
| 1978 | 95.1 | 87.4 | 19.9 | 9.2 | 48.2 | 17.5 | 34.2 | 5.2 | n.a. | 26.1 | 19 | 0.9 |
| 1979 | 111.5 | 90.9 | 26.0 | 18.2 | 47.7 | 16.4 | 40.6 | 6.2 | n.a. | 20.0 | 10 | 0.9 |
| 1980 | 125.2 | 91.4 | 28.4 | 20.7 | 47.7 | 15.3 | 45.1 | 7.3 | 31.3 | 14.9 | 4 | 0.9 |
| 1981 | 117.7 | 91.5 | 26.3 | 23.7 | 55.7 | 13.4 | 46.7 | 10.1 | 32.2 | 19.4 | 25 | 1.3 |
| 1982 | -- | -- | 34.6 | 28.1 | -- | 10.1 | 53.9 | -- | -- | -- | -- | -- |

Sources:

Col. (8):   Elaborated on the basis of data from F. Rojas.

Col. (9):   Superirtendencia de Bancos e Instituciones Financieras.

Col. (11):   Ffrench-Davis and Arellano (1983).

Others:   Data base World Bank project on liberalization and stabilization policies in the Southern Cone countries.

Notes:

n.a.   Not available.

a/   Real values. Corrected CPI Cortázar and Marshall (1980) was used.

b/   Financial costs = $\dfrac{\text{Financial Expenses}}{\text{Average debt which draws interest}} \times 100$

The sample of firms has been classified into two groups: those which went out of business during 1979-80, and those which did so during 1981-82; in other words, those firms that went bankrupt before the internal recession that occurred in the second semester of 1981 and the peso devaluation of 1982, and those that faced these shocks. In the case of the first group of companies, financial balances corresponding to the year 1977, 1978 and 1979 are being worked on. For the second group of enterprises financial balances from 1977 to 1980 have been made available. This classification makes it possible to study the differences in the reasons for bankruptcy between both groups of firms.

On another level, this methodology makes it possible to compare the behavior of the companies that went out of business during the period with those that did not.

The whole sample of bankrupt firms has been disaggregated by industrial sectors (2 digits, SIIC) and year of bankruptcy (see table A3 in appendix 1). This classification makes it possible to determine the extent to which industrial sectors behaved differently. It also makes it possible to investigate within each industrial sector if there was dissimilar behavior among firms which went bankrupt in different years during the period.

As in the case of the sample of non-bankrupt firms, the aggregation of individual balances for each group of firms was carried out by adding the balances.

### 4.5.1. Financial Behavior of the whole Sample of Bankrupt Firms

In order to analyze the results, a standard of reference is needed. We will comparatively analyze below adjustments made by surviving enterprises and by enterprises that went out of business during the 1977-82 period.

Table 5 presents the main results. Tables A4 and A5 in appendix 1 sum up the general balance and the profit and loss statements for the group of firms that went bankrupt in 1977-80 and for those firms which did so in 1981-82, respectively.

The information available does not offer evidence of very different behavior between both groups of companies. In general, one might infer that companies that went bankrupt in the years 1979-80 show similar, even more extreme behavior than companies that went bankrupt in 1981-82. As they appear, we will comment on the differences between both groups of companies that went out of business.

Table 5. COMPANIES THAT WENT OUT OF BUSINESS VERSUS COMPANIES THAT SURVIVED THE 1977-82 PERIOD.

| | Assets (1977=100) a/ | | as a % of total assets | | | | as a % of total debt | | | Total debt |
|---|---|---|---|---|---|---|---|---|---|---|
| | Total | Fixed | Financial assets | Assets in related firms | Total debt | Inventories | Debt with banks | Foreign currency debt (art.14) | Foreign currency debt with dom. fin. system | Net worth |
| | (1) | (2) | (3) | (4) | (5) | (6) | (7) | (8) | (9) | (10) |
| **Companies that went bankrupt 1979-80** | | | | | | | | | | |
| 1977 | 100.0 | 100.0 | 0.0 | 0.0 | 85.2 | 27.2 | 41.5 | 8.2 | n.a. | 5.8 |
| 1978 | 118.5 | 128.2 | 0.5 | 0.4 | 81.6 | 22.6 | 43.9 | 0.0 | n.a. | 4.4 |
| 1979 | 105.9 | 114.7 | 0.0 | 0.0 | 104.9 | 25.2 | 60.1 | 6.4 | n.a. | 4.0 |
| **Companies that went bankrupt 1981-82** | | | | | | | | | | |
| 1977 | 100.0 | 100.0 | 1.5 | 0.3 | 60.8 | 20.8 | 41.9 | 0.8 | n.a. | 1.6 |
| 1978 | 103.7 | 91.5 | 0.8 | 0.5 | 69.3 | 21.5 | 49.5 | 1.8 | n.a. | 2.3 |
| 1979 | 115.6 | 92.9 | 10.2 | 9.9 | 68.9 | 21.2 | 52.4 | 0.5 | n.a. | 1.4 |
| 1980 | 107.1 | 93.3 | 7.1 | 6.5 | 71.1 | 19.7 | 51.1 | 1.9 | 17.8 | 1.5 |
| **Total sample Companies that survived** | | | | | | | | | | |
| 1977 | 100.0 | 100.0 | 17.8 | 9.2 | 45.3 | 18.7 | 27.8 | 4.1 | n.a. | 0.8 |
| 1978 | 95.1 | 87.4 | 19.9 | 9.2 | 48.2 | 17.5 | 34.2 | 5.2 | n.a. | 0.9 |
| 1979 | 111.5 | 90.9 | 26.0 | 18.2 | 47.7 | 16.4 | 40.6 | 6.2 | n.a. | 0.9 |
| 1980 | 125.2 | 91.4 | 28.4 | 20.7 | 47.7 | 15.3 | 45.1 | 7.3 | 31.3 | 0.9 |
| 1981 | 117.7 | 91.5 | 26.3 | 23.7 | 55.7 | 13.4 | 46.7 | 10.1 | 32.2 | 1.3 |

Sources: See table 4.

Notes: n.a. Not available.
a/ Real values. Corrected CPI Cortázar and Marshall (1980) was used.

It is appropriate here to recall the analysis of the sample of manufacturing firms which adjusted and survived internal financial market liberalization as well as the rest of the reforms. It made it possible to deduce that these enterprises adjusted through asset recomposition, that is to say, through an increase in their financial assets which conditions at that time made more profitable, and through a decrease in their physical assets. This is not what happened to companies that declared bankruptcy during those years. These companies did not substantially alter the composition of their assets between financial assets and physical assets; this situation was even more evident in the case of companies that went bankrupt before 1981-82. For those firms the real value of their fixed assets increased in absolute terms from 100 in 1977 to 114.7 in 1979.

An alternative way of verifying this phenomenon is observing the fraction of total assets which were kept in the form of financial assets for those companies. Manufacturing companies that went bankrupt in 1979-80 did not keep financial assets during 1977 and 1979, and only 0.5% of total assets were financial assets in 1978. On the other hand, companies that went bankrupt in 1981-82 kept 1.5% of their assets in the form of financial assets in 1977; this figure dropped to 0.8% in 1978, and increased to 10.2% in 1979 and to 7.1% in 1980. These figures contrast with those for the surviving firms where 17.8% of total assets were held in the form of financial assets in 1977; this share increased up to 26.3% in 1981 (col. 3, table 5).

Another element that points in the same direction is the behavior of inventories as a proportion of total assets. Bankrupt firms barely altered the share of inventories in total assets; however, firms that survived the period experienced a significant decrease in the share of inventories in total assets throughout those years. It is likely that surviving firms adjusted to new economic conditions by reducing their trade-stock to the maximum and investing the money in the short-run capital market which offered high real interest rates.

An important fraction of the total assets of the companies that went out of business was made up of commercial credit furnished by the companies. Just like the case of the surviving companies, one can not see a decrease in commercial credit as a result of more pronounced intermediation brought about by financial market liberalization (see tables A4 and A5).

Companies that went bankrupt in 1979 and 1980 have the largest part of their assets in the form of short-term assets; this is not the case for companies that went bankrupt at a later time, whose long and short-term asset composition is similar to that of firms that survived (tables A1, A4 and A5). When looking at the liabilities of these companies, one can pinpoint important differences between the ones that survived and those that went bankrupt. In the first place, the proportion of debt-financed assets is far higher in the case of companies that went out of business, especially in the case of companies that went bankrupt in 1979-80 (col. 5). The greatest part of the assets here are financed with short-term debt. The rather insignificant importance of net worth as a source of financing for companies that went bankrupt is probably due to the negative profitability obtained by these companies throughout the period.

The short-term debt of manufacturing firms that went bankrupt in the 1977-82 period is fundamentally made up of debts with banks and financial institutions and commercial debt with suppliers. Commercial debt, while it financed a significant proportion of corporate assets, did not decrease throughout the period; i.e., there was apparently no substitution between bank debt and commercial debt in the case of companies that went bankrupt. The share of bank debt in total debt is notoriously higher in the case of companies that went bankrupt than in those that did not; this probably was the result of interest accumulation incurred by the companies that went bankrupt.

It is notable to compare the total leverage (short-term debt plus long-term debt/net worth) of companies that went bankrupt versus those that survived the period. Companies that went bankrupt in 1979-80, had reached a debt level in 1977 equivalent to 5.8 times their net worth. On the other hand, companies that went bankrupt in 1981-82 had a debt level equivalent to 1.6 times their net worth, whereas enterprises that survived the period had a debt level equal to 0.8 times their net worth; only in 1981 total debt exceeded the net worth of the surviving enterprises (see col. 10). Manufacturing firms that did not manage to survive the period studied, already showed in 1977 a debt-level that was hard to bear. Generally speaking, it is very difficult for a company to obtain new financing under reasonable conditions when its balance sheet casts total leverage higher than 1. Nevertheless, these enterprises kept on contracting debts at ever-increasing cost. The fact that credit was quite short-term and that, furthermore, the economic authorities permanently held that interest rate would be falling shortly made interest accumulation appear to be a marginal phenomenon.[24]

When comparing income statements for the companies which had to declare bankruptcy with the statements from surviving firms, one can see that the companies which went bankrupt had to allocate a larger share of their operational income to marketing and administrative expenses. Surviving companies adjusted to the new economic situation (growing competition and rise in credit cost among others) by reducing administrative and marketing expenses as an item of their income. Companies that went out of business in 1979-80 are the ones that had the highest administrative and marketing expenses. This is partly offset by a decrease in operational cost which was, however, insufficient to absorb growing negative non-operational results (see tables A4 and A5).

Available evidence indicates that operational costs (i.e. direct cost, e.g., labor), are not responsible for the serious problems these companies faced which eventually forced them to declare bankruptcy. High financial expenses which continued to grow in relation to sales income are responsible for the losses sustained each year for those firms that went bankrupt. Contrary to the financial expenses of surviving companies, which until 1981 decreased in proportion to sales, in the case of bankrupt companies financial expenses increased every year in regard to operational income.

Companies that went bankrupt in 1979-80 apparently tried to improve their impaired situation by obtaining income from activities outside the main turnover of the firm (other inflows and outflows), but this did not make up for the high financial expenses the companies were facing. On the other hand, companies that went bankrupt in 1981-82 managed to survive that far, by decreasing their net losses during 1978 and 1979; in 1980, however, losses once again reached an approximate 6% of their sales income.

Observing balance sheets and profit and loss statements for bankrupt firms does not allow us to determine why they contracted debt to the extent they did. It is certain that excessive debt contracting and the high cost of credit were what finally forced these firms out of business; this, however, may be only a reflection of other problems. It is conceivable that these companies contracted debt in order to survive a time when they were being hit by the sudden opening up to foreign trade and the 1975 internal recession; it is also feasible that thanks to that debt-contracting some managed to function up to 1979-80 and some others lasted until 1981-82. An analysis of the results of this study appears to point in that direction.

Information available for the whole industrial sector seems to support the aforementioned. There was an important increase in debt-contracting with the financial system in this sector between 1974 and 1977. Debt in national currency increased in real terms 2.4 times, and it grew 5 times in foreign currency between 1974 and 1977.[25] During those years the industrial sector had to adjust to growing foreign competition and an important drop in aggregate demand, the aftermath of the 1975 recession. The adjustment was probably undertaken through debt, and the larger debts triggered an ever growing debt-contracting cycle due to high interest-accumulation.

In fact, this behavior would contribute to explaining the evolution of the firms' bankruptcies during the 1974-82 period. Firms did not go out of business when important economic shocks hit them at the beginning of the period, but later when debts accumulated and new economic shocks developed.[26]

## 4.5.2. Financial Behavior of Bankrupt Firms, Disaggregated by Industrial Sectors

The total sample of bankrupt firms has been disaggregated by industrial sectors (2 digits, SIIC) and according to year of bankruptcy. Data from surviving firms disaggregated by industrial sectors is utilized as a standard of reference. This information was obtained for three years. Figures for 1978 and 1979 come from the Industrial Questionnaires of the Sociedad de Fomento Fabril (SOFOFA); figures for 1981 come from a study by Espinosa, González and Morales (1982). It is important to point out that financial ratios for surviving firms can not be compared through the years. There are two reasons for this: on the one hand, the samples are not the same; on the other, SOFOFA computes financial ratios by adding individual balances for each sector, while Espinosa, González and Morales (1982) obtain financial ratios as the weighted average of the ratios of individual firms; the weights are the firm net worth's share. Espinosa, González and Morales' sample includes all manufacturing firms in operation on September 30, 1981.

Tables 6 to 9 sum up the results for each industrial sector for which a sample of bankrupt firms was available. The results for the paper and paper product industry (34) and the non-metallic mineral products industry (36) are not included due to the small sample size which is hardly representative of the bankrupt firms of these sectors (see table A3 in appendix 1).

The results from this disaggregation by industrial sectors enable us to conclude that there are no significant differences among bankrupt firms according to year of bankruptcy. In general, as was the case with the whole sample of bankrupt firms, companies that went bankrupt earlier in the period show more extreme behavior, mainly with respect to the indebtedness level. These firms also faced higher financial expenses in relation to their sales level, probably due to the high risk involved in the credit granted to these companies.

The industrial sectors with a higher incidence of financial problems seem to be textiles, clothing and footwear (32) and electrical and non-electrical machinery, appliances and equipment (38). These sectors were the hardest hit by the trade liberalization policy and also suffered a significant drop in prices during the period.[27]

It is likely that the high leverage level of the sectors mentioned above could be explained by an attempt to survive the negative impact of trade openness and the drop in their products' prices. These sectors have the highest financial expenses in proportion to their sales level and thus the worst non-operational results, which are the results bearing no direct relation to the firm's main turnover (see appendix 2). Negative non-operational results more than offset positive operational results in the textile, clothing and footwear industry (see table 7). In the case of the machinery, appliances and equipment industry negative non-operational results strongly lessened the profits of the firms that went bankrupt in 1981, and to a large extent they explain the negative profits of the firms that went bankrupt in 1982 (see table 9).

In general, the story the figures tell us is quite the same for all industrial sectors. These manufacturing firms were faced with important liquidity problems during the period, probably due to a drop in their sales as a result of the 1975 internal recession and increased foreign competition. The liquidity problems could have induced firms to take out loans in order to acquire working capital, and possibly, although this can not be inferred from the results, to adjust to the new economic conditions. Firms took loans at extremely high real interest rates, which is confirmed by the significant share of financial expenses in firms' total sales. A question arises: Why did firms borrow at such high real interest rates? The answer is simple: they did not have many alternatives: Either they had to borrow money to obtain necessary working capital or they had to go out of business.[28] Moreover, expectations played an important role, since the government continually announced the imminent decline in interest rates and a very brief 1975 economic recession. A rational basis for a firm's behavior could also be found in the lack of credibility in the sustainability of the import liberalization process.

High financial expenses represent an increasing proportion of bankrupt firms' sales. This fact explains the negative non-operational results and the low profitability of these firms. The continual losses experienced by the firms forced them to take out new loans, reaching leverage levels where total debt exceeded the firms' net worth, leaving the firm in an extremely weak financial position.

Firms' losses diminish during 1978 and 1979 in relation to 1977, and increase again in 1980. These increases in firms' losses may be due to the effects of the fixed exchange rate policy followed by the government between June 1979 and June 1982, together with very low import tariffs. This policy had the same effect on domestic activities as further reductions in tariffs.

Table 6. SAMPLE OF MANUFACTURING FIRMS IN THE FOOD MANUFACTURING BEVERAGE AND TOBACCO INDUSTRIES. (31).

| | Enterprises that went bankrupt in 1981 | | | | Enterprises that went bankrupt 1982 | | | | Surviving enterprises | | |
|---|---|---|---|---|---|---|---|---|---|---|---|
| | 1977 | 1978 | 1979 | 1980 | 1977 | 1978 | 1979 | 1980 | 1978 | 1979 | 1981 |
| -Liquidity (acid test) | 0.32 | 0.68 | 0.40 | 0.14 | 0.62 | 0.54 | 0.29 | 1.08* | 0.75 | 0.82 | 0.81 |
| -Indebtedness | | | | | | | | | | | |
| Total debt/sales (%) | 42 | 41 | 55 | 80 | 21 | 31 | 48 | 43 | 50 | 63 | - |
| Total debt/net worth | 1.1 | 1.2 | 1.7 | 3.3 | 0.7 | 1.4 | 14.7* | 1.5 | 0.7 | 0.8 | 1.2 |
| Bank debt/total debt (%) | 39 | 12 | 83 | 34 | 39 | 51 | 48 | 62 | - | - | - |
| -Financial expenses/sales (%) | 5 | 9 | 16 | 23 | 1 | 2 | 13 | 9 | - | - | 14 |
| -Profitability | | | | | | | | | | | |
| Operational results (%) | | | | | | | | | | | |
| Sales | 2 | 17 | 13 | 12 | -3 | -1 | -15 | -6 | - | - | - |
| Non-operational results (%) | | | | | | | | | | | |
| Sales | -7 | -14 | -11 | -28 | 0 | -1 | -1 | 7 | - | - | - |
| Net profits (%) | | | | | | | | | | | |
| Sales | -6 | 2 | 1 | -17 | -3 | -3 | -17 | 2 | 5 | 7 | 1 |
| Net profits (%) | | | | | | | | | | | |
| Net worth | -15 | 7 | 2 | -67 | -10 | -12 | -517* | 6 | 6 | 12 | -10 |

Sources: - Bankrupt firms: Data base World Bank project on liberalization and stabilization policies in the Southern Cone countries.

- Surviving firms year 1978: Quarterly Industrial Questionnaires (SOFOFA). Indexes of profits over sales and profits over net worth consider firms that had profits (81.5% of the sample) and those that had losses (18.5% of the sample). All indexes are obtained from the sum of individual balances.

- Year 1979: Quarterly Industrial Questionnaire (SOFOFA). Indexes of profits over sales and profits over net worth only consider firms that had profits (84.4% of the sample). All indexes are obtained from the sum of individual balances.

- Year 1981: Espinosa, González and Morales (1982). All indexes are weighted average of the ratios of individual firms belonging to the sector, the weights are each firm's net worth share.

## Notes on table 6

Some results for the firms that went bankrupt in 1982 have been singled out with an asterisk because they require an explanation.

(a) The liquidity coefficient 1.08 for 1980 is explained by the fact that a large firm from the sample significantly decreased its short-term debt with banks and financial institutions and increased its short-term assets that year.

(b) Total leverage (total debt/net worth) for 1979 seems to be too high (14.7); the explanation is an important increase in total debt and a decline in net worth that year.

(c) The ratio of profits over net worth for 1979 (-517) is explained by a decrease in net worth and a significant increase in the industrial sector's losses.

Table 7. SAMPLE OF MANUFACTURING FIRMS IN THE TEXTILE, CLOTHING AND FOOTWEAR INDUSTRIES (32)

| | Enterprises that went bankrupt in 1979-80 | | | Enterprises that went bankrupt 1981 | | | | Enterprises that went bankrupt 1982 | | | | Surviving enterprises | | |
|---|---|---|---|---|---|---|---|---|---|---|---|---|---|---|
| | 1977 | 1978 | 1979 | 1977 | 1978 | 1979 | 1980 | 1977 | 1978 | 1979 | 1980 | 1978 | 1979 | 1981 |
| -Liquidity (acid test) | 0.64 | 0.83 | 0.74 | 0.88 | 0.80 | 0.67 | 0.60 | 0.50 | 0.49 | 0.56 | 0.79 | 0.69 | 0.74 | 2.52 |
| -Indebtedness | | | | | | | | | | | | | | |
| Total debt/sales (%) | 141 | 167 | 169 | 121 | 105 | 136 | 132 | 107 | 99 | 116 | 154 | 46 | 90 | 108 |
| Total debt/net worth | 6.2 | 4.6 | -230.2* | 2.5 | 3.9 | 1.5 | 5.3 | 4.6 | 7.7 | 15.0* | -61.5* | 0.7 | 0.8 | 0.5 |
| Bank debt/total debt (%) | 45 | 46 | 63 | 38 | 44 | 43 | 44 | 34 | 36 | 60 | 46 | - | - | - |
| -Financial expenses/sales (%) | 11 | 26 | 21 | 18 | 14 | 33 | 24 | 11 | 8 | 13 | 34 | - | - | 13 |
| -Profitability | | | | | | | | | | | | | | |
| Operational results (%) Sales | 6 | 13 | 9 | 14 | 14 | 16 | 5 | 1 | 8 | 5 | 7 | - | - | - |
| Non-operational results (%) Sales | -12 | -19 | -17 | -22 | -15 | -4 | -21 | -18 | -8 | -14 | -30 | - | - | - |
| Net profits (%) Sales | -5 | -6 | -9 | -8 | -1 | 2 | -17 | -17 | -2 | -9 | -23 | 1 | 2 | 0 |
| Net profits (%) Net worth | -22 | -18 | 1222* | -16 | -4 | 3 | -67 | -72 | -17 | -117* | 902* | 1 | 3 | -3 |

Sources:
- Bankrupt firms: Data base World Bank project on liberalization and stabilization policies in the Southern Cone countries.

- Surviving firms year 1978: Quarterly Industrial Questionnaires (SOFOFA). Indexes of profits over sales and profits over net worth consider firms that had profits (81.5% of the sample) and those that had losses (18.5% of the sample). All indexes are obtained from the sum of individual balances.

- Year 1979: Quarterly Industrial Questionnaire (SOFOFA). Indexes of profits over sales and profits over net worth only consider firms that had profits (84.4% of the sample). All indexes are obtained from the sum of individual balances.

- Year 1981: Espinosa, González and Morales (1982). All indexes are weighted average of the ratios of individual firms belonging to the sector, the weights are each firm's net worth share.

## Notes on table 7

Results requiring an explanation have been singled out with an asterisk.

1. Firms that went bankrupt in 1979-80.

(a) The leverage ratio (total debt/net worth) for 1979 (-230.2) is negative and extremely high. In effect, total debt increased that year; however, more important is the fact that net worth is negative and lower in absolute value than total debt.

(b) The ratio of profits over net worth for 1979 (122) is very high and positive; the explanation can be found in a significant increase in total losses and the existence of negative net worth, lower in absolute value than total losses.

2. Firms that went bankrupt in 1982.

(a) Total leverage is high for 1979 and very high and negative for 1980. In 1979 the sector's total debt increased and at the same time net worth declined, which explains the result obtained (15). In 1980 the result (-61.5) is explained by a significant decrease in net worth which turned negative.

(b) The ratio of profits over net worth is negative and very elevated in 1979, and high and positive in 1980. In 1979 losses increased and net worth declined, which explains the results for that year (-117). In 1980 losses continued increasing and the sector's net worth was negative which, in turn, explains the results for that year (902).

Table 8.   SAMPLE OF MANUFACTURING FIRMS IN THE CHEMICAL AND RUBBER PRODUCTS INDUSTRIES (35)

| | Enterprises that went bankrupt in 1981 | | | | Enterprises that went bankrupt 1982 | | | | Surviving enterprises | | |
|---|---|---|---|---|---|---|---|---|---|---|---|
| | 1977 | 1978 | 1979 | 1980 | 1977 | 1978 | 1979 | 1980 | 1978 | 1979 | 1980 |
| -Liquidity (acid test) | 0.54 | 0.59 | 0.64 | 0.23 | 0.45 | 0.51 | 0.48 | 0.53 | 0.91 | 0.42 | 1.4 |
| -Indebtedness | | | | | | | | | | | |
| Total debt/sales (%) | 103 | 108 | 143 | 260 | 130 | 95 | 91 | 81 | 33 | 109 | 23 |
| Total debt/net worth | 4.4 | 6.0 | 7.9 | 18.8 | 1.2 | 1.3 | 1.4 | 1.3 | 0.5 | 0.8 | 0.2 |
| Bank debt/total debt (%) | 20 | 19 | 5 | 6 | 52 | 67 | 60 | 62 | - | - | - |
| -Financial expenses/sales (%) | 1 | 4 | 15 | 41 | 6 | 11 | 5 | 5 | - | - | 1 |
| -Profitability | | | | | | | | | | | |
| Operational results (%) | | | | | | | | | | | |
| Sales | 0 | 0 | - 5 | - 26 | 7 | 5 | 11 | 9 | - | - | - |
| Non-operational results (%) | | | | | | | | | | | |
| Sales | - 1 | - 4 | 2 | 21 | - 17 | - 9 | - 10 | - 10 | - | - | - |
| Net profits (%) | | | | | | | | | | | |
| Sales | - 2 | - 4 | - 3 | - 4 | - 10 | - 3 | 1 | - 2 | 1 | 5 | - |
| Net profits (%) | | | | | | | | | | | |
| Net worth | - 6 | - 21 | - 18 | - 31 | - 9 | - 4 | 1 | - 3 | 1 | 11 | 3 |

Sources: - Bankrupt firms: Data base World Bank project on liberalization and stabilization policies in the Southern Cone countries.

- Surviving firms year 1978: Quarterly Industrial Questionnaires (SOFOFA). Indexes of profits over sales and profits over net worth consider firms that had profits (81.5% of the sample) and those that had losses (18.5% of the sample). All indexes are obtained from the sum of individual balances.

- Year 1979: Quarterly Industrial Questionnaire (SOFOFA). Indexes of profits over sales and profits over net worth only consider firms that had profits (84.4% of the sample). All indexes are obtained from the sum of individual balances.

- Year 1981: Espinosa, González and Morales (1982). All indexes are weighted average of the ratios of individual firms belonging to the sector, the weights are each firm's net worth share.

Table 9.   SAMPLE OF MANUFACTURING FIRMS IN THE ELECTRICAL AND NON-ELECTRICAL MACHINERY, APPLIANCE AND EQUIPMENT INDUSTRIES (38)

| | Enterprises that went bankrupt in 1979-80 | | | Enterprises that went bankrupt 1981 | | | | Enterprises that went bankrupt 1982 | | | | Surviving enterprises | | |
|---|---|---|---|---|---|---|---|---|---|---|---|---|---|---|
| | 1977 | 1978 | 1979 | 1977 | 1978 | 1979 | 1980 | 1977 | 1978 | 1979 | 1980 | 1978 | 1979 | 1981 |
| -Liquidity (acid test) | 0.49 | 0.54 | - | 0.76 | 0.90 | 0.89 | 0.74 | 0.68 | 0.58 | 0.73 | 0.78 | 0.83 | 0.97 | - |
| -Indebtedness | | | | | | | | | | | | | | |
| Total debt/sales (%) | 277 | 151 | - | 86 | 108 | 159 | 242 | 76 | 91 | 96 | 82 | 57 | 69 | 115 |
| Total debt/net worth | 5.2 | 1.3 | - | 4.6 | 7.7 | 7.3 | -10.4* | 1.2 | 2.4 | 3.1 | 2.7 | 0.9 | 1.1 | - |
| Bank debt/total debt (%) | 0 | 0 | - | 35 | 54 | 72 | 61 | 85 | 45 | 27 | 17 | - | - | - |
| -Financial expenses/sales (%) | 21 | 3 | - | 16 | 21 | 25 | 58 | 5 | 13 | 22 | 22 | - | - | - |
| -Profitability | | | | | | | | | | | | | | |
| Operational results (%) Sales | 31 | -1 | - | 17 | 22 | 2 | -9 | 2 | 3 | 13 | 17 | - | - | - |
| Non-operational results (%) Sales | -24 | 5 | - | -17 | -17 | -21 | -48 | -9 | -14 | -21 | -11 | - | - | - |
| Net profits (%) Sales | 7 | 3 | - | 1 | 5 | 4 | -58 | 2 | -12 | -7 | -1 | 5 | 5 | - |
| Net profits (%) Net worth | 13 | 3 | - | 3 | 33 | 18 | 248* | 3 | -32 | -23 | -3 | 7 | 8 | - |

Sources: - Bankrupt firms: Data base World Bank project on liberalization and stabilization policies in the Southern Cone countries.

- Surviving firms year 1978: Quarterly Industrial Questionnaires (SOFOFA). Indexes of profits over sales and profits over net worth consider firms that had profits (81.5% of the sample) and those that had losses (18.5% of the sample). All indexes are obtained from the sum of individual balances.

- Year 1979: Quarterly Industrial Questionnaire (SOFOFA). Indexes of profits over sales and profits over net worth only consider firms that had profits (84.4% of the sample). All indexes are obtained from the sum of individual balances.

- Year 1981: Espinosa, González and Morales (1982). All indexes are weighted average of the ratios of individual firms belonging to the sector, the weights are each firm's net worth share.

## Notes on table 9

Figures requiring an explanation have been singled out with an asterisk. They correspond to firms that went bankrupt in 1981.

(a) The total leverage for 1980 (-10.4), high and negative, is explained by a decrease in net worth which is negative that year. The drop in net worth more than offsets the decline in total debt.

(b) The ratio of net profits over net worth is extremely high and positive for 1980 (248). The explanation can be found in the existence of large losses and negative net worth which is lower in absolute value than the losses.

Comparing the financial ratios of bankrupt firms with those of surviving firms, it can be noted that the results tend to support what has been pointed out above.

Bankrupt firms had more serious liquidity problems than surviving firms. The latter also show lower indedtedness levels than bankrupt firms, as in only two sectors and in one year total debt slightly exceeded firms' net worth (see tables 6 and 9). Financial expenses as a proportion of total assets are higher for bankrupt firms than for firms which survived the period. This is true even when comparing 1980 figures for bankrupt firms (the year when domestic and external interest rates reached their lowest values during the 1977-82 period) with 1981 figures for non-bankrupt firms, a year when domestic and external interest rates increased, generating a general rise in financial expenses.

Non-bankrupt firms present greater profitability than the firms that went out of business, even though surviving firms show a decline in profitability in 1981, possibly as a result of the fixed exchange rate policy and the internal recession that started in the second semester of that year.

## 4.6. Summary and Conclusions

One of the main findings in this study is that the most important adjustment made by manufacturing companies which survived the 1977-82 period was the change in composition of their assets. The share of financial assets in total assets increased, while the share of physical assets in total assets decreased during the period. This phenomenon not only represents capitalization of interests accrued by financial assets, but also reflects a drop, in absolute terms, of fixed asset investment. For the whole sample of manufacturing firms, fixed assets dropped from a level equivalent to 100 in 1977, to 91.5 in 1981 (table 4). This means that market signals, mainly high interest rates, led productive enterprises to decrease their investment in physical capital and to increase financial intermediation. Financial liberalization, as it was implemented in the Chilean economy, made for decapitalization and speculation instead of real investment.

Moreover, when comparing the behavior of companies that survived the 1977-82 period with companies that went bankrupt, one can see that the latter did not alter the composition of their financial and physical assets as a way of adjusting to the new situation in the domestic financial market. It may be that these companies were incapable of adjusting by recomposing their assets as the rest of the manufacturing firms did, because they were facing serious economic difficulties. The impossibility of adjusting hindered them from taking advantage of profitable speculative opportunities offered by the market, which might eventually have reduced their losses.

In short, bankrupt firms which had the worst liquidity problems during the period did not reduce their investment in physical assets as surviving companies did. Hence, it can not be argued that the change in asset composition responds to a normal adjustment made by companies to minimize liquidity problems they encountered.

Therefore, in the financially liberalized Chilean economy the "competing-asset effect" dominated the "conduit effect". The greater attractiveness of financial assets due to the increase in the real interest rate inhibited accumulation of physical capital. This phenomenon was not exclusive to the industrial manufacturing sector, but applied to the Chilean economy as a whole where the increasing significance of financial investment as well as a low level of real investment can be observed during the 1977-82 period (see table A2). In other words, contrary to the postulation of advocates of financial liberalization in LDC's, domestic financial reform brought about a perverse financial deepening in the Chilean case.

In general, the manufacturing sector faced very high financial costs during the period. Financial cost for the sample of manufacturing companies which survived the period varied between 27.9% in 1977 and 14.9% in 1980; these are extraordinarily high figures when compared to the maximum real cost of bank credit in 1970 which amounted to 6.7%. High financial costs were accountable for the negative non-operational results of manufacturing firms during all of the years studied. Nevertheless, until 1981 firms did not sustain the heavy losses they started suffering in 1981. That year the manufacturing sector faced an important deterioration of its competitiveness in international markets, an abrupt increase in interest rates, and the initial consequences of the internal recession.

The sample of firms which survived the period presents an increase in debt contracting with banks and financial institutions, and in relative terms, a drop in commercial credit (suppliers' credit). The origin of this phenomenon is not quite clear, but it could be the result of an increase in financial intermediation as an effect of financial market liberalization, or it could be the result of an interest-accumulating process which was weighing heavily on the companies.

In regard to companies that went bankrupt during the 1977-82 period, available evidence indicates that there were no fundamental differences between the two groups into which bankrupt firms were classified, regarding both the reason for bankruptcy and the companies' financial behavior during the period. Nevertheless, companies that went bankrupt in 1979-80 show more extreme behavior than the companies that went bankrupt at a later date (1981-82), especially regarding the level of indebtedness.

Companies that went out of business during the period show extraordinarily high total leverage. The total debt of these firms amply exceeded their 1977 net worth; this situation showed no signs at all of improving in the following years. Available evidence indicates that it was excessive indebtedness which finally brought about their failure. The financial expenses paid by these firms were high and growing with respect to income obtained, thus generating losses in each one of the years studied. However, direct costs as a percentage of sales income were reduced annually, denoting that labor costs did not play a decisive role in the negative profitability and subsequent bankruptcy of these companies.

The short-run debt of bankrupt firms was composed by debts with banks and financial institutions and commercial debt (suppliers' credit). Commercial debts did not decline throughout the period; apparently there was no substitution between bank credit and commercial credit as a result of financial liberalization.

The analysis of bankrupt firms disaggregated by industrial sectors (2 digits, SIIC) shows that the textile, clothing and footwear industry (32) and the electrical and non-electrical machinery, appliance and equipment industry (38) are the ones with the most pronounced financial problems. These industrial sectors were strongly affected by trade reform, since they had traditionally enjoyed a high degree of protection; furthermore, these sectors suffered an important drop in prices during the period.

One question comes up. Why did bankrupt firms go into debt at the levels they did? It has been argued that the companies contracted debts when faced by growing foreign competition and the 1975 internal recession in order to overcome what they believed to be temporary difficulties. This debt contracting was possible due to domestic financial market liberalization. This behavior would contribute to explaining the evolution of bankruptcies during the 1974-82 period. Firms did not go out of business when important economic shocks hit them at the beginning of the period, but later when financial debts accumulated and new economic shocks developed. The results of this study point in this direction. Chapter 6 and 7 explore this issue in more detail.

APPENDIX 1

Table A1. TOTAL SAMPLE OF INDUSTRIAL ENTERPRISES THAT SURVIVED THE 1977-82 PERIOD.
(percentages)

Balance Sheet

|  | 1977 | 1978 | 1979 | 1980 | 1981 | 1982 |
|---|---|---|---|---|---|---|
| Assets | 100.0 | 100.0 | 100.0 | 100.0 | 100.0 | 100.0 |
| Short-term assets | 46.4 | 49.9 | 43.4 | 42.6 | 38.7 | 38.8 |
| Cash | 1.1 | 1.2 | 1.3 | 1.1 | 1.1 | 0.6 |
| Time deposits | 2.2 | 3.6 | 4.0 | 4.4 | 3.8 | 4.8 |
| Credits | 15.5 | 18.3 | 17.7 | 15.8 | 17.2 | 17.2 |
| Short-term investment | 6.3 | 7.1 | 2.4 | 3.9 | 1.8 | 1.7 |
| Inventories | 18.7 | 17.5 | 16.4 | 15.3 | 13.4 | 10.1 |
| Others | 2.3 | 2.2 | 1.6 | 2.1 | 1.4 | 3.7 |
| Long-term assets | 53.6 | 50.1 | 56.6 | 57.4 | 61.3 | 61.2 |
| Long-term credit related firms | 0.0 | 0.0 | 0.3 | 0.7 | 1.5 | 2.0 |
| Investment related firms | 7.8 | 6.7 | 15.4 | 17.4 | 17.7 | 18.5 |
| Fixed assets | 43.9 | 40.3 | 35.8 | 32.0 | 34.1 | 31.7 |
| Others 1/ | 1.9 | 3.1 | 5.1 | 7.3 | 8.0 | 9.0 |
| Short-term debt | 31.5 | 31.2 | 27.4 | 28.0 | 31.7 | 34.3 |
| Debt with public | 4.4 | 2.6 | 0.7 | 1.2 | 3.1 | 1.5 |
| Banks | 6.5 | 9.2 | 8.6 | 10.1 | 12.4 | 14.2 |
| Commercial | 13.0 | 12.7 | 11.1 | 9.9 | 8.8 | 11.5 |
| Others 2/ | 7.6 | 6.7 | 7.0 | 6.8 | 7.4 | 7.1 |
| Long-term debt | 13.8 | 17.0 | 20.3 | 19.3 | 23.6 | 25.9 |
| Banks | 6.0 | 7.2 | 10.9 | 11.4 | 13.6 | 18.3 |
| Debt with related firms | 0.0 | 0.0 | 2.0 | 2.5 | 3.7 | 1.7 |
| Others 3/ | 7.8 | 9.8 | 7.4 | 5.4 | 6.3 | 5.9 |
| Net worth | 54.7 | 51.8 | 52.3 | 52.7 | 44.7 | 39.8 |
|  |  |  |  |  |  |  |
| Profit and loss statement |  |  |  |  |  |  |
| Sales | 100.0 | 100.0 | 100.0 | 100.0 | 100.0 | 100.0 |
| Operational costs | - 69.1 | - 71.1 | - 69.5 | - 71.8 | - 74.8 | -69.1 |
| Gross margin | 30.9 | 28.9 | 30.5 | 28.2 | 25.2 | 30.9 |
| Marketing and administ. costs | - 20.1 | - 17.0 | - 17.2 | - 17.6 | - 19.3 | - 21.1 |
| Financial expenses | - 9.4 | - 7.1 | - 6.0 | - 5.5 | - 10.8 | - 19.3 |
| Other inflows and outflows | 6.1 | 4.4 | 3.6 | 2.3 | - 0.1 | 5.0 |
| Monetary correction | - 2.9 | - 1.9 | - 0.7 | 0.7 | - 1.0 | - 14.3 |
| Operational result | 10.7 | 11.9 | 13.3 | 10.6 | 5.9 | 9.8 |
| Non-operational result | - 6.1 | - 4.6 | - 3.1 | - 2.5 | - 11.8 | - 28.6 |
| Taxes | - 1.9 | - 3.2 | - 3.6 | - 2.9 | - 2.5 | - 2.0 |
| Net profits | 2.7 | 4.0 | 6.7 | 5.2 | - 8.4 | - 20.8 |

Source: Data base World Bank Project on liberalization and stabilization policies in the Southern Cone countries.

1/ Lower investment value, higher investment value, long-term debtors, intangible, amortization.

2/ Dividends to be paid, provisions, retentions, income tax, debt with related companies, income perceived in advance and deferred taxes.

3/ Documents payable in the long-term, debt with the public, other creditors, provisions.

Table A2.  REAL AND FINANCIAL INVESTMENT.

| Year | Gross investment in fixed assets | | | Investment in financial assets | | |
|------|----------------------------------|--|--|--------------------------------|--|--|
|      | Thousands of million 1977 pesos | 1977=100 | %GDP | Thousands of million 1977 pesos | a/ 1977=100 | %GDP |
| 1970 | 57.8 | 150.9 | 20.4 | 7.7 | 70.7 | 2.7 |
| 1977 | 38.3 | 100.0 | 13.3 | 10.9 | 100.0 | 3.8 |
| 1978 | 45.0 | 117.5 | 14.5 | 11.1 | 101.9 | 3.6 |
| 1979 | 52.6 | 137.3 | 15.6 | 28.0 | 256.9 | 8.3 |
| 1980 | 64.1 | 167.4 | 17.6 | 26.7 | 245.0 | 7.3 |
| 1981 | 74.8 | 195.3 | 19.5 | 22.6 | 207.3 | 5.9 |
| 1982 | 49.4 | 129.0 | 15.0 | 9.8 | 89.9 | 3.0 |

Sources:    ODEPLAN.  National Accounts  (new version).
            Central Bank of Chile.  Monthly Bulletin.

a/    Excludes public sector money and corporations' shares.

Table A3.   SAMPLE CLASSIFICATION OF INDUSTRIAL FIRMS THAT WENT BANKRUPT
DURING THE 1977-82 PERIOD.

| SIIC | Enterprises that went bankrupt in 1979-80 | Enterprises that went bankrupt 1981 | Enterprises that went bankrupt 1982 | Total |
|------|------|------|------|------|
| 31   | 0 | 2 | 3 | 5 |
| 311  | 0 | 2 | 3 |   |
|      |   |   |   |   |
| 32   | 7 | 4 | 6 | 17 |
| 321  | 4 | 1 | 2 |   |
| 322  | 1 | 3 | 2 |   |
| 323  | 1 | 0 | 0 |   |
| 324  | 1 | 0 | 2 |   |
|      |   |   |   |   |
| 34   | 0 | 1 | 1 | 2 |
| 342  | 0 | 1 | 1 |   |
|      |   |   |   |   |
| 35   | 0 | 3 | 6 | 9 |
| 351  | 0 | 1 | 0 |   |
| 352  | 0 | 1 | 1 |   |
| 355  | 0 | 1 | 1 |   |
| 356  | 0 | 0 | 4 |   |
|      |   |   |   |   |
| 36   | 1 | 0 | 0 | 1 |
| 362  | 1 | 0 | 0 |   |
|      |   |   |   |   |
| 38   | 1 | 2 | 6 | 9 |
| 381  | 1 | 1 | 3 |   |
| 382  | 0 | 1 | 1 |   |
| 383  | 0 | 0 | 2 |   |
|      |   |   |   |   |
| Total | 9 | 12 | 22 | 43 |

Table A4. TOTAL SAMPLE OF INDUSTRIAL COMPANIES THAT WENT BANKRUPT
DURING THE 1979-80 PERIOD.
(percentages)

Balance Sheet

|  | 1977 | 1978 | 1979 |
|---|---|---|---|
| Assets | 100.0 | 100.0 | 100.0 |
| Short-term assets | 66.6 | 65.6 | 65.1 |
| Cash | 2.1 | 1.0 | 1.3 |
| Time deposits | 0.0 | 0.0 | 0.0 |
| Credits | 32.2 | 36.9 | 36.4 |
| Short-term investment | 0.0 | 0.1 | 0.0 |
| Inventories | 27.2 | 22.6 | 25.2 |
| Others | 5.1 | 5.0 | 2.2 |
| Long-term assets | 33.4 | 34.4 | 34.9 |
| Long-term credit related firms | 0.0 | 0.0 | 0.0 |
| Investment related firms | 0.0 | 0.0 | 0.0 |
| Fixed assets | 30.7 | 32.0 | 32.8 |
| Others 1/ | 2.7 | 2.4 | 2.1 |
| Short-term debt | 63.0 | 55.6 | 59.3 |
| Debt with public | 0.0 | 0.0 | 3.5 |
| Banks | 27.0 | 19.8 | 19.8 |
| Commercial | 21.8 | 19.5 | 17.4 |
| Others 2/ | 14.2 | 16.3 | 18.5 |
| Long-term debt | 22.3 | 25.9 | 45.6 |
| Banks | 8.3 | 16.0 | 43.2 |
| Debt with related firms | 0.0 | 0.0 | 0.0 |
| Others 3/ | 14.0 | 9.9 | 2.4 |
| Net worth | 14.7 | 18.5 | - 4.9 |
| | | | |
| Profit and loss  statement | | | |
| Sales | 100.0 | 100.0 | 100.0 |
| Operational costs | - 70.0 | - 63.8 | - 66.7 |
| Gross margin | 30.0 | 36.2 | 33.3 |
| Marketing and administrative costs | - 24.6 | - 29.3 | - 26.4 |
| Financial expenses | - 9.2 | - 19.1 | - 22.1 |
| Other inflows and outflows | - 0.7 | 4.7 | 3.5 |
| Monetary correction | - 1.9 | 1.3 | - 0.7 |
| Operational result | 5.4 | 6.9 | 6.9 |
| Non-operational result | - 11.8 | - 13.1 | - 19.3 |
| Taxes | 0.0 | 0.0 | - 0.5 |
| Net profits | - 6.4 | - 6.2 | - 12.9 |

Source:     Data base World Bank Project on liberalization and stabilization policies
            in the Southern Cone countries.

1/    Lower investment value, higher investment value, long-term debtors, intangible,
      amortization.

2/    Dividends to be paid, provisions, retentions, income tax, debt with related
      companies, income perceived in advance and deferred taxes.

3/    Documents payable in the long-term, debt with the public, other creditors,
      provisions.

Table A5. TOTAL SAMPLE OF INDUSTRIAL COMPANIES THAT WENT BANKRUPT
DURING THE 1981-82 PERIOD.

(percentages)

Balance Sheet

|  | 1977 | 1978 | 1979 | 1980 |
|---|---|---|---|---|
| Assets | 100.0 | 100.0 | 100.0 | 100.0 |
| Short-term assets | 45.8 | 50.6 | 48.8 | 49.3 |
| Cash | 1.3 | 1.0 | 1.0 | 0.9 |
| Time deposits | 1.0 | 0.1 | 0.1 | 0.1 |
| Credits | 20.6 | 26.6 | 23.5 | 25.6 |
| Short-term investment | 0.2 | 0.2 | 0.1 | 0.5 |
| Inventories | 20.8 | 21.5 | 21.2 | 19.7 |
| Others | 1.9 | 1.3 | 2.8 | 0.9 |
| Long-term assets | 54.2 | 49.4 | 51.2 | 50.7 |
| Long-term credit related firms | 0.0 | 0.0 | 0.2 | 0.0 |
| Investment related firms | 0.3 | 0.5 | 9.3 | 5.0 |
| Fixed assets | 47.3 | 42.1 | 36.7 | 41.7 |
| Others 1/ | 6.6 | 6.8 | 5.0 | 4.0 |
| Short-term debt | 42.2 | 46.0 | 47.6 | 51.6 |
| Debt with public | 0.0 | 0.0 | 0.0 | 0.0 |
| Banks | 12.4 | 17.6 | 20.2 | 21.9 |
| Commercial | 19.3 | 18.9 | 17.4 | 18.2 |
| Others 2/ | 10.5 | 9.5 | 10.0 | 11.5 |
| Long-term debt | 18.7 | 23.3 | 21.3 | 19.5 |
| Banks | 13.0 | 16.8 | 16.0 | 14.5 |
| Debt with related firms | 0.0 | 0.0 | 0.1 | 0.9 |
| Others 3/ | 5.6 | 6.5 | 5.2 | 4.1 |
| Net worth | 39.1 | 30.7 | 31.1 | 28.9 |
|  |  |  |  |  |
| Profit and loss statement |  |  |  |  |
| Sales | 100.0 | 100.0 | 100.0 | 100.0 |
| Operational costs | - 75.1 | - 73.1 | - 72.0 | - 71.8 |
| Gross margin | 24.9 | 26.9 | 28.0 | 28.2 |
| Marketing and administrative costs | - 18.0 | - 19.7 | - 20.6 | - 21.5 |
| Financial expenses | - 8.0 | - 10.0 | - 13.0 | - 15.3 |
| Other inflows and outflows | - 4.3 | - 2.0 | - 2.1 | - 4.5 |
| Monetary correction | - 0.7 | 2.6 | 4.5 | 7.0 |
| Operational result | 6.9 | 7.2 | 7.4 | 6.7 |
| Non-operational result | - 13.0 | - 9.0 | - 10.6 | - 12.8 |
| Taxes | - 0.3 | - 0.4 | - 0.4 | - 0.3 |
| Net profits | - 6.4 | - 2.6 | - 3.6 | - 6.4 |

Source:    Data base World Bank Project on liberalization and stabilization policies
in the Southern Cone countries.

1/    Lower investment value, higher investment value, long-term debtors, intangible,
amortization.
2/    Dividends to be paid, provisions, retentions, income tax, debt with related
companies,   income perceived in advance and deferred taxes.
3/    Documents payable in the long-term, debt with the public, other creditors,
provisions.

# APPENDIX 2

In this appendix some concepts used throughout the chapter are defined, the contents of some financial statement-accounts made clear and the calculation of the companies' financial costs explained.

## 1. Other non-operational inflows and outflows

This refers to such income as royalties, bonuses, profits on the sale of fixed assets and income not proceeding from sales of the common company-turnover. Furthermore, income obtained through share-transfers as well as dividends earned through investment, presented under the heading of short-term investment and investment in other companies, is being considered.

Non-operational outflows consider losses incurred in investment and fixed-asset sales, excluding financial expenditures.

## 2. Financial expenses

Expenses incurred by the company when obtaining financial resources are being represented by the interest, subsidies and commissions resulting from any kind of debt.

The way interest is recorded in the financial expense account varies according to the type of debt:

(a) Debt expressed in UF[29]: In this case only the interest is registered in the financial expense account. Debt correction due to UF variation is recorded in the monetary correction account.

(b) Debt expressed in pesos at a fixed interest rate: In this case the amount equivalent to the nominal rate stipulated is the amount acknowledged; the CPI variation is deducted from it (when nominal interest is lower than the CPI variation, the latter is subtracted only up to the agreed amount of interest, i.e., at the maximum, financial expenses will be zero). CPI variation for the amount of the debt is recorded in the monetary correction account.

(c) Debt in foreign currency: Interest is calculated on the capital expressed in pesos, using the exchange rate in force at closure of the period covering the financial statements. Also, variation of the exchange rate during the period for the amount of the debt is recorded in the monetary correction.

## 3. Monetary correction

There are three large items which must be monetarily corrected in the companies' financial statements: real assets and liabilities; sales, administrative and marketing expenses and operational cost (income statement); and the net cash balances held by the companies.

Real assets and liabilities are monetarily adjusted according to CPI variation. Monetary correction associated with adjustment for the income statement and the companies' net cash balances are obtained by net worth difference. The difference between the adjusted initial net worth and the final net worth yielding the financial year's real profit is calculated. Monetary correction corresponding to the income statement adjustment and net monetary balances is equivalent to the difference between the financial year's real profit and the profit forecast by the income statement.

Until 1981, according to the Superintendencia de Valores y Seguros, companies would calculate amounts corresponding to the monetary correction account according to the procedure described above. That is to say, until that year the monetary correction account simultaneously reflected the effect of inflation on the company's net cash balances and the income statement monetary correction.

In 1981, the Superintendencia de Valores y Seguros decided to explicitly apply the monetary correction of the income statements. Therefore, sales, marketing and administrative expenses and operational costs are adjusted according to the monetary variation experienced by the CPI used to correct assets and liabilities. It is supposed that all transactions are undertaken by the last day of the month. This monetary correction applied to the profit and loss statement must be entered into accounts by means of charges and credits in the monetary correction account. After monetarily adjusting the profit and loss statement, the monetary correction account will only reflect the effect of inflation on net cash balances kept by the company.

Hence, as from 1981, the monetary correction account represents the real net result, the outcome of the variation suffered by money's purchasing power.

## 4. Financial assets

The following are considered financial assets: Bank deposits, tradable holdings (short-term investments), short-term documents and accounts receivable from related companies, investment in related companies, investment in other companies, long-term documents and accounts receivable from related-companies.

## 5. Assets in related companies

According to the criterion established by the Superintendencia de Valores y Seguros, investment in related companies corresponds to investment in shares or bonds in any other kind of firm exceeding 10% of the social capital of the issuing company or 5% of the investing entity's total assets.

## 6. Depreciation

Depreciation is deducted from fixed assets on the general balance sheet. The concept of depreciation being used is accumulated depreciation; i.e., the period's depreciation is unknown; information is only found in the statement of sources and uses of funds.

Depreciation is included in administrative and marketing expenses in the income statement (i.e., it is included in the company's indirect costs).

## 7. Financial cost

The financial cost reflects average conditions of access to credit on behalf of the company and the average debt explicitly earning interest.

$$\text{Financial cost} = \frac{\text{Financial expenses}}{(\text{debt}_{t-1}(1+\pi) + \text{debt}_t)1/2} \times 100$$

where $\pi$ is inflation for the period.

December to December CPI variation corrected by Cortázar and Marshall (1980) was considered because the official price index was manipulated and understates inflation.

Average debt was calculated on the basis of the existing debt-stock to December each year. Only that part of the debt explicitly earning interest is considered since it is the only interest recorded in the financial expenses. Whenever the debt does not explicitly earn interest, it is included in the debt-stock (for example, short-term suppliers' credit).

The debt explicitly earning interest is made up of the following accounts: Short-term liabilities with banking and financial institutions, long-term portion of the debt with banking and financial institutions falling due in less than one year, liabilities with the public (business effects), liabilities with the public (bonds), long-term liabilities due in one year, short-term documents and accounts payable to related companies, long-term liabilities with banks and financial institutions, long-term liabilities with the public (bonds), documents payable in the long-term, various long-term creditors, long-term documents and accounts payable to related companies.

## 8. Operational Result

This corresponds to the aggregate of all the accounts related to the main turnover of a firm. It includes sales income, operational costs, and marketing and administrative costs.

## 9. Non-operational Result

This is related to the aggregate of all accounts independent from the main turnover of a firm. It includes financial income, profits obtained from investment in related firms, other income outside the main firm turnover, losses from investment in related firms, financial expenses, other expenses outside the main turnover of the firm and monetary correction.

## 10. Acid Test

This is an index of a firm's liquidity which considers the fact that not all short-term assets can be easily converted into cash. For instance, inventories held by firms sometimes can not be sold because they become obsolete or their sale price is much lower than their price on the books. The acid test is computed in the following way:

$$\frac{\text{Short-term assets} - \text{inventories}}{\text{Short-term liabilities}}$$

## Notes

1. I would especially like to thank professor Vittorio Corbo who kindly allowed me to use this information.

2. The main reference for this section are: Cortázar, Foxley and Tokman (1984) and PREALC (1984).

3. See Cortázar, Foxley and Tokman (1984).

4. It is important to note that these figures underestimate the number of industrial bankruptcies because they do not include 1982. That year the Chilean economy had a record number of bankruptcies. See table 2.

5. The analysis of sources and uses of funds is commonly made by drafting a table with the net changes occurring in different assets, liabilities and equity between the current balance and the previous one. Variations in each account are categorized according to whether they correspond to sources or uses of funds.

6. In 1960 the maximum real cost of bank credit was 24.7%, an unusually high figure. In terms of sources of funds, the high real interest rate implied a decrease in the share of short-term debt that year to 23.7% and an increase in the share of net worth in the same year to 74.9%.

7. It should be remembered that in April 1975 commercial banks were authorized to freely contract for an interest rate. The real interest rate paid for deposits reached 21.9% in the second half of 1975.

8. Open stock corporations are companies that publicly offer their shares in accordance with Stock Market Law, where at least 10% of the subscribed capital belongs to a minimun of 100 shareholders, and there are 500 or more shareholders.

   Closed stock corporations are companies that do not fit the qualifications in the preceding paragraph; nevertheless they may freely submit to the norms governing open stock corporations.

9. By reason of the securities law of October $22^{nd}$, 1981, closed stock corporations are not required to send statements to the Superintendencia de Valores y Seguros.

10. This foreign currency debt corresponds to article 14 for foreign loans intermediated by the domestic banking system. Since September 1977 domestic banks have been allowed to intermediate foreign loans brought in under article 14. See chapter 3.

11. Article 14 of the Foreign Exchange Law establishes that private individuals or enterprises may freely intern capital guaranteeing them access to the foreign exchange market for their service, subject to legal norms in force at the time of the inflow.

12. I wish to thank Flavio Rojas, who allowed me to use this information.

13. Table A1 in appendix 1 sums up basic information arising from the balances and income statements for the total sample of firms.

14. According to the Superintendencia de Valores y Seguros' definition related-company investment corresponds to investment in shares or bonds in any type of company, above 10% of the social capital of the issuing company, or 5% of the whole of the investing company.

15. See appendix 2 for a definition of these concepts.

16. It can be argued that companies were adjusting their trade-stock accumulated during the 1975 internal recession towards an equilibrium level. However, this is not too probable since companies normally adjust their stock-level from year to year, and the results show a continuous stock-drop during the period.

17. The financial behavior of the companies that went bankrupt during the 1977-82 period is analyzed in the next section.

18. This was not a peculiar phenomenon in the industrial manufacturing sector. For the Chilean economy as a whole the increasing significance of financial investment and low level of real investment can be observed during the 1977-82 period. Table A3 in appendix 1 shows the evolution of real and financial investment of the whole economy during the 1977-82 period.

19. The internal real interest rate decreased from 39.4% in 1977 to 35.1% in 1978, 16.9% in 1979, and 12.2% in 1980; it increased to 38.8% in 1981 and 35.2% in 1982.

20. Real interest rates in pesos charged for credits in foreign currency were: -0.8% in 1977, 2.7% in 1978, -0.1% in 1979, -8.6% in 1980, 11.6% in 1981, and 46.9% in 1982 (considering the preferential exchange rate).

21. This estimate was obtained from Ffrench-Davis and Arellano (1983).

22. It strikes one that financial cost calculated for the sample of manufacturing firms are systematically larger than the estimate of the average cost of credit. The explanation lies in the fact that the average cost of credit does not necessarily represent a typical debtor's financial cost since not all economic agents have equal access to the cheapest credit. On the other hand, financial cost-calculation may be overestimated due to the fact that debts contracted at shorter than one-year terms do not appear on the balance-sheet even though interest paid throughout the year for the debt does appear. Finally, to the extent that enterprises prepay part of their debts on the days just prior to the balance-sheet (in order to improve it), the estimate of financial costs may be inflated.

23. The Superintendencia de Valores y Seguros establishes specific norms in relation to foreign currency debts held by stock corporations. In particular, the contracted interest value multiplied by the capital expressed in pesos is recorded as financial expenditure. The capital is expressed in pesos according to the exchange rate currently in force at the time of closure of the period the financial statements are covering. Next, the variation experimented by the exchange rate during the period multiplied by the amount of the debt is charged to the monetary correction account. See appendix 2.

24. Interest accumulation was far from being a marginal phenomenon in the Chilean economy. If interest collected for credits in national currency between 1977 and 1982 are accumulated, one reaches a figure equivalent to 72% of total debts in that currency at the end of 1982. See Arellano (1983).

25. Financial information. Superintendencia de Bancos e Institutiones Financieras.

26. Chapters 6 and 7 explore this issue in detail. Chapter 6 studies the financial behavior of a sample of import-competing, export and non-tradable manufacturing firms. Chapter 7 is a case study of a subsam-

ple of manufacturing firms whose balance sheets are analyzed in this chapter.

27. In fact, an important number of bankrupt firms belong to these sectors. See table A3 in appendix 1.

28. The decision to borrow to obtain working capital can not be postponed while waiting for a drop in interest rates as is the case for investment in fixed assets. If a firm does not take out loans, it has to go out of business.

29. UF= Unidad de Fomento. This is a readjustable money unit according to the consumer price index (CPI) showing monthly dephasing.

# 5. CAPITAL MARKET SEGMENTATION AND FINANCIAL LIBERALIZATION

## 5.1. Introduction

Financial repression involves rationing in the financial market, the existence of interest rates below market-equilibrium level causing the savings level to become lower than the desired investment level. Hence, the need to ration credit.[1] It is argued that financial repression would lead to segmented credit markets, since the maintenance of interest rates below the equilibrium would require credit allocation mechanisms outside the market (Fry, 1982). This commonly results in credit access for large enterprises with political and financial connections, whereas small, new, unknown enterprises would find credit severely restricted (Sheahan, 1980).

Financial market segmentation implies inefficient resource allocation, because firms with privileged access to cheaper credit make investments some of which yield returns barely above the ceiling interest rate, while other firms may have the potential for higher return investments, but are unable to obtain credit. Moreover, firms with preferential access to credit over-invest in plant capacity or over-mechanize their plants in order to make use of available financing. In contrast, expansion of activities with reduced access to cheap financing is inhibited. These activities, which are normally more labor-intensive, may be squeezed out from access to formal markets and forced into the more expensive informal credit market.[2] This is one factor that contributes to the technological dualism (formal-informal sectors) frequently observed in developed economies (Ramos, 1984).

The existence of segmented financial markets has negative effects on the employment level due to the insufficient amount of savings generated and the artificial financing restriction that a segmented credit market imposes on most firms.

Theories promoting financial liberalization argue that improvement of the financial intermediation process through increase in the deposit real interest rate would bring about an increase in the savings-flow, as well as more efficient allocation of any given level of savings-flow, which would benefit firms and sectors previously held back. The quantity and quality of investment would improve if the interest rate were the main rationing mechanism which would discriminate against inefficient investments (see chapter 2).

The objective of this chapter is to determine whether the financial reform implemented in Chile eliminated segmentation of the financial market, a characteristic of financially repressed economies, or whether large companies and firms connected with financial institutions maintained differentiated access to cheap credit.

In order to answer the above question I have analyzed access to foreign currency credit, which was substantially cheaper than domestic currency credit during the 1977-82 period.[3] The study is centered on foreign loans brought into the country under article 14 of the Foreign Exchange Law, because this channel of capital inflows was the one most used by the private sector during the period (see chapter 3).

The organization of the Chapter is the following: Section 2 describes the main features of the Chilean financial sector and analyzes the behavior of financial institutions in the liberalized domestic financial market. Section 3 presents the empirical evidence. First, the allocation of article 14 foreign loans among different economic sectors is examined. Second, the distribution of these loans in the industrial sector is studied. Finally, access to article 14 foreign loans is analyzed in a sample of manufacturing corporations; these corporations are classified according to their connections to economic groups and their size. Section 4 discusses the influence of differentiated access to cheap credit on firms' profitability and the financial adjustment undertaken by different groups of firms during the 1977-81 period. Section 5 summarizes the main conclusions.

## 5.2. The Liberalized Financial Market

### 5.2.1. Main Characteristics of the Chilean Financial Sector

One of the main features of the Chilean financial sector is the predominant position of the banking system as a financial intermediary.

As mentioned before, the pre-1973 financial sector consisted of a Central Bank, a number of commercial banks, a state commercial bank (Banco del Estado) and a savings and loan system (SINAP). As a result of major structural changes in the financial sector, the SINAP system was eliminated as a financial intermediary. Later on, due to a massive bankruptcy of the recently created financieras, a large shift of funds took place from the financieras to the banks, leaving the banking system as the major financial intermediary (see chapter 3).

Another feature of the financial structure of the Chilean economy is the small role played by the stock market. As Taylor (1979) points out, stock markets are virtually absent in most LDC's, and Chile is not an exception. Therefore, the banking system is the main source of funds for domestic firms to finance fixed and working capital needs.

Moreover, as Dahse (1979) has shown, since the financial reform of 1975, the Chilean capital market can be characterized by the existence of economic conglomerates - groups of firms organized around one or more domestic banks. At the end of 1973, most commercial banks were in state hands; during the last quarter of 1975 most of them were sold to their former owners and to the new economic groups.[4]

## 5.2.2. The Behavior of Banks

During the 1975-82 period domestic firms could ask for three types of loans:

(i) They could borrow directly in the international financial market, and bring these loans in under article 14 of the Foreign Exchange Law. Nevertheless, most of these loans were guaranteed by a bank; i.e., domestic banks played the role of indirect financial intermediaries.[5]

(ii) As of September 1977 the domestic financial sector was allowed to borrow abroad through article 14; therefore, banks acquired a larger role as a direct intermediary in private foreign borrowing. These loans, denominated in foreign currency, were transferred at their external cost plus a spread to domestic firms.[6]

(iii) Finally, firms could borrow in the domestic peso-loan market.

In the following a model showing the behavior of banks which operated in the liberalized financial market is presented. In order to do so I will differentiate between peso and foreign currency (mainly dollar) loan markets. Three reasons support this distinction: the currency denomination of the loans was different; the maturity of the loans was different, since there was a minimum maturity requirement of two years for foreign loans (see chapter 3); and the degree of competition in both markets was different.

This latter issue results from the fact that the better known, more established banks in the country had preferential access to private foreign borrowing. Hoffmann (1979) shows that the international private banking system prefers some specific domestic banks to lend money to directly or to guarantee loans to private domestic firms. In fact, table 1 exhibits the annual flows of article 14 foreign loans obtained by the banking sector throughout the 1977-82 period. The four largest banks in the country accounted for more than 50% of the foreign loans brought in under article 14 of the Foreign Exchange Law[7]. Therefore, there was relatively little competition in the foreign loan market. This was not the case in the peso-denominated loan market which was completely liberalized and more competitive.[8]

I will now focus on the foreign currency-denominated loan market, hereafter referred to as the "dollar-denominated" loan market. I want to show that credit rationing represents rational banking behavior, as long as there is uncertainty regarding loan repayments and banks can not discriminate adequately between firms. In this respect the bank-customer relationship,[9] the degree of competitiveness between banks which operate in the foreign loan market, and the fact that loans to different customers are different "goods" in the sense of implying different profits (i.e., banks loans can be viewed as a special kind of non-homogeneous goods) are all critical factors in determining the existence of rationing.

There are at least two senses in which banks can be said to ration credit to borrowers. According to the first definition, credit is rationed whenever a customer receives a smaller loan than he aspired to at the interest rate quoted by the bank. The second definition applies when the total number of loans requested exceeds the total number of loans provided by the banks, i.e., when some firms are able to obtain loans while other, identical firms are not.[10] Rationing in the first sense may occur if banks have market power, and there is imperfect price differentiation among customers (Jaffee and Modigliani, 1969). An alternative explanation for rationing in the first sense, which does not rely upon market power on the part of banks, considers that bank credits are non-homogeneous goods (Keeton, 1979). Rationing may occur in the second sense if there exist moral hazard problems, resulting from the lender's inability to monitor all the relevant characteristics of the borrower's investment project (see Stiglitz and Weiss, 1981).

In the Chilean case the first definition of credit rationing is the relevant one. We want to model a situation where different firms have differentiated access to foreign credit, in contrast to a situation where some firms are able to obtain foreign loans while other, identical firms are not. Moreover, the market structure of the dollar denominated loan market, the bank-customer relationship and the non-homogeneity of loans due to the different characteristics of differents customers are all important elements that help explain the behavior of the banks which operate in this market.

The analysis follows closely the lines of the work done by Hodgman (1960 and 1961), Kane and Malkiel (1965), Jaffee and Modigliani (1969), Jaffee (1971) and Keeton (1979).

Table 1.   ARTICLE 14.   ANNUAL FLOWS OBTAINED BY THE BANKING SECTOR.
(millions of current dollars and percentages)

| Banks | 1977 | 1978 | 1979 | 1980 | 1981 | 1982 |
|---|---|---|---|---|---|---|
| Group 1 | 10.7 | 140.2 | 273.2 | 1020.8 | 1602.3 | 362.9 |
|  | (51.9) | (53.6) | (55.0) | (63.9) | (49.1) | (47.1) |
| Del Estado |  |  |  |  |  |  |
| De Chile |  |  |  |  |  |  |
| De Crédito e Inversiones |  |  |  |  |  |  |
| De Santiago |  |  |  |  |  |  |
| Group 2 | 4.7 | 53.6 | 109.5 | 356.5 | 1008.8 | 149.4 |
|  | (22.6) | (20.5) | (22.0) | (22.3) | (30.9) | (19.4) |
| BHC |  |  |  |  |  |  |
| O'Higgins |  |  |  |  |  |  |
| Sud Americano |  |  |  |  |  |  |
| Del Trabajo |  |  |  |  |  |  |
| Concepción |  |  |  |  |  |  |
| De A. Edwards |  |  |  |  |  |  |
| BHIF |  |  |  |  |  |  |
| Group 3 | 5.3 | 66.2 | 97.2 | 157.3 | 461.9 | 156.9 |
|  | (25.5) | (25.3) | (18.7) | (9.8) | (14.2) | (20.4) |
| BUF |  |  |  |  |  |  |
| Colocadora Nacional de Valores |  |  |  |  |  |  |
| Internacional |  |  |  |  |  |  |
| Osorno y La Unión |  |  |  |  |  |  |
| Nacional |  |  |  |  |  |  |
| BICE |  |  |  |  |  |  |
| Español-Chile |  |  |  |  |  |  |
| Morgan Finansa |  |  |  |  |  |  |
| De Talca |  |  |  |  |  |  |
| Del Pacífico |  |  |  |  |  |  |
| Group 4 | - | 1.5 | 21.5 | 63.3 | 190.1 | 101.1 |
|  | - | (0.6) | (4.3) | (4.0) | (5.8) | (13.1) |
| Foreign banks |  |  |  |  |  |  |
| Total | 20.7 | 261.5 | 496.9 | 1597.9 | 3263.1 | 770.3 |
|  | (100.0) | (100.0) | (100.0) | (100.0) | (100.0) | (100.0) |

Source:   Elaborated on the basis of data obtained from F. Rojas.

Notes:    - Group 1:  Each bank in group 1 accounts for more than 5% of total loans in the financial system.

- Group 2:  Each bank in group 2 accounts for a percentage of total loans in the financial system which varies between 4.9% and 2.5%.

- Group 3:  Each bank in group 3 accounts for a percentage of total loans in the financial system which varies between 2.4% and 0.25%.

- Group 4:  In this group all foreign banks which operate in Chile (around 20 banks) are included.  These foreign banks perform the same transactions as domestic banks.  According to official figures they account for about 16% of the financial system's total loans.

It is assumed that banks maximize their expected profits, i.e., they are risk neutral. The bank's expected profits from granting a dollar loan to the $i^{th}$ firm can be written as:[11]

$$\Pi_i = R_i^* L_i^* \int_{R_i^* L_i^*}^{Y_M} f_i(y,v)dy + \int_{Y_m}^{R_i^* L_i^*} Y f_i(y,v)dy - I^*(L^*)L_i^*$$

$$= [R_i^* - I^*(L^*)]L_i^* - \int_{Y_m}^{R_i^* L_i^*} F_i(y,v)dy$$

where $R_i^* L_i^* = (1 + r^*)L_i^*$ is the principal and interest on the loan. Y is the outcome of the firm's investment project, $Y_M$ is the maximum possible outcome and $Y_m$ is the minimum possible outcome of the project. $f_i(y,v)$ is the bank's subjective evaluation of the probability of different outcomes. This probability distribution not only depends upon the outcome of the firm's project, but also varies with the bank's estimate of the quality of the relationship established with the firm. This relationship is represented by the shift parameter $v$. $I^*(L^*) = (1+i^*)L^*$ is the opportunity rate factor. Although the country under analysis is small with respect to the world capital market and therefore, in that particular sense, faces an exogenously given international interest rate, the banks may find their relevant opportunity cost rising as their demand for foreign credit increases.[12]

Notice that the second term in the above expression represents the bank's evaluation of risk of granting a loan to the $i^{th}$ customer. This expression depends on the possible outcome of the project the firm is financing and on the quality of the bank-customer relationship. The point here is that there are some customers for which the denial of a loan request lessens the bank's expected profits because the bank fears it may lose these customers and more importantly their deposits. In this sense the expected profits obtained from granting a loan are related to the borrower's characteristics and, therefore, banks are not indifferent to the way total lending is distributed among customers. The bank's total expected profits depend not only on the total volume of its lending but also on the distribution of credit.

The optimal loan offer curve of the bank is obtained by maximizing expected profits with respect to the amount of the loan.

$$(\partial \Pi_i / \partial L_i^*) = R_i^*[1 - F_i(R_i^* L_i^*, v)] - I^*(L^*) - L_i^* I^{*'}(L^*) = 0$$

The above equation defines the optimal loan offer $\hat{L}_i^*$ as a function of the rate factor, the opportunity cost, and the density function $F_i()$.

The properties of the optimal loan offer are:

(i) $\hat{L}_i^* = 0$ for $R^* < I_0^*$ (since $I^*(L^*) \geq 0$, see footnote 10)

(ii) $\hat{L}_i^* > 0$ for $I_0^* < R^* < \infty$

(iii) $\lim_{R_i^* \to \infty} \hat{L}_i^* = 0$

The reason for this result is that default becomes virtually certain when the size of the contracted repayment $R_i^* L_i^*$ becomes sufficiently large.

It can be easily shown that a single bank free to discriminate between borrowers by charging each firm its monopolistic rate would not ration credit by non-price devices. The same conclusion is reached if there is more than one bank, and collusive action to maximize joint profits is exerted. Expected profit maximization would lead a monopolistic bank to raise the interest rate it charges on loans to the point where excess demand for loans would be eliminated.[13]

I want to argue that the monopolistic solution was not feasible in the dollar-denominated loan market given the prevailing institutions in the Chilean financial market. Banks can not openly collude, although they share a common desire to maintain interest rates as close as feasible to the collusive optimum. Therefore, in order to minimize competitive underbidding of interest rates they would need tacit agreement as to the appropriate rate structure for different firms. Besides, there are direct costs associated with a more detailed and complex rate system.[14] As a result, the banks would tend to limit the spread between the rates they charge and instead the would classify firms into different categories, charging a common rate for each category. On the one hand, the classification scheme should be based on readily verifiable objective criteria such as type of industry, asset size and other standard financial measures so that all banks can follow the rules. On the other hand, the bank-customer relationship is a crucial element in the bank's classification of different customers.

Jaffee and Modigliani (1969) have shown that the common interest rate for each class of customer will be between the highest and the lowest rate a discriminating monopolist will charge to the firms in that category. They also show that it will not be profitable for the banks to ration firms whose optimal monopolistic rate is lower than the class rate, but it might be profitable to ration firms whose optimal monopolististic rate is higher than the class rate; specifically those firms for whom the class rate is lower than the rate that equilibrates supply and demand will be profitably rationed.

Therefore, it is rational banking behavior to ration foreign credit to small firms without a special bank-customer relationship.

Given the characteristics of the Chilean financial sector, firms rationed in the dollar-denominated loan market have the peso-denominated loan market as the only alternative source of funds.

However, one important question comes up. Why is it that firms rationed in the dollar-loan market are not rationed in the peso-loan market?

There are different reasons for this behavior. In the first place, the degree of competitiveness in the peso-loan market is higher than in the dollar-loan market. Since 1977 there has been strong competition for market shares in the banking industry. One of the elements which explains this fact is the significant growth of the banking industry. New banks were responsible for around 45% of the credit expansion during the 1977-82 period (see Arellano, 1983). This increased competition, however, did not manifest itself in price competition; banks did not increase deposit interest rate and decrease lending rates in order to maintain or increase their market shares.[25] On the contrary, increased competition evinced a relaxation of standards and quality of collateral required. This is a well known phenomenon in the banking industry. Structural changes in banking systems that lead to increased competition are causal factors responsible for increased risk. Revell (1980) has analyzed this issue.[16] He argues that most banking crises have in common an upsurge of competition a few years before a crisis, partly from new banks and partly from new management. In the beginning the new banks and new management are responsible for speculative business and bad banking, because such practices are profitable for a while; however, after some time even established and respectable banks are tempted to relax their standards. He concludes that competition in the banking industry can not be finely tuned to achieve just the desirable results of improving efficiency and lowering prices. In many cases competition brings about a relaxation of banking practices.[17]

Another important fact to explain banking behavior in the peso-loan market is the "portfolio liberalization" brought about by domestic financial reform, that is, the elimination of regulations governing credit allocation.

Finally, if the rationing of firms in the dollar-loan market takes the form of a limit in the size of loan made available rather than outright rejection of the loan request, the applicant could be expected to shift to the peso-loan market in need of supplemental financing, after the bulk of the financing has already been provided in the dollar-loan market. In this case the likelihood of rationing in the peso-loan market is less certain.

Therefore, it is hypothesized that domestic banks with preferential access to foreign credit transferred these funds to domestic firms closely linked to them and to special customers at the external interest rate plus spread. Credit rationing of foreign loans was common practice, and therefore, domestic firms had differential access to this type of credit. Firms rationed in the dollar-loan market were compelled to take out expensive loans in the peso-loan market. The next section tests this hypothesis empirically.

## 5.3. Financial Market Segmentation

The aim of this section is to test empirically the hypothesis that during the period of financial liberalization some economic sectors and groups of firms had preferential access to new, cheaper foreign credit. During the 1975-82 period the differential between peso-loan and dollar-loan interest rates surpassed 30% annually.

In order to test the above hypothesis access to foreign credit during the 1977-82 period is examined. The study is centered on foreign loans brought into the country under article 14 of the Foreign Exchange Law, because this channel of capital inflows was the one most used by the private sector during the period.

In the first place, the allocation of article 14 foreign loans among different economic sectors is examined. In the second place, the distribution of these loans within the industrial sector is discussed. Finally, direct and indirect (through the domestic banking sector) access to article 14 foreign loans is studied by means of a sample of industrial manufacturing corporations. These corporations have been classified according to their connections to the economic groups and thereby to financial institutions, and also according to their size.

Table 2 presents the allocation by economic sectors of foreign credits brought into the country through article 14 of the Foreign Exchange Law during the 1976-82 period. Most of these foreign loans were concentrated in the industrial sector and the non-financial service sector up to 1977. From 1978 on the financial sector obtained most of these loans. The explanation rests in the fact that commercial banks were authorized to utilize article 14 of the Foreign Exchange Law for their capital inflows as of that year.

As can be seen, only a few sectors benefited from access to cheaper foreign credit during the 1975-82 period. Given the fact that the industrial sector had relatively easier access to external credits it is appropriate to

analyze what happened in this sector. Specifically, it is interesting to examine the allocation of foreign loans between industrial firms connected with
economic groups and the rest of the industrial firms.

Table 2. ARTICLE 14. ALLOCATION OF ANNUAL FLOWS BY ECONOMIC SECTORS.

| Years | Total (mill. current dollars) | Agric. | Mining | Indust. | Constr. | Non-financ. Services | Financ. Services |
|-------|------|--------|--------|---------|---------|------------|----------|
| | | (p e r c e n t a g e s)   1/ | | | | | |
| 1975 | 58.8 | | | | | | |
| 1976 | 262.6 | 8.8 | 1.4 | 43.4 | 11.6 | 30.9 | 4.0 |
| 1977 | 336.4 | 6.6 | 3.4 | 45.6 | 8.6 | 27.6 | 8.3 |
| 1978 | 780.2 | 3.8 | 1.8 | 22.8 | 7.9 | 22.0 | 41.7 |
| 1979 | 1245.2 | 4.1 | 1.1 | 22.5 | 4.7 | 18.1 | 49.7 |
| 1980 | 2503.7 | 1.4 | 0.9 | 20.0 | 1.3 | 8.2 | 68.3 |
| 1981 | 4516.7 | n.a. | n.a. | 7.6 | n.a. | n.a. | 72.9* |
| 1982 | 1770.8 | n.a. | n.a. | 5.8 | n.a. | n.a. | 44.8* |

Source:  Central Bank of Chile. "Créditos liquidados: Artículo 14", different numbers.

Notes:   1/  The national distribution of foreign credits among sectors was estimated on
             the basis of the distribution in Santiago.
         *   Only includes banks and financial institutions.

Table 3.  ARTICLE 14.  ANNUAL FLOWS OBTAINED BY INDUSTRIAL
FIRMS BELONGING TO ECONOMIC GROUPS
(millions of current dollars)

| Economic groups | 1977 | 1978 | 1979 | 1980 | 1981 | 1982 |
|-----------------|------|------|------|------|------|------|
| BHC | 14.1 | 19.1 | 29.7 | 48.8 | 45.0 | 9.6 |
| Cruzat-Larraín | 6.7 | 24.1 | 45.4 | 153.3 | 162.5 | 10.0 |
| Luksic | 6.1 | 4.5 | 1.0 | 10.5 | 5.4 | 0.0 |
| Yarur | 5.0 | 3.9 | 1.5 | 35.8 | 0.0 | 0.0 |
| Edwards | 5.3 | 4.7 | 2.0 | 0.9 | 27.5 | 0.0 |
| Matte-Alessandri | 4.0 | 2.5 | 3.1 | 1.6 | 41.7 | 12.5 |
| Total economic groups | 41.2 | 58.8 | 82.7 | 250.5 | 282.1 | 32.1 |
| Total industrial sector | 153.2 | 178.2 | 280.0 | 500.2 | 344.7 | 102.4 |
| Art. 14 credits obtained by the groups as a percentage of total art. 14 obtained by the industrial sector | 27 | 33 | 30 | 50 | 82 | 31 |
| Art. 14 credits obtained by BHC and Cruzat-Larraín as a percentage of total art. 14 obtained by the industrial sector | 14 | 24 | 27 | 40 | 60 | 19 |

Source:  Rojas (1983)  and Central Bank of Chile.  "Créditos Liquidados: Artículo 14",
         different numbers.

Table 3 shows that the industrial manufacturing firms belonging to the six most important economic groups in the country concentrated a significant amount of the direct external credits the industrial sector brought into the country under article 14. Furthermore, the two largest economic groups in the country enjoyed extraordinarily privileged access to these loans. In 1980, 50% of the direct external credits brought in by the industrial sector were destined for the industrial enterprises belonging to the six most important economic conglomerates; moreover, 40% of these credits were allocated to the industrial enterprises of two of these conglomerates: the BHC group and Cruzat-Larraín. In 1981 the figures are even more dramatic, as 82% of the direct external credits to the industrial sector were concentrated in firms connected to economic groups; 60% of the credits were obtained by firms belonging to the BHC and Cruzat-Larraín conglomerates.

Therefore, a significant fraction of the cheaper foreign credit obtained directly by the industrial sector during the 1977-82 period was allocated to firms connected with the largest economic groups in the country.

Nevertheless, as mentioned before, from 1978 on most of the direct external credits brought into the country under article 14 were channelled through the financial sector. Consequently, it is important to investigate the destination of foreign credits intermediated by the domestic banking system. Unfortunately, the information only makes it possible to study what happened to loans obtained by the industrial sector.

The source of information is the same sample of 190 publicly-held industrial corporations utilized in chapter 4. The information from the financial statements was supplemented with information on the companies' debt in foreign currency. On the one hand, direct debt of the companies in the international financial market is considered, debt that has been contracted through article 14 of the Foreign Exchange Law. On the other hand, debt in foreign currency with the national financial system is taken into account. This debt corresponds to article 14 foreign loans intermediated by the domestic banking system. This information has been available only since 1980.[18]

In order to determine whether different groups of firms had differentiated access to foreign credit during the 1977-81 period, the company sample was classified according to two relevant criteria: their connections to economic groups and their size.[19] The size-classification was carried out according to the companies' sales values. Firms whose sales were in the top 25% bracket were defined as large, enterprises whose sales were in the next 50% bracket were considered medium, and the remaining 25% were ranked as small. Firms were also classified according to their "connections", i.e., companies belonging to economic groups and independent companies. Table 4 sums up the classification of the sample.

Table 4. SAMPLE CLASSIFICATION

|                        | Large | Medium | Small | Total |
|------------------------|-------|--------|-------|-------|
| Without "connections"  | 25    | 78     | 42    | 145   |
| With "connections"     | 25    | 20     | 0     | 45    |
| Total                  | 50    | 98     | 42    | 190   |

Table 5 presents the main results for companies with and without "connections". Table 6 presents the results for large, medium, and small companies. Tables A1 to A5 in the appendix sum up balance-sheet financial structures and the profit and loss statements for the different groups of firms.[20]

Looking at the results for companies with and without connections to economic groups, we can see that the financial cost facing independent companies was higher every year than the financial cost for companies with connections to economic groups (col. 10, table 5). This differential is fundamentally due to favored access to credit in foreign currency on the part of companies with connections.[21] The percentage of the total debt of these firms corresponding to debts directly contracted with foreign banks by virtue of article 14, increased from 5.0% in 1977 to 11.4% in 1981. Meanwhile, companies without links to economic groups reached the highest percentage of debt contracted through article 14 in 1980 with 3.4% (col. 8 table 5). This very same phenomenon may be observed regarding credit in foreign currency intermediated by domestic banks. During the years 1980 and 1981, 39.5% and 41.3% respectively of the total debt for companies with connections was a foreign currency debt with the internal financial system; figures corresponding to non-connected companies were 26% in 1980 and 25.8% in 1981.

When comparing financial costs facing large, medium and small firms, one may see that throughout all those years the small companies were facing the highest financial cost. Although it is true that from the banks' point of view there are higher operational costs for some firms, this does not justify the dispersion observed in financial cost for each of the three groups considered. For instance, a study cited by Dornbusch (1983a) about the conditions for short-term credits offered by the U.S. private banking sector presents a range of variation of interest rates not exceeding three percentage points.

It is interesting to point out that small companies independent of economic groups faced higher financial costs than independent firms of different size, the size of the firm also influenced the cost of credit (col. 10, table 6). Once again, the explanation for these differentials in the cost of credit lies in the access companies had to loans in foreign currency. The percentage of total debt which is debt in foreign currency contracted through article 14 varies between 3.6% in 1977 and 9.2% in 1981 in the case of large firms. For small companies these percentages vary between 1.8% in 1977 and 5% in 1979, and then decrease to 2% and 2.6% in 1980 and 1981 respectively. The hypothesis of differentiated access to cheap credit in foreign currency is strengthened when one observes column 9 in table 6. The percentage of total debt which is foreign currency debt with the domestic financial system is 35.4% in 1980 for large firms and 21.3% for small ones; in 1981 these figures are 37.6% for the large firms and 21.4% for the small ones.

The magnitude of the impact that access to credit in foreign currency had on the companies' financial cost is illustrated by Ffrench-Davis (1983b). The companies that went into debt in the domestic peso-loan market between 1977 and 1981 paid excess interest above a real "normal" 8% annual interest rate for an amount equivalent up to 133% of the initial loan. If an enterprise which was actually paying the creditor 8% a year were to renew the principal and capitalize the interests in excess of 8%, it would have a debt more than 2.3 times the initial amount in constant purchasing-power money at the end of 1981. In contrast, the firm indebted abroad under equal circumstances would have a real debt 27% smaller in 1981 than the debt contracted in 1977, and it would be equivalent to one third the liability for the firm indebted in pesos. The company indebted in foreign currency, would have ended up after the 1982 devaluation with a debt equal to the initial one. This calculation is sensitive to the year the credit was contracted; e.g. companies which took out loans in foreign currency in 1981, suffered serious losses after having to absorb the real devaluations of 1982.[22]

The results commented upon in previous paragraphs furnish sufficient evidence to allow one to conclude that there was indeed important segmentation in the financial market. The large companies that belonged to economic groups had preferential access to cheap credit in foreign currency. Domestic banks transferred foreign loans contracted under article 14 of the Foreign Exchange Law to domestic firms with close ties and special customers. By contrast, small independent enterprises had to contract debt mainly in the internal peso-loan market and pay the high real interest rates prevalent in the market.

Table 5. COMPANIES RELATED TO ECONOMIC GROUPS VERSUS INDEPENDENT COMPANIES

| | Assets (1977=100) a/ | | as a % of total assets | | | | as a % of total debt | | | Financial costs b/ | Total debt / Net worth |
|---|---|---|---|---|---|---|---|---|---|---|---|
| | Total | Fixed | Financial assets | Assets in related firms | Total debt | Inventories | Debt with banks | Foreign currency debt (art.14) | Foreign currency debt with dom. fin. system | | |
| | (1) | (2) | (3) | (4) | (5) | (6) | (7) | (8) | (9) | (10) | (11) |
| Companies with "connections" | | | | | | | | | | | |
| 1977 | 100.0 | 100.0 | 29.9 | 15.5 | 46.3 | 17.3 | 25.8 | 5.0 | n.a. | 21.9 | 0.9 |
| 1978 | 99.6 | 95.7 | 29.7 | 13.8 | 48.3 | 14.9 | 36.1 | 7.6 | n.a. | 21.3 | 0.9 |
| 1979 | 122.7 | 103.1 | 31.6 | 26.6 | 46.9 | 13.6 | 44.5 | 9.5 | n.a. | 17.3 | 0.9 |
| 1980 | 147.7 | 116.6 | 36.0 | 28.3 | 46.8 | 12.1 | 48.1 | 9.7 | 39.5 | 13.4 | 0.9 |
| 1981 | 142.5 | 116.9 | 33.7 | 32.2 | 56.0 | 10.6 | 50.8 | 11.4 | 41.3 | 18.4 | 1.3 |
| Companies without "connections" | | | | | | | | | | | |
| 1977 | 100.0 | 100.0 | 4.4 | 2.4 | 43.8 | 20.3 | 29.7 | 2.9 | n.a. | 35.5 | 0.8 |
| 1978 | 89.7 | 81.0 | 8.0 | 3.6 | 47.5 | 20.7 | 31.9 | 2.2 | n.a. | 32.6 | 0.9 |
| 1979 | 100.0 | 81.8 | 12.8 | 6.7 | 48.5 | 20.3 | 35.6 | 1.6 | n.a. | 24.0 | 0.9 |
| 1980 | 100.0 | 72.4 | 16.2 | 8.4 | 48.8 | 20.5 | 40.5 | 3.4 | 26.0 | 17.0 | 1.0 |
| 1981 | 90.6 | 72.6 | 13.5 | 8.9 | 54.7 | 18.0 | 39.0 | 1.0 | 25.8 | 21.2 | 1.2 |

Sources: Col. (8): Elaborated on the basis of data from F. Rojas
Col. (9): Superintendencia de Bancos e Instituciones Financieras.
Others: Data base World Bank project on liberalization and stabilization policies in the Southern Cone countries.

Notes: a/ Real values. Corrected CPI Cortázar and Marshall (1980) was used.

b/ Financial costs = $\dfrac{\text{Financial Expenses}}{\text{Average debt which draws interest}} \times 100$

Table 6. LARGE, MEDIUM AND SMALL COMPANIES

| | Assets (1977=100) a/ | | Financial assets | Assets in related firms | Total debt | Inventories | Debt with banks | Foreign currency debt (art.14) | Foreign currency debt with dom. fin. system | Financial costs b/ | Total debt / Net worth |
| | Total | Fixed | as a % of total assets | as a % of total assets | as a % of total assets | | as a % | as a % of total debt | as a % of total debt | | |
| | (1) | (2) | (3) | (4) | (5) | (6) | (7) | (8) | (9) | (10) | (11) |
| **Large companies** | | | | | | | | | | | |
| 1977 | 100.0 | 100.0 | 18.4 | 9.5 | 45.8 | 18.7 | 27.6 | 3.6 | n.a. | 29.1 | 0.9 |
| 1978 | 93.3 | 87.5 | 20.6 | 9.4 | 48.0 | 17.1 | 34.0 | 5.1 | n.a. | 26.4 | 0.9 |
| 1979 | 108.7 | 89.7 | 24.4 | 18.6 | 47.9 | 16.2 | 40.6 | 6.7 | n.a. | 19.5 | 0.9 |
| 1980 | 123.0 | 89.9 | 28.8 | 20.9 | 48.2 | 15.4 | 44.9 | 8.1 | 35.4 | 13.5 | 0.9 |
| 1981 | 116.5 | 90.8 | 26.7 | 24.1 | 57.2 | 13.1 | 46.7 | 9.2 | 37.6 | 18.6 | 1.3 |
| **Medium companies** | | | | | | | | | | | |
| 1977 | 100.0 | 100.0 | 16.0 | 9.7 | 46.3 | 19.1 | 27.2 | 6.7 | n.a. | 20.1 | 0.9 |
| 1978 | 103.0 | 87.5 | 17.9 | 9.3 | 52.5 | 20.0 | 34.0 | 5.0 | n.a. | 22.1 | 1.1 |
| 1979 | 131.4 | 101.4 | 20.8 | 17.7 | 49.8 | 17.9 | 40.3 | 1.1 | n.a. | 21.2 | 1.0 |
| 1980 | 143.0 | 105.0 | 24.7 | 18.5 | 46.8 | 16.1 | 49.2 | 3.6 | 34.5 | 20.4 | 0.9 |
| 1981 | 134.6 | 103.0 | 24.5 | 22.2 | 49.8 | 15.3 | 47.5 | 0.2 | 32.8 | 25.2 | 1.0 |
| **Small companies** | | | | | | | | | | | |
| 1977 | 100.0 | 100.0 | 8.1 | 0.7 | 30.8 | 16.9 | 40.2 | 1.8 | n.a. | 36.8 | 0.4 |
| 1978 | 106.6 | 86.9 | 11.5 | 2.7 | 35.5 | 16.2 | 41.3 | 3.1 | n.a. | 44.6 | 0.6 |
| 1979 | 85.6 | 71.9 | 14.7 | 1.7 | 35.5 | 15.1 | 45.8 | 5.0 | n.a. | 31.0 | 0.6 |
| 1980 | 68.2 | 48.9 | 29.9 | 9.2 | 40.8 | 11.2 | 39.6 | 2.0 | 21.3 | 34.8 | 0.7 |
| 1981 | 44.6 | 37.7 | 11.5 | 9.3 | 53.7 | 11.5 | 40.2 | 2.6 | 21.4 | 26.2 | 1.2 |

Sources: Col. (8): Elaborated on the basis of data from F. Rojas

Col. (9): Superintendencia de Bancos e Instituciones Financieras.

Others: Data base World Bank project on liberalization and stabilization policies in the Southern Cone countries.

Notes: a/ Real values. Corrected CPI Cortázar and Marshall (1980) was used.

b/ Financial costs = $\dfrac{\text{Financial Expenses}}{\text{Average debt which draws interest}} \times 100$

Therefore, during the financial liberalization period the completely deregulated domestic peso-loan market played a similar role to the role played
by informal credit markets in financially repressed economies.

## 5.4. Financial Market Segmentation, Profitability and Financial Adjustment

The aim of this section is to examine the influence the differentials in
the cost of credit had on the firms' profitability. A further objective is
to compare the financial adjustment made by the different entrepreneurial
groups during the period of financial liberalization.

Differentials in the cost of credit facing companies during the 1977-81
period had influenced their profitability. The profit and loss statement
shows high profitability for companies belonging to economic groups. This
situation changes dramatically in 1981, basically due to an abrupt rise in
financial expenses (see table A1 in appendix).[23]

Performance of independent companies is less satisfactory from the start;
the reason for this is the high financial cost these firms had to face and, to
a lesser degree, high operational costs in relation to total sales. Hence, the
low performance in terms of profitability for the independent firms is largely
explained by non-operational results, i.e., results not directly related to the
firm's main turnover (see table A2 in appendix).

On the other hand, the statement of profit and loss for small companies shows that they only made profits in 1978. Losses as a percentage of
total sales vary between 7% and 29%. These losses are fundamentally explained by negative non-operational results, where financial expenses play
an important role. This situation worsened when operational results also
deteriorated during 1980 and 1981 as a consequence of the increase in operational cost and administrative and marketing expenses. Administrative
and marketing expenses are higher and rising in relation to sales for small
companies compared to large ones. This is a typical form of behavior since
small companies suffer from greater inflexibility in their administration and
sales cost, because there is a reduced division of labor and less possibility
of taking advantage of economies of scale in sales and advertising.

During 1977 and 1978, however, it is non-operational results which determined profitability problems for small firms, in particular the results
yielded by the monetary correction account. The monetary correction account reflects the effects of inflation on the companies' net cash balances
and the monetary correction of the income statement. It is probable that
the high level attained by that account in 1977 and 1978 is reflecting the

effect of inflation on bank deposits held by these firms, encouraged by high real interest rates paid in the short-term capital market (see table A5).[24]

We will analyze next the financial adjustment to new conditions in the domestic financial market made by different entrepreneurial groups. We will compare first the adjustment made by firms according to whether they do or do not belong to economic conglomerates. Secondly, we will compare the changes in companies' financial structure according to their size.

Observing the results of related and unrelated companies, the preponderance of financial assets in proportion to total assets calls one's attention. Whereas firms belonging to economic groups kept 29.9% of their assets in financial assets in 1977, unrelated companies only kept 4.4% of their assets in financial assets. During 1981 the share of financial assets in total assets corresponded to 33.7% for related companies and 13.5% for unrelated companies. (col. 3, table 5).

Throughout the period trade-stock diminished in proportion to total assets in the case of firms belonging to economic groups. Unrelated companies barely altered the asset-share maintained in inventories.

Independent firms show a decrease in fixed assets in absolute terms during the period. They descended from a 100 level in 1977 to 72.6 in 1981. In the case of firms related to economic groups, fixed assets decreased in absolute terms from 1977 to 1978; however, further along in the period one may notice an increase in fixed assets. Nevertheless, in view of the amount of resources available to the economic groups and in view of the greatly lower cost of these resources, it is only modest fixed-asset growth.

In general, the companies belonging to economic groups chose to invest a large proportion of their assets in financial assets, in particular in related companies. This was a mechanism used to artificially increase the assets for the whole group. Once the operation was completed, the investing company could show an asset-increase and the issuing company could show a net-worth increase. Assets with related companies represented 15.5% of their total assets in 1977; this proportion reached 32.2% in 1981. By contrast, companies that were unrelated to economic groups invested 2.4% of their assets in related companies in 1977, and 8.9% in 1981 (see col. 4, table 5).

Consequently, during the period firms belonging to economic conglomerates utilized an important part of the cheap credit they obtained to buy shares in existing firms.[25] The rational basis for this behavior can be found in the fact that these firms were maximizing the objective function of the whole conglomerate rather than the objective function of the individual firm. The aim of the conglomerate was to build up the group and amplify its scope.

Moreover, it can be hypothesized that some firms with privileged access to foreign credit transformed themselves into financial intermediaries and lent in pesos to the other firms at the high interest rate in force in the market. Support for this hypothesis can be found in the fact that commercial credit did not decline throughout the period despite increased financial intermediation (see tables A1 and A2). This could have turned out to be an important source of profits for firms with access to external credit. The existence of this profitable, liquid investment opportunity can also help explain why investment in real assets experienced only a modest increase, despite the significant amount of resources "related" firms had access to during the period.

It can be argued that this kind of behavior on the part of firms that had access to foreign credit should have led to interest rate arbitrage. However, the spread between domestic and external interest rates remained very high throughout the whole period. The explanation is provided by the fact that the supply of domestic credit was never sufficient to lower the peso-interest rate, because there was an important increase in the demand for credit. This greater demand for credit was directed toward consumption in imported durable goods, investment opportunities offering high returns, and mainly toward firms that hoped to avoid bankruptcy. Unrelated firms borrowed in the short-term peso-loan market to obtain working capital while waiting for a decline in the domestic interest rate in the near future. However, the interest rate did not decline and firms had to take out new loans to service their expiring debts (see chapters 4, 6 and 7). In a world where part of the demand for short-term financing reflects capitalization of interest, a rise in the short-term interest rate may increase the demand for short-term loans, and this can lead to further increases in short-term interest rates.

In regard to liabilities, related and unrelated firms show similar behavior. The proportion of assets financed with debt and net worth are similar. Nevertheless, this is only an apparent similarity when one considers the fact that the purchase of debt-financed shares was a generalized procedure among companies related to banks and financial institutions. The same applies when considering the intercrossing of companies' properties.[26]

Looking at the results for companies of different sizes one notices, as regards liabilities, larger asset-proportion for small companies being financed with net worth, when compared to the other two size-groups of firms. The fact that small companies normally run into greater difficulty in obtaining indirect external financial resources (bank loans) explains the importance of net-worth in their financial structure.[27] In 1980, and especially in 1981, the fraction of assets financed with net worth decreased, probably due to the negative performance in terms of profitability observed during those years.

In contrast to the other two groups of companies, small firms tend to increase short-term assets compared to long-term ones. This occurred despite the fact that trade-stock diminished throughout the whole period. In 1977 trade-stock represented 16.9% of total assets, whereas in 1981 it only represented 11.5% of total assets. This decrease in the relative importance of trade-stock is offset by an important increase in time deposits. This change in asset composition was to be expected in view of the high interest rates prevalent in the financial market which encouraged enterprises to reduce their trade-stock, invest their assets in the short-term capital market and thus obtain a high return. It strikes one that medium and large companies, even though they also showed a decrease in the relative importance of trade-stock, did not increase their time deposits with the same intensity that small ones did. It makes sense to believe that the reason for this behavior is linked to the fact that medium and large companies had better alternative opportunities for financial investment, i.e., investment in related companies (see col. 4, table 6).

Small firms as well as large ones registered a decline in fixed assets in absolute terms, and only in the case of medium firms did fixed assets remain more or less constant during the whole period. Small companies showed a very steep drop in fixed assets; they diminished from a level of 100 in 1977 to 37.7 in 1981 (col. 2, table 6). By contrast, financial assets increased their participation in total assets during the period. Large companies kept 18.4% of their assets in the form of financial assets in 1977; this percentage rose to 26.7% in 1981. Small companies on the other hand kept 8.1% of their assets in financial assets in 1977 and 11.5% in 1981 (col. 3, table 6).

Hence, when observing the sample of manufacturing firms classified according to their relations and size one arrives at a conclusion similar to the conclusion in chapter 4, namely that the financial market liberalization process did not encourage real investment (in fixed assets) on behalf of productive companies. On the contrary, persistently high real interest rates encouraged decapitalization and speculative investment in financial assets. This phenomenon is explicable under conditions where the real interest rate systematically exceeds the real rate of return on productive investment, and when the market at the same time presents other more profitable and liquid investment opportunities.

## 5.5. Conclusions

Theories promoting financial liberalization in LDC's argue that segmentation is one of the characteristics of repressed financial markets. This means that some usually capital-intensive economic sectors (for instance, mining and industry versus agriculture and construction) and some firms within each sector (the large firms with political and financial connections versus the medium and small firms), enjoy privileged access to cheap credit. In this study the finding is that the Chilean liberalization process did not eliminate the financial market segmentation characteristic of financially repressed economies. When the differential between internal and foreign real interest rate surpassed an annual 30%, foreign currency credit brought into the country under article 14 of the Foreign Exchange Law became concentrated in a few economic sectors. These included the industrial sector up to 1977, and thereafter the financial sector.

In can be reasoned that there is nothing wrong with the fact that most of the external credit became concentrated in the financial sector, since its role is precisely to allocate these resources. However, as Dahse (1979) has shown, since the financial reform of 1975, the Chilean capital market can be characterized by the existence of economic conglomerates, groups of firms organized around one or more domestic banks. Under these conditions financial intermediaries pursued the objectives of the economic group to which they belonged rather than the objectives of their depositors and creditors. Present research confirms this hypothesis; large companies with connections to economic groups had privileged access to cheaper foreign credit. Domestic banks transferred the foreign credit contracted under article 14 to domestic firms with close ties to them and to special customers. In other words, credit rationing of foreign loans was a common practice in the liberalized financial market.

The differential access to credit led small firms without connections to borrow in domestic currency in the recently liberalized internal financial market, and to pay the persistently high real interest rates in force in this market. This implied that different types of firms faced different costs. For example, companies unrelated to economic groups faced higher financial cost than related firms. Likewise, small firms suffered higher financial cost than medium or large ones. It is interesting to point out that small companies unrelated to economic groups faced higher financial costs than differently sized companies without connections, i.e., the size of the company also influenced the cost of credit.

Differentials in the cost of credit facing companies during the 1977-81 period influenced their profitability. The profit and loss statements show high profitability for companies belonging to economic groups until 1981. That year they suffered losses due to an increase in the external interest rate which implied an abrupt rise in financial expenses. The performance of non-related companies is less satisfactory, mainly due to the high financial cost these firms had to face. The case of small firms is even more dramatic, inasmuch as only in 1978 did they make any profits. Their losses are fundamentally explained by negative non-operational results, where financial expenses play an important role. Companies with restricted access to cheap credit in foreign currency and therefore greater financial cost suffered significant losses during the period studied.

Therefore, the completely deregulated domestic peso-loan market played a role similar to the role of informal credit markets in financially repressed economies. In the Chilean peso-loan market firms willing to pay high interest rates could contract loans. The behavior of the peso-loan market is explained by the elimination of regulations governing credit allocation, brought about by financial liberalization, and by the strong competition for market share in the banking industry during the period. Both phenomena implied a relaxation of the criteria used to select debtors, and a lowering of the standards and quality of collateral required. Increased competition in the banking sector during the period did not bring about a decrease in lending rates and an increase in deposit rates but instead a rise in the risk of the bank's portfolios. The perverse behavior of the domestic credit market belies a very weak financial structure liable to go bankrupt at any time.

Analyzing the adjustment made by different groups of firms during the period, one arrives at the same conclusion as in chapter 4; the financial market's liberalization process did not encourage real investment on behalf of productive firms. On the contrary persistently high real interest rates encouraged decapitalization, financial intermediation and speculative investment in financial assets. Only firms belonging to economic groups had an increase in fixed assets during the period. However, in view of the amount of resources available to the groups and the greatly lower cost of these resources, fixed- asset growth remains modest. Firms connected with economic groups chose to invest a significant proportion of their assets in financial assets, particularly in related companies. The objective was to build up the conglomerate and amplify its scope.

The financial reform as implemented in Chile during the last decade did not contribute to improving resource allocation. Moreover, the significant financial market segmentation led to a greater concentration of wealth.

APPENDIX

Table A1. SAMPLE OF INDUSTRIAL COMPANIES RELATED TO ECONOMIC GROUPS
(percentages)

Balance Sheet

|  | 1977 | 1978 | 1979 | 1980 | 1981 |
|---|---|---|---|---|---|
| Assets | 100.0 | 100.0 | 100.0 | 100.0 | 100.0 |
| Short-term assets | 48.2 | 51.2 | 40.0 | 37.3 | 35.4 |
| Cash | 0.9 | 0.9 | 1.1 | 0.7 | 0.9 |
| Time deposits | 2.8 | 3.3 | 3.0 | 3.1 | 3.2 |
| Credits | 14.5 | 18.4 | 17.4 | 13.9 | 16.8 |
| Short-term investment | 11.6 | 12.6 | 3.7 | 5.7 | 2.5 |
| Inventories | 17.3 | 14.9 | 13.6 | 12.1 | 10.6 |
| Others | 1.2 | 1.0 | 1.2 | 1.8 | 1.4 |
| Long-term assets | 51.8 | 48.8 | 60.0 | 62.7 | 64.6 |
| Long-term credit related firms | 0.0 | 0.0 | 0.4 | 0.9 | 2.1 |
| Investment related firms | 13.4 | 10.9 | 23.3 | 24.5 | 24.5 |
| Fixed assets | 36.1 | 34.7 | 30.4 | 28.5 | 29.6 |
| Others 1/ | 2.2 | 3.3 | 5.9 | 8.8 | 8.4 |
| Short-term debt | 32.4 | 33.2 | 26.6 | 27.0 | 31.7 |
| Debt with public | 5.9 | 4.3 | 1.0 | 1.4 | 4.8 |
| Banks | 5.8 | 9.2 | 7.2 | 8.5 | 12.2 |
| Commercial | 16.2 | 14.3 | 12.7 | 11.4 | 9.0 |
| Others 2/ | 4.5 | 5.4 | 5.7 | 5.7 | 5.7 |
| Long-term debt | 13.8 | 15.1 | 20.3 | 19.5 | 24.3 |
| Banks | 6.1 | 8.3 | 13.6 | 14.0 | 16.3 |
| Debt with related firms | 0.0 | 0.0 | 0.3 | 0.5 | 1.2 |
| Others 3/ | 7.7 | 6.8 | 6.4 | 5.0 | 6.8 |
| Net worth | 53.7 | 51.7 | 56.5 | 57.4 | 48.4 |
|  |  |  |  |  |  |
| Profit and loss statement |  |  |  |  |  |
| Sales | 100.0 | 100.0 | 100.0 | 100.0 | 100.0 |
| Operational costs | -67.6 | -67.0 | -66.6 | -72.1 | -75.2 |
| Gross margin | 32.4 | 33.0 | 33.4 | 27.9 | 24.8 |
| Marketing and administ. costs | -16.9 | -18.1 | -18.5 | -16.9 | -18.5 |
| Financial expenses | - 8.9 | - 7.1 | - 6.5 | - 5.7 | -13.3 |
| Other inflows and outflows | 7.6 | 4.8 | 7.2 | 5.3 | - 0.6 |
| Monetary correction | - 2.0 | - 0.4 | - 1.1 | 1.7 | - 0.8 |
| Operational result | 15.5 | 14.9 | 14.9 | 11.0 | 6.3 |
| Non-operational result | - 3.2 | - 2.7 | - 0.4 | 1.4 | -14.8 |
| Taxes | - 2.1 | - 3.9 | - 3.5 | - 3.0 | - 2.0 |
| Net profits | 10.2 | 8.2 | 11.0 | 9.4 | -10.5 |

Source: Data base World Bank Project on liberalization and stabilization policies in the Southern Cone countries.

1/ Lower investment value, higher investment value, long-term debtors, intangible, amortization.

2/ Dividends to be paid, provisions, retentions, income tax, debt with related companies, income perceived in advance and deferred taxes.

3/ Documents payable in the long-term, debt with the public, other creditors, provisions.

Table A2. SAMPLE OF INDUSTRIAL COMPANIES UNRELATED TO ECONOMIC GROUPS
(percentages)

Balance Sheet

|  | 1977 | 1978 | 1979 | 1980 | 1981 |
|---|---|---|---|---|---|
| Assets | 100.0 | 100.0 | 100.0 | 100.0 | 100.0 |
| Short-term assets | 44.0 | 48.1 | 47.8 | 50.9 | 44.2 |
| Cash | 1.2 | 1.4 | 1.6 | 1.6 | 1.5 |
| Time deposits | 1.5 | 4.0 | 5.4 | 6.7 | 4.9 |
| Credits | 16.4 | 17.9 | 17.9 | 18.7 | 17.6 |
| Short-term investment | 0.5 | 0.4 | 0.6 | 0.9 | 0.4 |
| Inventories | 20.3 | 20.7 | 20.3 | 20.5 | 18.0 |
| Others | 4.1 | 3.6 | 2.0 | 2.5 | 1.8 |
| Long-term assets | 56.0 | 51.9 | 52.2 | 49.1 | 55.8 |
| Long-term credit related firms | 0.0 | 0.0 | 0.2 | 0.3 | 0.5 |
| Investment related firms | 1.7 | 1.5 | 4.6 | 5.7 | 6.0 |
| Fixed assets | 52.8 | 47.6 | 43.4 | 37.9 | 42.3 |
| Others 1/ | 1.5 | 2.8 | 4.0 | 5.2 | 7.1 |
| Short-term debt | 30.2 | 27.9 | 27.8 | 29.4 | 30.7 |
| Debt with public | 2.7 | 0.4 | 0.4 | 0.7 | 0.3 |
| Banks | 7.2 | 9.2 | 9.9 | 12.5 | 12.5 |
| Commercial | 9.4 | 10.7 | 8.9 | 7.1 | 8.5 |
| Others 2/ | 10.9 | 7.6 | 8.6 | 9.1 | 9.4 |
| Long-term debt | 13.6 | 19.5 | 20.7 | 19.0 | 22.8 |
| Banks | 5.9 | 5.9 | 7.4 | 7.2 | 8.8 |
| Debt with related firms | 0.0 | 0.0 | 4.4 | 5.9 | 8.2 |
| Others 3/ | 7.7 | 13.6 | 8.9 | 5.9 | 5.8 |
| Net worth | 56.2 | 52.5 | 51.5 | 51.6 | 46.5 |
| | | | | | |
| Profit and loss   statement | | | | | |
| Sales | 100.0 | 100.0 | 100.0 | 100.0 | 100.0 |
| Operational costs | -70.6 | -75.3 | -72.4 | -71.5 | -74.5 |
| Gross margin | 29.4 | 24.7 | 27.6 | 28.5 | 25.5 |
| Marketing and administ. costs | -23.1 | -16.0 | -15.7 | -18.4 | -20.1 |
| Financial expenses | - 9.8 | - 7.0 | - 5.4 | - 5.3 | - 8.3 |
| Other inflows and outflows | 4.9 | 4.1 | 0.4 | - 1.1 | 0.6 |
| Monetary correction | - 3.5 | - 3.2 | - 0.2 | - 0.4 | - 1.1 |
| Operational result | 6.3 | 8.7 | 11.9 | 10.1 | 5.4 |
| Non-operational result | - 8.3 | - 6.1 | - 5.2 | - 6.7 | - 8.8 |
| Taxes | - 1.7 | - 2.5 | - 3.6 | - 2.7 | - 3.1 |
| Net profits | - 3.7 | 0.1 | 3.0 | 0.7 | - 6.5 |

Source:      Data base World Bank Project on liberalization and stabilization policies
             in the Southern Cone countries.

1/   Lower investment value, higher investment value, long-term debtors, intangible,
     amortization.
2/   Dividends to be paid, provisions, retentions, income tax, debt with related
     companies,   income perceived in advance and deferred taxes.
3/   Documents payable in the long-term, debt with the public, other creditors,
     provisions.

**Table A3.** SAMPLE OF LARGE INDUSTRIAL COMPANIES
(percentages)

Balance Sheet

|  | 1977 | 1978 | 1979 | 1980 | 1981 |
|---|---|---|---|---|---|
| Assets | 100.0 | 100.0 | 100.0 | 100.0 | 100.0 |
| Short-term assets | 46.3 | 49.4 | 42.4 | 42.2 | 38.1 |
| Cash | 1.0 | 1.1 | 1.3 | 1.0 | 1.1 |
| Time deposits | 2.2 | 3.2 | 4.2 | 4.6 | 4.0 |
| Credits | 14.9 | 17.7 | 16.7 | 15.2 | 16.6 |
| Short-term investment | 6.7 | 7.9 | 2.5 | 4.0 | 1.9 |
| Inventories | 18.7 | 17.1 | 16.2 | 15.4 | 13.1 |
| Others | 2.7 | 2.3 | 1.5 | 2.0 | 1.4 |
| Long-term assets | 53.7 | 50.6 | 57.6 | 57.8 | 61.9 |
| Long-term credit related firms | 0.0 | 0.0 | 0.3 | 0.5 | 1.6 |
| Investment related firms | 8.1 | 6.7 | 15.9 | 17.6 | 17.9 |
| Fixed assets | 43.9 | 41.1 | 36.2 | 32.1 | 34.1 |
| Others 1/ | 1.7 | 2.8 | 5.2 | 7.6 | 8.3 |
| Short-term debt | 32.7 | 31.2 | 27.1 | 27.5 | 31.7 |
| Debt with public | 4.8 | 3.0 | 0.7 | 1.0 | 3.4 |
| Banks | 6.6 | 9.2 | 8.0 | 9.8 | 12.6 |
| Commercial | 13.7 | 12.9 | 11.5 | 10.0 | 8.4 |
| Others 2/ | 7.6 | 6.1 | 6.9 | 6.7 | 7.3 |
| Long-term debt | 13.1 | 16.8 | 20.8 | 20.1 | 25.0 |
| Banks | 6.0 | 7.1 | 11.6 | 11.8 | 14.1 |
| Debt with related firms | 0.0 | 0.0 | 2.4 | 3.1 | 4.0 |
| Others 3/ | 7.1 | 9.7 | 6.8 | 5.2 | 6.9 |
| Net worth | 54.2 | 52.0 | 52.1 | 52.4 | 43.3 |
|  |  |  |  |  |  |
| Profit and loss statement |  |  |  |  |  |
| Sales | 100.0 | 100.0 | 100.0 | 100.0 | 100.0 |
| Operational costs | -69.5 | -73.0 | -70.6 | -72.9 | -76.6 |
| Gross margin | 30.5 | 27.0 | 29.4 | 27.1 | 23.4 |
| Marketing and administ. costs | -20.2 | -15.7 | -15.8 | -16.4 | -18.0 |
| Financial expenses | -10.3 | - 7.5 | - 5.9 | - 5.1 | -11.0 |
| Other inflows and outflows | 7.2 | 4.9 | 4.2 | 2.3 | - 0.4 |
| Monetary correction | - 2.0 | - 1.4 | - 0.5 | 0.7 | - 1.3 |
| Operational result | 10.3 | 11.3 | 13.5 | 10.8 | 5.3 |
| Non-operational result | - 5.1 | - 4.1 | - 2.3 | - 2.1 | -12.6 |
| Taxes | - 1.9 | - 3.3 | - 3.7 | - 2.8 | - 2.5 |
| Net profits | 3.4 | 3.9 | 7.6 | 5.9 | - 9.8 |

Source: Data base World Bank Project on liberalization and stabilization policies in the Southern Cone countries.

1/ Lower investment value, higher investment value, long-term debtors, intangible, amortization.

2/ Dividends to be paid, provisions, retentions, income tax, debt with related companies, income perceived in advance and deferred taxes.

3/ Documents payable in the long-term, debt with the public, other creditors, provisions.

Table A4.    SAMPLE OF MEDIUM INDUSTRIAL COMPANIES
(percentages)

Balance Sheet

|                              | 1977   | 1978   | 1979   | 1980   | 1981   |
|------------------------------|--------|--------|--------|--------|--------|
| Assets                       | 100.0  | 100.0  | 100.0  | 100.0  | 100.0  |
| Short-term assets            | 47.1   | 51.9   | 47.4   | 46.4   | 43.2   |
| Cash                         | 1.4    | 1.3    | 1.3    | 1.4    | 1.2    |
| Time deposits                | 1.5    | 4.3    | 1.7    | 2.6    | 2.9    |
| Credits                      | 18.3   | 20.1   | 22.2   | 20.0   | 20.1   |
| Short-term investment        | 4.9    | 4.3    | 2.4    | 4.0    | 1.7    |
| Inventories                  | 19.1   | 20.0   | 17.9   | 16.1   | 15.3   |
| Others                       | 1.9    | 1.9    | 1.9    | 2.3    | 2.0    |
| Long-term assets             | 52.9   | 48.1   | 52.6   | 53.6   | 56.8   |
| Long-term credit related firms | 0.0  | 0.0    | 0.6    | 1.4    | 1.3    |
| Investment related firms     | 8.1    | 7.7    | 14.1   | 14.5   | 16.6   |
| Fixed assets                 | 41.8   | 35.5   | 32.3   | 30.7   | 32.0   |
| Others  1/                   | 3.0    | 4.9    | 5.6    | 7.0    | 6.9    |
| Short-term debt              | 27.8   | 32.1   | 29.5   | 30.0   | 32.0   |
| Debt with public             | 3.0    | 1.0    | 0.9    | 1.4    | 1.2    |
| Banks                        | 6.4    | 9.7    | 10.9   | 12.6   | 12.0   |
| Commercial                   | 11.1   | 13.2   | 10.2   | 9.3    | 11.1   |
| Others  2/                   | 7.3    | 8.2    | 7.5    | 6.7    | 7.7    |
| Long-term debt               | 18.5   | 20.4   | 20.3   | 17.3   | 17.7   |
| Banks                        | 6.2    | 8.2    | 9.2    | 10.9   | 11.7   |
| Debt with related firms      | 0.0    | 0.0    | 0.7    | 0.4    | 1.2    |
| Others  3/                   | 12.3   | 12.2   | 10.5   | 6.0    | 4.8    |
| Net worth                    | 53.7   | 47.5   | 50.2   | 52.7   | 50.3   |
|                              |        |        |        |        |        |
| Profit and loss   statement  |        |        |        |        |        |
| Sales                        | 100.0  | 100.0  | 100.0  | 100.0  | 100.0  |
| Operational costs            | -67.1  | -65.3  | -64.3  | -66.8  | -67.7  |
| Gross margin                 | 32.9   | 34.7   | 35.7   | 33.2   | 32.3   |
| Marketing and administ. costs| -20.2  | -21.4  | -22.1  | -22.1  | -23.4  |
| Financial expenses           | - 5.5  | - 5.2  | - 6.2  | - 6.9  | - 9.8  |
| Other inflows and outflows   | 2.2    | 1.8    | 1.5    | 2.8    | 2.3    |
| Monetary correction          | - 5.8  | - 2.5  | - 1.0  | 0.8    | 0.2    |
| Operational result           | 12.7   | 13.3   | 13.5   | 11.1   | 8.9    |
| Non-operational result       | - 9.2  | - 6.0  | - 5.7  | - 3.3  | - 7.3  |
| Taxes                        | - 2.1  | - 2.9  | - 3.1  | - 3.3  | - 2.7  |
| Net profits                  | 1.4    | 4.5    | 4.7    | 4.5    | - 1.0  |

Source:      Data base World Bank Project on liberalization and stabilization policies
in the Southern Cone countries.

1/   Lower investment value, higher investment value, long-term debtors, intangible,
amortization.
2/   Dividends to be paid, provisions, retentions, income tax, debt with related
companies,   income perceived in advance and deferred taxes.
3/   Documents payable in the long-term, debt with the public, other creditors,
provisions.

**Table A5.** SAMPLE OF SMALL INDUSTRIAL COMPANIES
(percentages)

Balance Sheet

|  | 1977 | 1978 | 1979 | 1980 | 1981 |
|---|---|---|---|---|---|
| Assets | 100.0 | 100.0 | 100.0 | 100.0 | 100.0 |
| Short-term assets | 43.5 | 53.3 | 52.0 | 49.6 | 47.8 |
| Cash | 1.1 | 1.4 | 1.8 | 2.2 | 2.3 |
| Time deposits | 5.8 | 10.3 | 12.4 | 20.3 | 6.9 |
| Credits | 15.3 | 23.5 | 20.4 | 13.7 | 25.3 |
| Short-term investment | 2.0 | 0.9 | 0.7 | 0.6 | 0.2 |
| Inventories | 16.9 | 16.2 | 15.1 | 11.2 | 11.5 |
| Others | 2.4 | 1.0 | 1.6 | 1.6 | 1.6 |
| Long-term assets | 56.5 | 46.7 | 48.0 | 50.4 | 52.2 |
| Long-term credit related firms | 0.0 | 0.0 | 0.2 | 0.1 | 0.4 |
| Investment related firms | 0.4 | 0.4 | 1.5 | 8.9 | 4.1 |
| Fixed assets | 53.9 | 43.9 | 45.3 | 38.6 | 45.6 |
| Others 1/ | 2.2 | 2.4 | 1.0 | 2.8 | 2.2 |
| Short-term debt | 20.2 | 27.3 | 26.9 | 30.5 | 42.3 |
| Debt with public | 0.0 | 0.0 | 0.0 | 0.0 | 0.1 |
| Banks | 6.2 | 8.7 | 10.6 | 9.4 | 16.1 |
| Commercial | 6.9 | 9.7 | 7.6 | 8.4 | 10.7 |
| Others 2/ | 7.1 | 8.9 | 8.7 | 12.7 | 15.4 |
| Long-term debt | 10.6 | 8.2 | 8.6 | 10.3 | 11.4 |
| Banks | 6.2 | 6.0 | 5.7 | 6.8 | 5.5 |
| Debt with related firms | 0.0 | 0.0 | 0.1 | 0.3 | 0.0 |
| Others 3/ | 4.4 | 2.2 | 2.8 | 3.2 | 5.9 |
| Net worth | 69.2 | 64.5 | 64.5 | 59.2 | 46.3 |
|  |  |  |  |  |  |
| Profit and loss statement |  |  |  |  |  |
| Sales | 100.0 | 100.0 | 100.0 | 100.0 | 100.0 |
| Operational costs | -69.4 | -60.8 | -71.0 | -74.9 | -72.0 |
| Gross margin | 30.6 | 39.2 | 29.0 | 25.1 | 28.0 |
| Marketing and administ. costs | -19.4 | -22.8 | -25.8 | -26.5 | -29.3 |
| Financial expenses | - 8.9 | - 7.8 | - 9.0 | -10.9 | -10.2 |
| Other inflows and outflows | 1.4 | 6.1 | 1.1 | - 6.9 | -14.5 |
| Monetary correction | - 9.5 | - 8.6 | - 3.4 | - 0.7 | - 2.4 |
| Operational result | 11.2 | 16.4 | 3.3 | - 1.4 | - 1.4 |
| Non-operational result | -17.0 | -10.2 | -11.3 | -18.5 | -27.1 |
| Taxes | - 1.2 | - 2.5 | - 1.1 | - 1.2 | - 1.0 |
| Net profits | - 7.0 | 3.7 | - 9.1 | -21.1 | -29.5 |

Source: Data base World Bank Project on liberalization and stabilization policies in the Southern Cone countries.

1/ Lower investment value, higher investment value, long-term debtors, intangible, amortization.
2/ Dividends to be paid, provisions, retentions, income tax, debt with related companies, income perceived in advance and deferred taxes.
3/ Documents payable in the long-term, debt with the public, other creditors, provisions.

Notes

1. Rationing is a characteristic of financial markets due to the risk of default. It is extremely difficult for a bank to monitor all the relevant characteristics of the borrower's investment project; therefore, financial institutions establish limits on the amount a customer can borrow, independently of his/her willingness to pay a higher interest rate (see Stiglitz and Weiss, 1981). On the other hand, there are selective credit policies which, for instance, attempt to favor productive activities in opposition to consumption activities. These types of rationing differ from rationing that originates in the artificially low cost of credit. In the latter case credit rationing induces inefficient resource allocation and makes extraordinary profits possible for those who enjoy preferred access to cheap credit.

2. Available estimates indicate that annual nominal interest rates in the LDC's informal financial markets vary around 24-50%, while interest rates in the formal credit market vary around 10-12%. See Chandavarkar (1971).

3. Table 1 in chapter 3 shows the large spread existent during the entire period between the peso-loan interest rate and the dollar-loan interest rate, despite relaxation of international capital controls. In order to explain the existence of these spreads, it is important to consider the significant increase in demand for credit during the period, as well as the fact that domestic and foreign credit were not perfect substitutes in the Chilean economy. As will be shown in this chapter, the differential access to foreign credit by economic agents implied important segmentation in the financial market. It is likely that external credit contributed to mitigating the demand for credit in the domestic market, but due to existing segmentation it did not bring about interest rate arbitrage. On the other hand, the exchange rate risk does not seem to have been an important element in explaining the differentials between both rates. The existing evidence indicates that until 1981 there were no expectations of devaluations in the Chilean economy.

4. See Dahse (1979) for a description of these conglomerates.

5. In some cases only the first loan of a firm was guaranteed by a domestic bank. Afterwards, the firm operated directly with the foreign bank.

6. Since these loans were denominated in foreign currency the banks did not run the exchange risk.

7. It is important to note that three of these banks belong to economic conglomerates and the other is a commercial state bank. See table 4 in chapter 3.

8. However, as will be discussed later greater competition in the peso-loan market did not manifest itself in price competition but rather in a relaxation of banking standards.

9. The bank-customer relationship is an extremely relevant factor in the Chilean case due to the existence of important economic conglomerates.

10. Rationing in the first sense does not necessarily imply complete rejection of the loan requested by a borrower but rather a limit on the size of the loan. Moreover, observationally identical borrowers receive identical loans.

    Rationing in the second sense implies that among observationally identical borrowers some receive loans and others do not. Credit restrictions in this case take the form of limiting the number of loans the bank will make, rather than limiting the size of each loan, or making the interest rate charged an increasing function of the magnitude of the loan as in other cases of credit rationing.

11. In order to simplify, we separate the bank's decision to grant dollar loans to firms from the decision about peso loans. These would actually be made jointly as part of an overall profit maximization decision.

12. It is assumed that:
    (i) $I^*(0) = I_0^*$
    (ii) $\partial I^*(L^*)/\partial L^* = I^{*\prime}(L^*) \geq 0$
    (iii) $\partial^2 I^*(L^*)L^*/\partial L^{*2} = I^{*\prime}(L^*) + L^* I^{*\prime\prime} \geq 0$.

13. Please note that this does not necessarily imply price discrimination in the usual sense of this term, i.e, the setting of different prices for different customers, depending on their demand elasticities, regardless of identical costs. The price differentiation involved here may just as well be explained by the different risk characteristics of different customers.

14. An analogy for the practice of charging a uniform interest rate would be the postal system's practice of charging identical rates for a letter going across town and one travelling the length of the continent.

15. The net spread between active and passive real interest rates in the peso-loan market averaged 14.6% during the 1967-82 period. This net spread is obtained after subtracting the bank's cost of attracting funds which is:

$$\frac{\text{Interest rate paid for deposits - interest for bank reserves}}{\text{1-legal reserve requirement}}$$

16. Revell (1980) compares the banking crisis in the $19^{th}$ Century in Britain and the "fringe" banking crisis in 1973-74.

17. The Chilean case offers empirical support for Revell's argument. One of the new entrants in the banking industry during the period was the Banco de Santiago. This bank increased its market share from 0.9% in 1977 to 12% in 1982. In January 1983 the Banco de Santiago, among others, was intervened by the government due to the existence of serious deficiencies in its administration. The large number of credits of uncertain recoverability endangered the solvency and liquidity of the bank.

18. Information on the firm's balance sheets was provided by the World Bank project on liberalization and stabilization policies in Southern Cone countries. Information on article 14 direct foreign loans was obtained from F. Rojas, and information on foreign loans intermediated by the domestic banking system was obtained from the Superintendencia de Bancos e Instituciones Financieras. The sample represents 56% of the total assets of establishments having 50 or more employees, based on the 1977 Manufacturing Industry Census. The sample is also quite representative as regards the industrial sector contracting debt in foreign currency. The percentage of debt with the financial system corresponding to debt in foreign currency was 56.4% for the total industrial sector, and 69.3% for the 1980 company sample. The figures were 62.6% and 69% in 1981 for the industrial sector and the company sample respectively.

19. The classification was made by the World Bank.

20. It is important to note that when comparing various groups of corporations we are underestimating the differences among industrial firms. A more relevant comparison would be between publicly held corporations and family companies; however, the information to carry out such a study is not available.

21. It is important to note that the financial cost differentials for the various groups of firms are underestimated due to the fact that financial expenses associated with foreign currency credit are entered into accounts in nominal terms, whereas financial expenses associated with peso credits are entered into accounts in real terms in the companies' financial statements. See appendix 2 in chapter 4.

22. If 1976 is taken as the starting year for the calculation, differences in financial costs for debtors in pesos and foreign currency are even more striking.

23. The real interest rate in pesos charged for credits in foreign currency increased from -8.6% in 1980 to 11.6% in 1981.

24. Bank deposits of companies accrue as income in the form of a nominal interest rate from which the price index variation of the period covering the financial statements must be deducted. The proportion corresponding to inflation acknowledgement must be entered into accounts by charging the monetary correction account, and the real interest earned must be entered as non-operational income during the period.

25. Chapter 7 illustrates this issue.

26. A classic case in point was CRAV and CRAVAL.

27. There are three financing sources for companies: Internal sources made up of non-distributed profits and depreciation allowances; indirect external sources consisting of debt with banks and financial institutions; and direct external sources corresponding to share-issues.

# 6. TRADE LIBERALIZATION AND FINANCIAL REFORM

## 6.1. Introduction

McKinnon (1973 and 1981) argues that repression of the financial sector is paralleled by the use of tariffs and quotas in an effort to promote development by manipulating the foreign trade sector. He claims that successful liberalization of the domestic capital market permits a radical restructuring of tariffs, quota and licensing restraints on foreign trade. The case for free trade is clear when the domestic capital market is working freely. Moreover, if existing protective tariffs and quota restrictions were eliminated, an enormous implicit burden on export activities would be lifted and, therefore, the need to give them preferred access to low cost credit would be avoided. Hence, a more effective strategy for economic growth would proceed from a thorough liberalization of financial markets and the lifting of restraints on foreign trade (see chapter 2).

Moreover, McKinnon (1973 and 1982) points out that the order of economic liberalization is crucial to attain successful results. The main question is which market should be liberalized first. He argues that trade liberalization should proceed simultaneously with liberalization of domestic finances. However, liberalization of the current account of the balance of payments should precede the elimination of exchange controls on the capital account. The capital and current accounts of the balance of payments should not be opened simultaneously, and capital inflows should be tightly controlled during the transition period after trade has been liberalized.

The reasoning is as follows.[1] Once the domestic financial market has been liberalized, the opening of the capital account may result in large inflows of foreign capital triggered by substantial interest rate differentials. If such capital inflows are absorbed in real terms, this could force a trade deficit and real exchange rate appreciation on the economy. Since financial markets adjust much faster than goods markets, this real appreciation will be quite abrupt, implying severe anti-protection in the production of tradable goods.

Therefore, there is an important inconsistency in liberalizing the current account and the capital account of the balance of payments simultaneously. While the opening of the capital account may generate real appreciation of domestic currency, many economists have argued that successful liberalization of the trade account will require real depreciation to help the export sector expand and facilitate the adjustment process in previously protected import-competing industries.

The Chilean case provides an example of comprehensive economic liberalization in the Third World. Chile followed the McKinnon order almost to the letter (see McKinnon, 1982). It simultaneously liberalized the domestic financial market and the foreign trade sector, and opened the capital account only after tariffs had reached their final goal of 10% (see chapter 3). Nevertheless, the Chilean experience during the 1973-82 period was not a success.

The fixing of the exchange rate with respect to the dollar in June 1979 when domestic inflation remained substantially higher than external inflation, together with a massive inflow of foreign capital in 1980 and 1981, generated great real appreciation that resulted in an important loss of com petitiveness in the tradable goods sector.[2] The magnitude of the capital flows which followed the opening up of the capital account destabilized the economy. This situation was aggravated by extremely high real interest rates in the domestic financial sector. Contrary to the economic authorities' expectations, the domestic interest rate did not decline as a result of massive inflows of external capital.

The objective of this chapter is to investigate the effects the interaction of liberalization reforms had on the Chilean manufacturing sector. In chapter 4 one of the findings was that some industrial manufacturing firms contracted a significant amount of debt at very high interest rates. There it was suggested that the companies borrowed in the recently liberalized financial market in order to survive a time when they were being hit by the 1975 internal recession and growing foreign competition due to the opening up of the economy to foreign trade and, later, due to the overevaluation of the exchange rate. This chapter examines this issue; specifically, it attempts to answer the following question: to what extent did import-competing firms choose to contract debt at the high interest rates in force in the domestic financial market in order to adjust and survive increasing foreign competition?

The main source of information used consists of the financial balances and income statements of a sample of 128 publicly held corporations in the Chilean manufacturing sector. These corporations annually submit their financial statements to the Superintendencia de Valores y Seguros (Superintendency of Holdings and Securities). The sample includes both the companies that survived the period and the ones that went bankrupt during the 1977-82 period.[3] The companies have been classified into exporters, import-competing firms, and producers of nontradable goods, according to their sales orientation.

The organization of the chapter is the following: The second section discusses the effects of the opening up of the economy on the industrial sector during the 1974-82 period. It specifically illustrates the impact of trade liberalization on import-competing firms. The third section investigates empirically the financial behavior of export firms, import-competing firms, and firms producing nontradables during the 1977-82 period. It also attempts to determine to what point firms hard-hit by increased foreign competition borrowed in the liberalized financial market in order to remain in operation. The fourth section summarizes the main conclusions.

## 6.2. Commercial Openness and its Effects on the Industrial Sector

### 6.2.1. Trade Liberalization and the 1975 Internal Recession

Foreign trade liberalization was not the only shock that affected the Chilean industrial sector during the 1974-82 period. In particular, the 1975 internal recession, appreciation of foreign currency, and the increase in financing costs had significant negative effects on domestic industry.[4]

It is very difficult to separate the effects on the industrial sector of the decrease in aggregate demand from the effects of rapid tariff cuts during the period. A very rough estimate of both effects will be given as follows.[5]

In table 1, column 2 presents the evolution of the available supply of industrial goods (both domestic and imported) during the 1969-82 period, measured in millions of 1977 dollars.[6] The potential supply of industrial goods is estimated in column 1. In order to obtain these estimates it is assumed that the industrial supply of goods in 1969 corresponds to a normal year, and the supply for the 1970-73 period is obtained by applying to 1969 the average growth rate of the total supply of industrial goods during the 1960-69 period (5.1%). Moreover, it is also assumed that 1974 is a normal year, and the potential supply of industrial goods for the 1975-82 period is obtained by applying the average growth rate for the 1960-69 period (5.1%) to 1974. The method of considering the effective capacity of industrial production in 1974 equal to potential capacity does not overestimate the capacity of industrial production that year; on the contrary, it underestimates it, because in the second semester of 1974 contraction of aggregate demand was already affecting the level of annual industrial production. Finally, the third column presents effective domestic industrial production (industrial GDP), i.e., it does not include industrial imports.

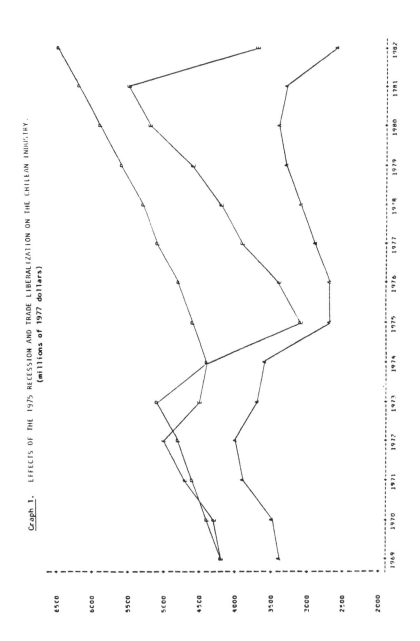

Graph 1. EFFECTS OF THE 1975 RECESSION AND TRADE LIBERALIZATION ON THE CHILEAN INDUSTRY. (millions of 1977 dollars)

Table 1. EFFECTS OF THE 1975 INTERNAL RECESSION AND TRADE LIBERALIZATION

ON THE CHILEAN MANUFACTURING INDUSTRY.

(millions of 1977 dollars)

|  | Potential supply of industrial goods | Available supply of industrial goods | Domestic industrial production (GDP) |
|---|---|---|---|
|  | (1) | (2) | (3) |
| 1969 | 4177.1 | 4177.1 | 3383.0 |
| 1970 | 4390.1 | 4331.6 | 3450.0 |
| 1971 | 4614.0 | 4711.1 | 3918.4 |
| 1972 | 4849.3 | 5017.2 | 4006.0 |
| 1973 | 5096.7 | 4522.9 | 3696.4 |
| 1974 | 4382.8 | 4382.8 | 3602.1 |
| 1975 | 4606.3 | 3146.8 | 2652.4 |
| 1976 | 4841.3 | 3363.2 | 2722.5 |
| 1977 | 5088.2 | 3919.6 | 2905.0 |
| 1978 | 5327.3 | 4174.5 | 3090.2 |
| 1979 | 5620.4 | 4627.8 | 3308.9 |
| 1980 | 5907.0 | 5231.1 | 3390.0 |
| 1981 | 6208.3 | 5453.5 | 3337.7 |
| 1982 | 6524.9 | 3663.8 | 2616.7 |

Sources: Industrial imports 1960-69: Odeplan.

Industrial imports 1970-82: Central Bank of Chile.

Industrial product 1960-73: National accounts.

Industrial product 1974-81: Meller et. al. (1984), 1982 National Accounts.

Graph 1 shows the evolution of these three variables throughout the 1969-82 period. The line represented by the P's shows the evolution of the potential supply of industrial goods (according to historical standards), while the line represented by the E's shows the evolution of the available supply of industrial goods. The difference between these two lines represents roughly the loss in industrial production due to contraction in aggregate demand. This is very clear in 1975-76 due to the internal recession in those years and also in 1982 when a new recession developed.[7] The line represented by the A's shows the evolution of domestic industrial production. Therefore, the difference between this line and the available supply of industrial goods represents the behavior of industrial imports during the period. Graph 1 illustrates that at the beginning of the 1974-82 period the contraction in aggregate demand was the main negative source of shock to the industrial sector; however, as of 1978 increasing competition from imports strongly impacted the industrial sector, mainly during 1980 and 1981. In 1982 the decrease in aggregate demand due to the new internal recession explains the poor industrial performance that year.

What table 1 and graph 1 show, in terms of timing and the impact of different shocks on the industrial sector, is consistent with the entrepreneurs' perceptions of the severity with which different shocks affected firms' behavior. Evidence regarding these perceptions during the 1977-80 period is found in the industrial questionnaires prepared by the Sociedad de Fomento Fabril (SOFOFA).[8]

These industrial questionnaires include about 80% of the firms in the industrial index of the Sociedad de Fomento Fabril. The firms surveyed represent around 47% of industrial GDP and 40% of industrial employment (considering establishments having 10 or more employees). In every case the general manager of the respective firm was interviewed with a standard questionnaire.

Survey data is always somewhat suspect, because one can never be sure of the motives or care taken by a subject who states a position on a questionnaire. It may be the case that the subject is more concerned with the image he or she wants to project than with an accurate answer to a specific question. Nevertheless, the evidence regarding entrepreneurs' perceptions that emerged from the survey of businessmen is consistent with the results obtained by sectorial studies of the industrial sector during the period (see Vergara, 1980 and Sherman, 1980).

The first survey made in October 1977, the second in April 1978, the fourth in August 1979, and the fifth in July 1980 include information about the entrepreneurs' sales expectations. Specifically, those firms which expected a decline in sales or at best maintenance of sales, were asked about the reasons for their forecasts.[9] Five possible reasons were considered: Import competition, lack of internal demand, financial problems, technical production problems, and lack of production capacity. Every firm had to decide on the most important reason to expect lower or constant sales in the future. Table 2 summarizes the answers; only the three main reasons considered by the entrepreneurs are tabulated here.

It can be seen that the two main explanations were increased import competition and the lack of internal demand. These evolved in a different way throughout the years. In 1977 48.6% of the firms singled out the restriction in aggregate demand as the main reason for low sales, and only 18.9% of the firms thought increased external competition was the main cause of their problems. However, in 1979 and 1980 the situation turned out to be the reverse. In 1979 43.1% of the firms which expected no rise in sales believed the main reason for stagnation was the increase in import competition, while 22.4% of the firms thought lack of internal demand was the main reason for this situation. Similar numbers were obtained for 1980.

Table 2. MAIN CAUSES WHICH EXPLAIN THE EXPECTATIONS OF CONSTANT OR LOWER INDUSTRIAL SALES: 1977-80. a/

|                          | Oct-Dec 1977 % | 1978 % | 1979 % | 1980 % |
|--------------------------|---------------|--------|--------|--------|
| Lack of internal demand  | 48.6          | 34.0   | 22.4   | 20.8   |
| Import competition       | 18.9          | 34.0   | 43.1   | 39.6   |
| Financial problems       | 8.5           | 4.5    | 6.9    | 4.2    |

Source:    SOFOFA.  Industrial Questionnaires I, II, IV and V.

Notes:    a/  The figures are percentages of the total number of firms which expected sales to be maintained or to decline in the future.

Therefore, according to the affected parties, internal factors associated with the contraction of aggregate demand were the main cause of low sales at the beginning of the period. Later on factors associated with increased foreign competition started to become more and more important in relative terms.

Table 3 presents similar results, but disaggregated by industrial sectors. This table allows us to see how these two shocks affected different industrial sectors. Unfortunately, disaggregate information was available only for 1979 and 1980; hence, it is not possible to observe the evolution throughout the period of the relative importance of each shock.

By mid-1979 the process of commercial opening up had finished, and from that date on the nominal exchange rate was pegged to the dollar. Moreover, on April 1980 all quantitative restrictions on international capital inflows were eliminated. The only remaining restrictions were the limit on all foreign borrowing and minimum maturity requirement of two years. The result of these measures was sustained capital inflow and rapid appreciation of the real exchange rate. These policies strongly affected firms dealing in tradables (see chapter 3).

Table 3. MAIN CAUSES WHICH EXPLAIN THE EXPECTATIONS OF CONSTANT

OR LOWER INDUSTRIAL SALES. DISAGGREGATED AT TWO DIGIT

LEVEL OF SIIC. 1979-80. a/

| Type of industry (SIIC code) | Import Competition | | Lack of Internal Demand | |
|---|---|---|---|---|
| | 1979 | 1980 | 1979 | 1980 |
| 31 Food manufacturing, beverages and tobacco | 16.6 | 25.0 | 16.6 | 33.3 |
| 32 Textiles, clothing and footwear | 61.1 | 68.0 | 16.7 | 16.0 |
| 33 Wood, wood products, furniture and fixtures | 33.3 | 12.5 | 66.7 | 25.0 |
| 34 Paper, paper products, printing and publishing | - | 25.0 | - | - |
| 35 Chemicals and rubber products | 30.0 | 33.3 | 39.0 | 33.3 |
| 36 Non-metallic mineral products | 100.0 | 42.9 | - | 28.6 |
| 37 Base metal and metal products | - | 0.0 | 66.7 | 50.0 |
| 38 Electrical and non-electrical machinery, appliances and equipment | 33.3 | 66.7 | 33.3 | 11.1 |

Source:   SOFOFA. Fourth and Fifth Industrial Questionnaires.

Notes:   a/ The figures are percentages of the total number of firms which expected their sales to be maintained or to decline in the future.

Table 3 shows that in 1979 and 1980 two industrial sectors were more affected by lack of internal demand than by import competition. They were the wood and wood products industry (33) and base metals and metal products (37). The import-competing firms singled out the increase in external competition as the main problem they were facing at that time. In 1980 68% of the firms interviewed which belonged to the textile, clothing and footwear industries (32) believed import competition was the main cause of their low level of sales while only 16% of firms thought lack of internal demand was causing their problems. Similar percentages were obtained for the electrical and non-electrical machinery, appliance and equipment industries (38); 66.7% of the firms felt that external competition was the main obstacle they were facing, while 11.1% of firms thought lack of internal demand was the main difficulty. Finally, 42.9% of the firms belonging to the non-metallic mineral products industry (36) declared that import competition was the major cause of their pessimistic expectations.

The next subsection will attempt to illustrate the impact trade liberalization had on firms producing import-competing goods.

### 6.2.2. The Impact of Trade Liberalization on Import-Competing Firms

The second industrial survey, conducted in April 1978, also shows that the industries most affected by import competition were textiles, clothing and footwear (32), electrical and non-electrical machinery, appliances and equipment (38), and non-metallic mineral products (36). In this survey businessmen were asked about the percentage of their firm's normal market share that was being taken over by imports at that moment.[10] Table 4 presents these results: 55% of the firms interviewed declared they were affected by external competition. These firms represented 61.6% of total sales, and they also said that 15.3% of their market was being supplied by imports. In the textile, clothing and footwear industry 63.3% of the firms interviewed declared that they were negatively affected by import competition and that 22.4% of their market was supplied by imports. The figures for the electrical and non-electrical machinery, appliance and equipment industry are similar; 65% of the firms declared that they were affected by external competition and that 27.7% of their market was supplied by imports at that moment. In the case of the non-metallic mineral products industry 76.9% of the firms were affected by import competition, and 14.3% of their market was being supplied by imports.

Furthermore, the evolution of goods prices produced by import-competing industries illustrates how much increased external competition, due to the rapid decrease in import tariffs and the fixed exchange rate policy followed since 1979, affected the companies during the 1974-82 period. Graphs 2 to 7 show the evolution of relative prices with respect to the consumer price index (CPI) of the textile, footwear, non-electrical machinery, electrical machinery, professional equipment and transport equipment industries respectively.[11] The evolution of these prices can be compared to the prices in the export industries. A good example is the wood industry, which benefited from the decrease in import tariffs, since it produced exportable goods with a comparative advantage; graph 8 presents wood industry prices with respect to CPI.

Table 4.  SHARE OF THE MARKET SUPPLIED BY IMPORTS: APRIL 1978

| Type of industry  (SIIC code) | % of firms being negatively affected by import competition | % of the market supplied by imports a/ |
|---|---|---|
| 31 Food manufacturing, beverages and tobacco | 38.3 | 12.6 |
| 32 Textiles, clothing and footwear | 63.3 | 22.4 |
| 33 Wood, wood products, furniture and fixtures | 22.2 | 9.4 |
| 34 Paper, paper products, printing and publishing | 50.0 | 15.7 |
| 35 Chemicals and rubber products | 62.5 | 14.5 |
| 36 Non-metallic mineral products | 76.9 | 14.3 |
| 37 Base metal and metal products | 75.0 | 6.4 |
| 38 Electrical and non-electrical machinery, appliances and equipment | 65.0 | 27.7 |
| 39 Other manufacturing industries | - | - |
| Total  b/ | 55.0 | 15.3 |

Source:     SOFOFA.  Second Industrial Questionnaire.

Notes:
a/     Refers to     firms which declared they were being affected by import competition.
b/     The aggregate result was obtained as the weighted average of all industries, the weights were  the industry sales' share.

The import-competing industries strongly affected by a decrease in prices were the non-electrical machinery (382, SIIC) and electrical machinery industries (383, SIIC) as well as the producers of professional and scientific equipment (385, SIIC). The evolution of these prices presents a strong contrast to the evolution of wood prices (331. SIIC) which show an increasing trend with respect to the CPI during the entire period under consideration; however, it can be noted that the rate of relative price increase declined around 1978-79 when the exchange rate started to be used as an anti-inflationary device.

Graph 2. TEXTILE INDUSTRY.

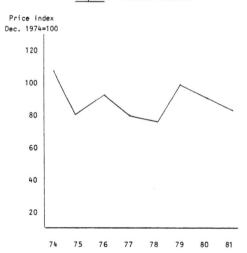

Graph 3. FOOTWEAR INDUSTRY.

Graph 4. NON-ELECTRICAL MACHINERY.

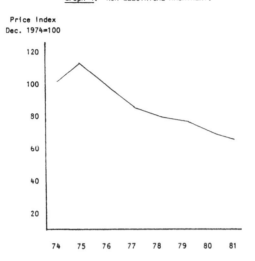

Graph 5. ELECTRICAL MACHINERY.

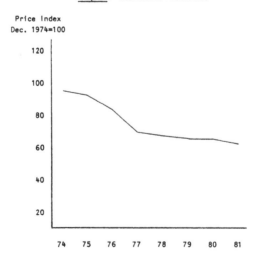

Graph 6. PROFESSIONAL EQUIPMENT.

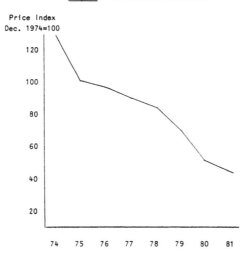

Graph 7. TRANSPORT EQUIPMENT.

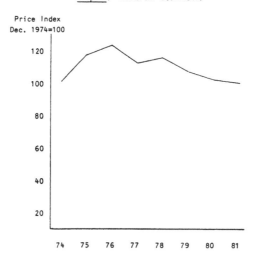

Graph 8. WOOD INDUSTRY.

To summarize, liberalization of international trade was not the only shock the Chilean industrial sector had to face during the 1974-82 period. In particular, an important drop in aggregate demand due to the 1975 internal recession strongly affected industrial firms. For industrial entrepreneurs as a whole the internal factors associated with the contraction of aggregate demand were the main obstacle they had to confront at the beginning of the period. Later on after 1978, the factors associated with increased import competition became more and more important. The rapid tariff cuts and fixed exchange rate policy followed by the government between mid-1979 and mid-1982 severely hit import-competing firms.

### 6.3. The Effects of Trade and Financial Reforms on Industrial Firms' Financial Behavior

During the 1974-82 period there was an important increase in the industrial sector's indebtedness, both in domestic and foreign currency. Table 5 presents evidence which supports this fact; the total debt of the industrial sector as a percentage of the sector's gross domestic product (GDP) increased from an average of 5.3% during 1973-75 to 31.5% during 1977-79. During this period the average tariff rate was reduced from 94% in 1973 to 10.1% in 1979, and there was an important overvaluation of the real exchange rate. It is likely that more than one factor explains this significant increment in the industrial sector's indebtedness; nevertheless, the significant decrease in the average cost of imports during the period played an outstanding role in industrial behavior during the 1970's.[12] The average cost of imports decreased from 100 in 1974 to 47.6 or 28.1 in 1981, depending on the deflator used to compute the real exchange rate.

Table 5. TOTAL MANUFACTURING INDUSTRY, AVERAGE TARIFF, REAL EXCHANGE RATE, AVERAGE COST OF IMPORTS AND INDEBTEDNESS: 1973-82.

| | Average tariff | Real exch. rate deflated by | | Average cost of imports 1974=100 | | Total debt c/ Industrial GDP |
| | % a/ | CPI | Wage index | CPI | Wage index | % |
| | (1) | (2) | (3) | (4) | (5) | (6) |
|---|---|---|---|---|---|---|
| 1973 | 94 | | | | | 1.8 |
| 1974 | 67 | 23.4 | 27.9 | 100.0 | 100.0 | 5.3 |
| 1975 | 44 | 32.1 | 39.4 | 118.2 | 121.7 | 8.9 |
| 1976 | 27 | 25.9 | 29.9 | 84.1 | 81.5 | 18.8 |
| 1977 | 15.7 | 21.5 | 21.5 | 63.7 | 53.4 | 20.8 |
| 1978 | 13.9 | 23.8 | 21.5 | 67.0 | 50.9 | n.a. |
| 1979 | 10.1 | 23.2 | 19.3 | 65.2 | 45.5 | 42.1 |
| 1980 | | 20.1 | 15.4 | 56.6 | 36.5 | 42.5 |
| 1981 | | 16.9 | 11.9 | 47.6 | 28.1 | 41.6 |
| 1982 | | 19.6 | 13.9 | 55.2 | 32.8 | 61.0 |

Sources:  Col. (1): Ffrench-Davis (1980)
Col. (2) and (3): Ffrench-Davis (1983,b). In col. (2) the nominal exchange rate was deflated by the CPI, in col. (3) it was deflated by the wage index.
Col. (4): Obtained from col. (1) and (2).
Col. (5): Obtained from col. (1) and (3).
Col. (6): Superintendencia de Bancos. "Financial Information", various numbers.

Notes:  a/ Rates on CIF import values in effect during December each year.
b/ Pesos per 1977 dollars.
c/ Corresponds to total debt with the domestic financial system.

Microeconomic financial data from an extensive representative sample of industrial firms will be analyzed as follows. The objective is to examine the financial behavior of different groups of industrial firms according to the type of goods produced and to determine whether or not industrial firms hard-hit by increased external competition borrowed in the financial market to remain in operation.

The source of information consists of the financial statements from a sample of 128 publicly held corporations in the Chilean manufacturing sector. These corporations submit their financial balances to the Superintendencia de Valores y Seguros annually. The sample includes both those companies that survived and those that went bankrupt during the 1977-82 period. Table 6 presents the number of firms for which information was available each year. Notice the significant decline in the number of import-competing firms during the last two years of the period.

Table 6. SAMPLE CLASSIFICATION

|                                   | 1977 | 1978 | 1979 | 1980 | 1981 | 1982 |
|-----------------------------------|------|------|------|------|------|------|
| Import-competing firms            | 79   | 79   | 79   | 79   | 43   | 40   |
| Export firms                      | 30   | 30   | 30   | 30   | 26   | 24   |
| Firms producing nontradables      | 19   | 19   | 19   | 19   | 18   | 18   |
| T o t a l                         | 128  | 128  | 128  | 128  | 87   | 82   |

This sample represents 50% of the total assets of establishments with 50 or more employees, based on the 1979 Manufacturing Industry Census. The sample also represents 56% of the industrial sector that contracted debt with the financial sector in foreign and domestic currency during 1981.

Companies have been classified into exporters, import-competing establishments and producers of nontradable goods, according to their sales orientation. Firms classified as exporters were those that sold more than 30% of their production in foreign markets; import-competing firms were those where 50% or more of their products directly competed with imports, and the remaining companies were defined as nontradables. Table 6 sums up the classification of the sample.

Table 7 presents the main results of the three groups of firms.

In terms of profitability import-competing firms did the worst, which was to be expected given the adverse conditions those companies faced throughout the whole period. In the beginning they had to adjust to the fast opening up to foreign trade and then to a loss in competitiveness due to the drop in the real exchange rate, all in the context of high financial costs. Export companies made profits up to 1981, as they enjoyed very positive conditions at the beginning of the period, due to tariff reduction and periodic exchange rate devaluations. Moreover, the negative impact of the fixed nominal exchange rate was offset by export-favoring international prices until 1980. Nevertheless, accumulated peso appreciation, together, with the export-price decrease and the 1981 interest rate increase, meant that only companies producing nontradable goods avoided losses in 1981 (see col. 9 and 10).[13]

Firms producing nontradables had the best results in terms of profitability during the 1977-82 period. Their losses in 1982 can be explained by the devaluation of domestic currency that year and the strong internal recession which started at the end of 1981. It is interesting to notice that during a period when an outward-looking development strategy was being implemented, the producers of tradable goods experienced lower profitability than firms producing nontradables.

The policies of opening the current account of the balance of payments on the one hand, and fixing the nominal exchange rate and opening the economy to inflows of foreign capital on the other hand, exerted pressures for resources to move in opposite directions, because these policies imply conflicting movements in the real exchange rate. The appreciation of the exchange rate generated an expansion of firms producing nontradables and a contraction of import-competing and export firms.[14]

Although they were suffering important losses in percentages of total assets and percentages of net worth, import-competing firms do not seem to have had problems obtaining loans from the domestic financial system. Their financial leverage was high, and in 1980 the amount of their total debt began to exceed their net worth (see col. 8). Import-competing firms' ratio of total debt to total assets increased more rapidly than that of export firms or firms producing nontradables. However, most of their debt was denominated in domestic currency. The percentage of their total debt which was foreign-currency denominated (article 14 loans and foreign currency debt contracted with the domestic financial system) and their high financial expenses in terms of percentage of total sales confirms this fact (col. 5, 6 and 7). It is likely that import-competing firms did not meet the minimum requirements for obtaining credit in foreign currency due to the difficult situation they were in.

Table 7 also shows that firms producing nontradable goods were the ones with the highest financial leverage until 1979. From then on their indebtedness fell in relation to import-competing firms. Financial expenses of the producers of nontradables as a percentage of total sales are lower than the financial expenses of export and import-competing firms. Companies producing nontradable goods have the lion's share of debt contracted directly with foreign banks through article 14 as part of their liabilities.

This result seems to contradict the textbook case where, given an upward-sloping supply of foreign funds, firms producing tradables are expected to have easier access to foreign credit than firms producing nontradables, because of their ability to generate foreign exchange to pay back their debt. However, in the Chilean case the result is explained by the real appreciation of the exchange rate which encouraged resources to move toward firms producing nontradable goods.[15]

During the 1977-82 period import-competing firms underwent an important decrease of fixed assets in absolute terms. Fixed assets dropped from a level equivalent to 100 in 1977 to 78.3 in 1980 (col. 2).[16] Export firms suffered a decrease in fixed assets at the beginning of the period, but later they recovered their 1977 level. Firms producing nontradables registered an important increase in fixed assets, growing from a 100 equivalent level in 1977 to 206.8 in 1982.

That is to say, during the 1977-82 period industrial firms producing nontradable goods experienced a significant increase in their investment in fixed assets, while industrial firms producing tradable goods did not. This is an undesirable result in an economy where a trade liberalization reform is being implemented. Successful trade liberalization requires higher, more rapid growth in the tradable goods sector. This implies a reallocation of resources toward this sector throughout the years. Therefore, it requires higher profitability in the traded goods sector than in the nontradables sector to help the export sector to expand.

Although import-competing firms show an important decrease in fixed assets, they also exhibit significant indebtedness during the period. This fact suggests that import-competing companies hard-hit by the trade liberalization policy took out loans to survive the increasing foreign competition. Let us explore this issue more closely.

Following Krumm (1983), I examine a cross section time-series data set of Chilean manufacturing firms to test whether changes in bank debt are in fact correlated to losses in the case of import-competing firms.

Ordinary least squares cross section time-series regressions are run for each group of firms. The dependent variable is the change in bank debt, and the independent variables are losses and investment. Figures on total assets of individual firms are used to correct for heteroscedasticity, and time dummies are included to adjust for possible contemporaneous correlation between firms' error terms due to changes in the macroeconomic variables over the period.

Table 7.  SAMPLE OF COMPANIES THAT SELL EXPORTABLE GOODS, IMPORT-COMPETING GOODS, AND NONTRADABLE GOODS.

| | Assets (1977=100) | | Total debt / Total assets | Debt with banks | as a % of total debt Foreign currency debt (art.14) | Foreign currency debt with dom. fin. system | Fin. expen. / Sales | Tot.debt / Net worth | Profits / Av. assets | Profits / Average net worth |
|---|---|---|---|---|---|---|---|---|---|---|
| | Total | Fixed a/ | | | | | | | | |
| | (1) | (2) | (3) | (4) | (5) | (6) | (7) | (8) | (9) | (10) |
| **Import-competing firms** | | | | | | | | | | |
| 1977 | 100.0 | 100.0 | 45 | 26 | 0.2 | n.a. | 16.8 | 0.8 | - | - |
| 1978 | 88.0 | 82.3 | 47 | 37 | 1.0 | n.a. | 11.9 | 0.9 | 0.6 | 1.0 |
| 1979 | 97.1 | 78.6 | 46 | 46 | 2.7 | n.a. | 10.0 | 0.8 | 2.5 | 4.6 |
| 1980 | 109.6 | 78.3 | 50 | 49 | 2.4 | 29.9 | 9.1 | 1.0 | - 2.1 | - 4.0 |
| 1981 | - | - | 55 | 47 | 0.5 | 29.6 | 13.0 | 1.2 | -10.9 | -22.7 |
| 1982 | - | - | 69 | 65 | 0.2 | 29.6 | 20.1 | 2.3 | -19.1 | -50.1 |
| **Export firms** | | | | | | | | | | |
| 1977 | 100.0 | 100.0 | 45 | 27 | 2.9 | n.a. | 5.7 | 0.8 | - | - |
| 1978 | 98.5 | 94.2 | 45 | 38 | 2.0 | n.a. | 5.5 | 0.8 | 7.2 | 13.2 |
| 1979 | 118.3 | 103.1 | 46 | 46 | 4.0 | n.a. | 5.2 | 0.9 | 8.5 | 15.8 |
| 1980 | 133.7 | 108.4 | 45 | 52 | 3.7 | 38.3 | 6.1 | 0.8 | 5.2 | 9.5 |
| 1981 | 127.3 | 107.1 | 49 | 56 | 6.1 | 35.3 | 12.1 | 1.0 | - 3.4 | - 6.1 |
| 1982 | 154.7 | 105.3 | 60 | 72 | 2.5 | 36.3 | 19.1 | 1.5 | - 6.4 | -14.1 |
| **Firms producing nontradables** | | | | | | | | | | |
| 1977 | 100.0 | 100.0 | 48 | 36 | 8.6 | n.a. | 6.2 | 0.9 | - | - |
| 1978 | 119.4 | 101.5 | 56 | 51 | 5.2 | n.a. | 5.0 | 1.3 | 6.2 | 13.0 |
| 1979 | 165.8 | 121.3 | 54 | 54 | 6.9 | n.a. | 5.6 | 1.2 | 6.0 | 13.4 |
| 1980 | 200.3 | 138.1 | 51 | 64 | 9.8 | 30.5 | 5.3 | 1.0 | 6.0 | 12.5 |
| 1981 | 229.3 | 152.2 | 57 | 60 | 18.6 | 31.4 | 8.1 | 1.3 | 5.1 | 11.0 |
| 1982 | 309.5 | 206.8 | 70 | 62 | 0.8 | 29.8 | 10.7 | 2.3 | - 8.3 | -23.3 |

Sources:   Superintendencia de Valores y Seguros

Notes:   a/ Real values.  CPI Cortázar and Marshall (1980) was used.

It has been assumed that bank loans are an important source of finance for manufacturing firms. The numbers given in table 7 support this assumption. Bank debt has been defined as including short and long-term bank lending; both have been added because during this period most short-term bank loans were constantly rolled over. Investment is defined as the change in fixed assets from which depreciation allowances are subtracted. The reason for using net investment instead of gross investment as an independent variable rests in the fact that bank loans finance a significant proportion of net investment[17] while a major source of gross investment financing is depreciation. Losses are defined as the absolute value of negative profits, or else as the negative value of positive profits.

Table 8 presents the results for the 1977-82 period. It is interesting to note that only in the case of import-competing firms losses constitute significant variables which explain the change in bank debt. The partial correlation between losses of import-competing firms and changes in bank debt is positive (0.27) and statistically significant. Bank borrowing by import-competing firms went to finance not only investment but also operating losses.

Since bank loans are an important source of investment financing in LDC's, it is not surprising that for the three groups of firms the partial correlation coefficients between the change in bank debt and the change in fixed assets are significantly positive. This is especially true in the case of the export sector.

The year 1982 is a very special one, as in that year an unexpected devaluation of the peso struck a severe blow at firms that had foreign-currency denominated debts.[18] Also the second worse internal recession of the century developed, and most firms suffered important losses. Due to this fact the same regressions were estimated but excluded the year 1982. Table 9 summarizes the results. As in the case where 1982 is included, the only group of companies which shows a significant positive partial correlation between losses and the change in bank debt are the import-competing firms. The main difference between both groups of results is the change in the sign of the partial correlation coefficient between losses and change in bank debt for the export firms, although in none of the cases is it statistically significant. It is likely that export firms attempted to finance part of their losses with bank loans during 1982.

Hence, the empirical evidence presented shows that import-competing firms were able to and did borrow in the financial market in order to cover current operating losses and remain in the running.[19] This was an important mechanism used by these firms to survive the new economic conditions.[20]

**Table 8.** RELATIONSHIP BETWEEN CHANGES IN BANK DEBT AND LOSSES

FOR A SAMPLE OF CHILEAN MANUFACTURING FIRMS: 1977-82.

Dependent variable:  change in bank debt/total assets.

|  | Import-competing firms | Export firms | Firms producing nontradables |
|---|---|---|---|
| Constant | 0.11 (5.28)*** | 0.09 (2.62)*** | 0.17 (3.83)*** |
| Losses/total assets | 0.27 (3.46)*** | 0.11 (1.11) | 0.14 (0.89) |
| Change in fixed assets / Total assets | 0.47 (7.32)*** | 0.30 (46.6)*** | 0.61 (5.43)*** |
| 1979 dummy | - 0.05 (1.62)* | 0.02 (0.38) | - 0.09 (1.43) |
| 1980 dummy | - 0.07 (2.27)** | - 0.04 (0.87) | - 0.14 (2.28)** |
| 1981 dummy | - 0.13 (3.47)*** | - 0.07 (1.43)* | - 0.13 (2.13)** |
| 1982 dummy | 0.03 (0.77) | 0.06 (1.15) | - 0.02 (0.32) |
| $R^2$ | 0.23 | 0.98 | 0.33 |
| SE | 0.19 | 0.18 | 0.19 |

Source:    Pooled cross-section time-series data set for a sample of Chilean manufacturing firms.  Superintendencia de Valores y Seguros.

Notes:

(i)    Absolute value of t-statistics in parentheses *, ** and *** indicating significance at 90%, 95% and 99% level respectively.

(ii)    Total assets are computed at the beginning of the period for each period.

(iii)    Losses are defined as the absolute value of negative profits and the negative value of positive profits.

This behavior suggests that firms' losses were believed to be temporary. Import-competing firms borrowed in the recently liberalized financial market to cover their current losses and overcome what they foresaw as only transitory difficulties.

There is evidence which seems to support the above hypothesis. The second industrial questionnaire organized by SOFOFA in April 1978 presents the entrepreneurs' expectations about the effect of trade liberalization on industrial firms. In April 1978, when more than one year remained in the pre-announced liberalization schedule, in every industrial sector, including the import-competing sectors, most respondents said they expected their competitive position to remain the same or improve by 1978, but not to continue to deteriorate as should have been the case had they professed credibility in the sustainability of the import liberalization process (see table 10).[21]

Table 9.  RELATIONSHIP BETWEEN CHANGES IN BANK DEBT AND LOSSES

FOR A SAMPLE OF CHILEAN MANUFACTURING FIRMS:  1977-81.

Dependent variable:  change in bank debt/total assets.

|  | Import-competing firms | Export firms | Firms producing nontradables |
|---|---|---|---|
| Constant | 0.11 (5.45)*** | 0.07 (2.18)** | 0.17 (3.94)*** |
| Losses/total assets | 0.22 (2.49)*** | - 0.04 (0.39) | 0.18 (0.92) |
| Change in fixed assets / Total assets | 0.43 (6.80)*** | 0.31 (44.18)*** | 0.87 (6.07)*** |
| 1979 dummy | - 0.05 (1.60)* | 0.02 (0.36) | - 0.10 (1.68)** |
| 1980 dummy | - 0.07 (2.26)** | - 0.03 (0.75) | - 0.15 (2.50)*** |
| 1981 dummy | - 0.12 (3.49)*** | - 0.05 (1.09) | - 0.14 (2.37)** |
| $R^2$ | 0.19 | 0.98 | 0.39 |
| SE | 0.18 | 0.18 | 0.18 |

Source:     Pooled cross-section time-series data set for a sample of Chilean manufacturing firms.  Superintendencia de Valores y Seguros.

Notes:

(i)        Absolute value of t-statistics in parentheses *, ** and *** indicating significance at 90%, 95% and 99% level respectively.

(ii)       Total assets are computed at the beginning of the period for each period.

(iii)      Losses are defined as the absolute value of negative profits and the negative value of positive profits.

However, liberalization continued on schedule until reaching the flat tariff of 10% in June 1979. This fact plus further overvaluation of the exchange rate squeezed profitability in the import-competing sector. Firms could not pay back their debts contracted at the high interest rates in force in the domestic market and continued borrowing to refinance them (see chapter 7). To the extent that debts accumulated and the interest rate did not decline to normal levels moral-hazard-type behavior became highly likely by the end of the period.

Table 10.  THE EXPECTED IMPACT OF TARIFF DECREASE ON

FIRMS' COMPETITIVENESS: 1978.

(percentage of firms)

| Type of industry  (SIIC code) | Competitiveness will improve | Competitiveness will remain the same | Competitiveness will worsen |
|---|---|---|---|
| 31 Food manufacturing, beverages and tobacco | 8.7 | 78.3 | 13.0 |
| 32 Textiles, clothing and footwear | 4.2 | 54.2 | 41.6 |
| 33 Wood, wood products, furniture and fixtures | 29.2 | 54.2 | 41.6 |
| 34 Paper, paper products, printing and publishing | 6.2 | 68.8 | 25.0 |
| 35 Chemicals and rubber products | 11.3 | 67.6 | 21.1 |
| 36 Non-metallic mineral products | 0.0 | 54.5 | 45.5 |
| 37 Base metal and metal products | 9.1 | 63.6 | 27.3 |
| 38 Electrical and non-electrical machinery, appliances and equipm. | 5.3 | 52.6 | 42.1 |
| 39 Other manufacturing industries | 16.7 | 50.0 | 33.3 |
| Total  a/ | 9.6 | 62.7 | 27.7 |

Source:    SOFOFA.  Second Industrial Questionnaire.

Notes:

a/          The aggregate result was obtained as the weighted average of all industries; the weights were the industry sales' share.

It can also be argued that even if firms believed in trade liberalization reform, the extremely high level of interest rates they faced, together with the overvalued exchange rate, prevented them from adjusting to the new economic conditions. Import-competing firms had extremely high financial costs throughout the whole period. Thus, firms that may have planned on taking out loans to invest in newly profitable areas may well have ended up borrowing to finance losses generated by high interest payments and the further loss of competitiveness brought about by real exchange rate appreciation.

## 6.4. Conclusions

Domestic financial market liberalization was only one of the structural changes which industrial manufacturing firms had to adjust to during the 1977-82 period. Trade liberalization reform also influenced the behavior of industrial firms; rapid reduction of import tariffs confronted firms with increasing foreign competition. Moreover, the fixed exchange rate policy, together with massive foreign capital inflows in 1980 and 1981 resulting from the opening up of the capital account, implied a further loss of competitiveness in the industrial sector. In this chapter the effect of the interaction of these reforms on the manufacturing companies has been analyzed.

The results support the hypothesis that import-competing firms, especially the ones hard hit by increased external competition, chose to contract debt at high existing interest rates in the domestic financial market in order to survive against the increasing foreign competition. Bank borrowing by import-competing firms went to finance not only investment but also current operating losses. In the case of export firms and firms producing nontradable goods, losses are not a statistically significant determinant of bank debt.

Evidence obtained from a survey of businessmen suggests that import-competing firms borrowed in the recently-liberalized financial market in order to overcome what they foresaw as only transitory difficulties. However, their losses were far from temporary, and further loss of competitiveness brought about by real appreciation of domestic currency prevented the firms from servicing their debts. Hence, firms had to continue borrowing in order to refinance their obligations.

It can also be argued that even if firms believed in trade liberalization reform, the extremely high level of interest rates they faced throughout the whole period, together with the exchange rate appreciation, prevented them from adjusting to the new economic conditions.

The results also show that there was an important inconsistency in the liberalization policies followed during this period. One of the most important consequences of opening up the capital account was a further appreciation of the peso due to massive capital inflows. Real appreciation of domestic currency implied severe anti-protection of firms producing traded goods. Therefore, there was an important contradiction in the economic model that was implemented. At a time when an outward looking development strategy was being implemented firms producing tradable goods, which theoretically should have been the dynamic engine of the new economic model, suffered an important decline in profitability. On the contrary, producers of nontradables enjoyed very positive conditions.

Firms producing nontradables show the best results in terms of profitability during the 1977-82 period. Also, these firms registered an important increase in fixed assets in absolute terms. In contrast, import-competing firms suffered a significant decline in fixed assets, and export firms ended up the period with a level of fixed assets similar to those they had had in 1977.

Moreover, firms producing nontradable goods in general faced lower financial expenses in regard to sales income than export firms. The explanation rests in the fact that producers of nontradables had easier, more fluid access to direct foreign credit contracted under article 14 of the Foreign Exchange Law. Import-competing firms faced very restricted access to cheaper foreign credit and, therefore, extremely high financial expenses. In the Chilean case the real appreciation of the exchange rate encouraged resources to move toward firms producing nontradable goods and prevented the expansion of firms producing tradables.

This same phenomenon was experienced with greater intensity by the aggregate economy. An important proportion of funds obtained abroad were used to finance nontradables, especially in the construction sector. Moreover, there was unbalanced economic growth during this period between the tradable and nontradable sectors. The tradable goods sector's average growth rate of real GDP was 5% during the 1977-81 period, while the average growth rate of real GDP for the nontradable goods sector reached 8.4% during the same period (see Muñoz, 1982).

Therefore, in the Chilean case the interaction of domestic financial liberalization with foreign trade and external financial liberalization resulted in perverse resource allocation. Loan demand satisfied by the recently liberalized domestic banking sector was caused not only by standard investment demand, but also significantly by losses incurred by existing import-competing firms. Moreover, as pointed out above an important proportion of cheap foreign credit was allocated to the nontradable goods sector.

A question comes up. Does the Chilean experience imply that the order of economic liberalization recommended by McKinnon is incorrect? I think that the Chilean experience does not imply that the order is incorrect, but that there is a big difference between a textbook case and a real economy, especially a developing fragmented economy.

In a simple textbook case resources immediately move from one sector to another in response to price signals. In a real economy it is necessary to consider the existence of adjustment costs, externalities and market imperfections. In these conditions resource reallocation will take place more slowly.

The Chilean experience, for example, indicates that complete liberalization of the domestic financial market does not ensure a competitive market. Moreover, the opening up of the capital account of the balance of payments does not ensure full integration between domestic and international financial markets, and does not necessarily bring about interest rate arbitrage. Therefore, a massive capital inflow takes place in response to interest rate differentials. These inflows of capital tend to destabilize the domestic economy. The Chilean case also indicates that successful trade liberalization requires greater, more rapid growth in the tradable goods sector. This implies a reallocation of resources toward this sector throughout the years, and, therefore, a relatively higher return in the tradable sector than in the nontradable goods sector. Hence, a successful opening up to foreign trade requires a change in the productive structure. Tariff cuts are only a tool which needs to be complemented with investment in infrastructure (transport and communications), research and development, and human capital. Also, exchange rate policy is crucial in successful trade reform. This policy should ensure a stable real exchange rate in order to make the traded goods sector permanently profitable and competitive.

Notes

1. This line of reasoning has been followed by Dornbusch (1983b) and Frenkel (1982), among others.

2. The main goal behind the fixing of the nominal exchange rate was control of domestic inflation. However, it is not necessary to have a fixed exchange rate to obtain real appreciation following external capital inflows. Under a fixed exchange rate these inflows will be monetized and will result in inflation and real appreciation of the domestic currency. Under a floating exchange rate the inflows will result in an appreciation of nominal and real exchange rates.

3. This company sample was obtained directly from the Superintendencia de Valores y Seguros. In this chapter the World Bank company sample is not being used, because the firms that went bankrupt are not included in the same data set as all other firms in existence at the beginning of the period. Since I would like to test the hypothesis that import-competing firms borrowed to survive the period, I should not perform the test on a sample consisting only of firms that did not later go bankrupt. That would be sample selection bias.

4. The reduction in aggregate demand due to contractionary fiscal and monetary policies, and the increased financial costs faced by domestic firms due to freed interest rates, lay behind the big recession in 1975. See chapter 3.

5. The methodology used in this estimation follows Ffrench-Davis (1980).

6. Available supply of goods includes domestic production of industrial goods plus imports of industrial goods.

7. The difference between the potential supply of goods and the available supply of goods can also be explained by a low level of national investment during the 1974-82 period and by a change in demand composition due to the income concentration process and import competition.

8. This section draws on the work done by Jaime Gatica with the industrial questionnaires. See Gatica (1989).

9. In 1978 13.5% of the firms interviewed expected no increase in their sales level; figures for 1979 and 1980 were 18.8% and 27.5% respectively.

10. Let us remember that in April 1978 the maximum nominal tariff was 25%, the average tariff was 15.3%, and the government had already announced that in June 1979 there would be a flat tariff of 10%.

11. Relative prices with respect to the CPI are used to account for domestic inflation during the 1974-81 period. The Cortázar and Marshall (1980) CPI is used, because the official price index was manipulated and understated inflation.

12. The industrial sector was not the only economic sector which increased its indebtedness during the period. Specifically, the construction sector presents an extraordinary increase in total debt during the 1979-82 period, when there was a construction boom in the country.

13. A Banco Central estimate of the average price of Chilean export-products points to a 16% drop between the second half of 1980 and the second half of 1981.

14. It is interesting that this phenomenon can be noticed in the industrial sector even though this sector as a whole is normally classified as a traded goods sector.

15. This phenomenon manifested itself in the whole Chilean economy. After the capital account of the balance of payments was opened, an important fraction of the massive capital inflows was used to finance the expansion of the construction sector.

16. Due to the important number of bankrupt firms in 1981 and 1982, it is not possible to obtain the evolution of the absolute level of fixed assets for those years.

17. During this period bank loans were also used to finance firms' investment in financial assets. See chapter 4.

18. This devaluation marked the end of reliance on the economic model based on the open economy monetary approach to the balance of payments, also called global monetarism. See chapter 3.

19. The fact that a significant proportion of the demand for credit comes from the firms' need to cover operating losses implies a demand for credit which is very inelastic with respect to the interest rate, or a demand for credit with perverse behavior in relation to the interest rate. Any of these phenomena would help explain the persistently

high real interest rates experienced by the Chilean economy during the 1975-82 period.

20. Other adjustment mechanisms used by import-competing firms were the merger of firms and the transformation of firms' production lines into commercial lines; i.e., import-competing firms started to import goods they had formerly produced, using their previously established commercial networks. See Ffrench-Davis (1980) and Vergara (1980).

21. There are two facts that could have damaged public credibility in the trade liberalization reform implemented during the 1974-82 period in Chile. In the first place the history of Chilean foreign trade policies from the Great Depression until 1970 is full of attempts to liberalize foreign trade. Nevertheless, none of these liberalizations were sustained, and regression to more repressive tariffs and exchange controls was commonplace. In the second place, the reform implemented during the 1974-82 period can be characterized as a rapid and erratic opening up to international trade. Moreover, there was a lack of consistency on the part of economic authorities when the reduction of tariffs was not compensated for with an increase in the real exchange rate, as promised (see chapter 3). If economic agents perceive policies to be inconsistent, they expect the reform attempt to be discontinued or reversed in the future.

# 7. FINANCIAL BEHAVIOR OF COMPANIES IN A LIBERALIZED CAPITAL MARKET: SOME CASE STUDIES

## 7.1. Introduction

The aim of this chapter is to attain a better understanding of the way productive firms reacted to the structural changes that took place in the Chilean financial market during the 1975-82 period.

In pursuing this goal a case-study approach is taken. The study is based on a deliberately chosen sample of Chilean industrial manufacturing corporations. The firms were selected from a larger sample of publicly held corporations whose balance sheets and income statements have been analyzed in previous chapters.

Analysis of the corporations' financial statement sheds some interesting light on the problems they faced and the adjustment they made during the period of financial liberalization, but it also emphasizes the need for a closer look at some of the issues. Financial statements show the firms' results throughout one year, and if one analyzes them over a longer period, they also reveal changes in the firms' asset and liability structures. Nevertheless, they can not acquaint us with specific problems the firms faced, the businessmen's expectations and perceptions, or the reasons for making a certain decision. These are the types of issues addressed in this case-study.

Specifically, we are interested in the relationship between firms and banks in the context of a liberalized financial market. To what extent do firms believe the banks fulfilled their role as financial intermediaries during the 1975-82 period? Were there important differences among banks during the period? Did banks ration credit using some other kind of mechanism besides interest rates such as collateral requirements? We are also concerned with the financial decisions made by firms. Why did firms increase their financial leverage during the period? What type of loans were the firms able to obtain and in what conditions? Did firms experience changes in their asset and cost structures? Moreover, the role of expectations is extremely important in a liberalized economy. In this sense, we intend to shed some light on the role played by expectations in firms' decisions. More concretely, what did firms expect regarding the evolution of the domestic interest rate? Did expectations of future devaluations of the peso with respect to the dollar influence firms' decisions about foreign loans? And what were their expectations about the future of business activities? Finally, since the period can be characterized by a massive wave of bankruptcies, we should find out why certain firms in particular went bankrupt.

The chapter is organized in the following way: The second section discusses the methodology utilized. The third section presents the results obtained; these are organized around the main questions posed above. The fourth section contains some final remarks. Furthermore, an appendix is attached, presenting the questionnaire used in the interviews with the firms.

## 7.2. Methodology

As we have already indicated, this study intends to examine, as if through a magnifying glass, a sub-sample of the group of firms whose balance sheets were studied in previous chapters. Twelve firms were deliberately selected; four of them belonged to economic conglomerates, four of them were unrelated to economic groups, and the remaining four went bankrupt during this period. The criteria used to select these three groups of firms proceed from the previous studies. The analysis of the financial statements from a large sample of industrial corporations indicates that this classification is the most relevant for the type of issues being investigated.

The general manager or the financial manager in charge of the firms during the 1975-82 period was personally interviewed in every case. Each interview was conducted with a standard questionnaire in order to homogenize the data obtained.[1]

Table 1 summarizes the main characteristics of the firms studied.

The case-study approach has limitations as well as advantages. Because of the non-standardized way data is collected in a case-study, it is not generally useful for statistical treatment. In other words, there is a more impressionistic interpretation of data; therefore, it is difficult to use qualitative data to support a specific theory. Nevertheless, this type of methodology is extremely helpful when the researcher wants to probe issues in depth that can not be observed through quantitative data. Difficult-to-quantify variables are probably less distorted by unstructured observation and interviewing than by abortive attempts to operationalize them for quantification.

Table 1. SAMPLE CHARACTERISTICS.

| | SIIC code | Total sales as a % of their product market | Number of workers | Size of firms according to sales 1/ | Orientation of sales | Does it belong to economic conglomerate ? | State particip. % | Foreign particip. % |
|---|---|---|---|---|---|---|---|---|
| **Firms related to economic groups** | | | | | | | | |
| 1 | 313 | 40-42 / 99-100 2/ | 2.300 | large | nontradables | yes | no | no |
| 2 | 382 | 60 | 1,200 | large | import-competing | yes | no | no |
| 3 | 352 | 98 | 40 | medium | import-competing | yes 65% | no | yes 5% 3/ |
| 4 | 362 | 80 | 390 | large | import-competing | yes | no | no |
| **Firms not related to economic groups** | | | | | | | | |
| 5 | 311 | 50 | 600 | large | nontradables | no | no | no |
| 6 | 381 | 70-75 | 200 | medium | import-competing | no | no | no |
| 7 | 382 | 68-70 | 42 | medium | export oriented | no | no | yes 100% |
| 8 | 321 | 10 | 100 | small | import-competing | no | no | no |
| **Bankrupt firms** | | | | | | | | |
| 9 | 322 | 5 | 180 | --- | import-competing | no 4/ | no | no |
| 10 | 322 | 6-7 | 250 | --- | import-competing | no | no | no |
| 11 | 381 | 17 | 300 | --- | import-competing | no | no | no |
| 12 | 355 | 25 | 310 | --- | import-competing | no | no | yes 70% |

Notes:
1/ Classification of firms according to their total sales is the same used in chapter 5.
2/ Firm 1 produces two types of goods.
3/ 65% of the firm belongs to an economic conglomerate, 5% to foreign investors, and the remaining 30% to many small stockholders.
4/ In 1981 this firm was sold to an economic conglomerate.

Another problem faced by the case-study approach is the likelihood of bias. There is a danger that the researcher will guide the inquiry in accordance with wrong impressions he/she has gotten from the first informants contacted, or else the first hypothesis that emerges attracts the researcher to conclusions that confirm these notions and blinds him/her to data that points in other directions. Moreover, the researcher can never be sure of the reason why a subject states a particular position on a questionnaire. It is difficult for the researcher to tell just how representative the picture is that he/she is getting. This limitation in the case-study approach can be successfully avoided if field research is combined with a more general approach which uses standardized data. If this option is taken, the case-study will enrich and add new dimensions to the findings of more standardized research.

### 7.3. Results

### 7.3.1. Firm-Bank Relationship

In this section we intend to determine what kind of relationship firms maintained with banks during the financial liberalization period and what factors determined this relationship. We are also interested in the perceptions firms have about the role played by banks as financial intermediaries during the 1975-82 period.

a) The banks' role as financial intermediaries.

Firms have different perceptions about the role played by banks during this period. Two of the bankrupt firms think the banks did not satisfactorily provide all the services firms required of them.

*Since the purchase of banks was completely financed by debt, banks did not have enough capital to operate; therefore, they had to collect important amounts of money to be able to lend to firms. Operational expenses were extremely high, and hence the spreads between lending and borrowing interest rates were also high (firm 10).*

*During this period the banks worked for economic groups and not for the rest of the firms (firm 11).*

Firms belonging to economic groups, with the exception of firm 2, argued that banks did provide all the necessary services required of them during this period. Nevertheless, they all agreed that the banks were not prepared to operate in a liberalized financial market, mainly because they did not consider and evaluate the risks involved in their operations.

*Firm 1, which belonged to one of the two biggest economic conglomerates in the country, thinks the banks made important efforts to offer a satisfactory supply of services, due to the strong competition they faced. However, it argues that there were inadequate regulations in the financial market; specifically, the maximum limit on banks' lending capacity was too low. According to firm 1, banks were too restricted in their ability to lend.*

Two of the other firms, 5 and 2, think the banks improved their services throughout this period, mainly after the government authorized foreign banks to operate in Chile. According to these firms the increased competitiveness post-1977 induced national banks to offer more and better services.

b) Were there differences among banks with respect to credit conditions?

All the firms interviewed agreed that they did not find differences among banks in relation to the interest rates they charged, terms of credit, or guarantees required. However, firms 2 and 4 consider there were important differences associated with the level of modernization and business attitude among the banks. Specifically, newly established banks were more modern and aggressive than traditional ones. According to firm 2 it took years to modernize the Banco de Chile because of its size, among other things.[2]

Other interviewees pointed out that there were no differences in the credit conditions offered by different banks to one firm. Nevertheless, important differences could, in fact, be found in credit conditions, depending on the firm's relationship with economic conglomerates and therefore with the banks.

*Firm 10, which went bankrupt during the period, argued that its relationship with all banks was similar; they charged high interest rates and asked for real guarantees. However, there were differences in the banks' policies towards group-firms versus non-group firms.*

Indeed, there were enormous discrepancies depending on the firm-group relationship in terms of the collateral banks required of applicants. For instance, firms 1, 2 and 4 which had direct access to the international financial market did not provide collateral for the loans obtained. They merely had to sign a contract with the foreign banks where some minimum requirements regarding specific financial indicators were set and where it was stipulated that none of the firm's creditors was to be preferred in terms of payment. This was not the case for firms independent of the groups.

*Firm 6 had to mortgage the whole company in 1979 to obtain a foreign currency credit intermediated by a domestic bank.*

*Firm 8 had to mortgage an industrial plot of land they owned in order to obtain a foreign-currency loan intermediated by the local banking system. This was not the case for peso-denominated loans which the firm could secure without putting up important collateral.*

c) Why did firms choose specific banks for their financial operations?

Firms can be divided into two groups according to their answers to the above question. On the one hand, firms belonging to economic groups said they chose banks because of their credit facilities and because of the contacts they had through the group.

*"They (the banks) treated us like a relative" said firm 3's General Manager.*

Moreover, only firms related to economic groups included foreign banks (without branches in Chile) among the list of banks with which they normally operated; the only exception was firm 3. These firms explained that being accepted as a client by foreign banks depended on their relationship with the economic conglomerate.

*The manager of firm 2 commented that the fact that the firm belonged to one of the two biggest economic groups in the country made foreign banks open their doors. Actually, he personally had two important meetings with the main executives of foreign banks where he outlined the firm's current situation and perspectives. In 1978 he reported on the history of the firm and its future projects; two years later in 1980 the results were evaluated. Two elements were very important in these presentations: the firm's credibility and the fact that it belonged to one of the largest Chilean economic conglomerates.*

On the other hand, firms without connections to economic groups stressed elements such as the size of the bank, the traditional role of some banks, and the fact that certain banks had local branches in the neighborhood.

The Banco de Chile and the Banco del Estado (state bank) are the banks which fulfill these conditions, as they are the oldest and largest banks in the country.

*Firm 5 stated that they chose the Banco de Chile and the Banco Continental because they had branches two blocks away. The Banco de Chile was also chosen for its size, since firm 5 is large, very liquid, and handles important amounts of money.*

*The only commercial relationship firm 7 had with banks during this period was through its checking account in the Banco de Chile and Banco Internacional y de Comercio Exterior (BICE). They never asked for credit. The main reason for choosing the Banco de Chile was the traditional aspect of this bank and its location near the firm.*

*Firm 8 has worked more than 20 years with the Banco de Chile and Banco del Estado. They chose them because these banks have branches throughout the country.*

*25% of firm 11 belonged to its workers. This firm operated with the Banco de Chile and the Banco del Estado "because of their traditional importance" and with Fintesa, a financial institution which supported worker-owned companies.*

Firms normally operated with one or two banks during the period preceding financial reform. During the 1975-82 period the number of banks firms operated with increased enormously.

*Firm 6 traditionally operated with two banks: the Banco de Chile and the Banco del Estado. The continuous need for credit during the 1975-82 period forced the firm to enlarge its creditors' portfolio. The firm had financial operations with fifteen financial institutions during those years.*

*Until 1976 firm 10 operated only with the Banco del Estado. After 1976 it was necessary to borrow from other banks in order to pay interest and survive. The firm then contacted Banespa Bank and Sudameris Bank.*

## 7.3.2. Firms' Financial Decisions

In this section financial decisions made by firms during the financial liberalization period are discussed.

a) Structure of firms' liabilities and cost of credit.

The composition of firms' liabilities has many similarities among the different groups. Firms belonging to economic conglomerates are the only ones which included direct foreign loans contracted under article 14 of the Foreign Exchange Law among their liabilities; the exception was firm 3. In fact, more than 50% of their liabilities were direct foreign debts. These firms were also the only ones that sold very short-term debentures as a means of financing; i.e., they were directly indebted to the public. Both types of debt were notoriously cheaper than the alternatives; the interest rate charged by foreign banks on their direct lending to firms varied between libor plus 1% and libor plus 2%. On the other hand, the interest rate paid to brokers was equivalent to the deposit rate in the domestic financial market, which was much lower than the banks' lending rate. There was an important spread between passive and active interest rates which averaged 14.6% during the 1976-82 period.

Furthermore, only firms 1 and 2 sold equity capital at the beginning of the period in 1975, and only firms 1 and 4 used their own funds as a partial means of financing. Firm 3 shows slightly different behavior. Its liabilities consisted of 50% foreign loans intermediated by domestic banks; the interest rate charged on these loans was libor plus 5%. The remaining 50% was commercial credit from suppliers. The fact that firm 3 only had foreign-currency loans intermediated by domestic banks contrasted with the rest of the group-firms, such as, for instance, firm 2 which used foreign-currency loans intermediated by domestic banks only as short-term bridge financing (90 days) between two direct foreign loans.

Some firms' debt structure changed throughout the period, especially around mid-1981 when the international interest rate rose, and direct foreign lending declined. At the same time, some firms altered their credit composition from direct external credit to internal credit, i.e., peso and foreign-currency denominated loans intermediated by domestic banks.

*Firm 1 is a good example. In 1975 the new owners increased the firm's equity capital. The firm also utilized its own funds as a source of financing. However, most of its liabilities were direct external loans. It paid interest rates of libor plus 1% or $1\frac{1}{2}$% for these loans. Firm 2 also contracted some foreign-currency loans intermediated by domestic banks; the interest rate on these was between libor plus 3% and libor plus 5%. Around 1981 when conditions in international financial markets changed, firm 1 altered its credit composition from direct to internal credit (peso and foreign-currency denom-*

*inated). They also increased their debt with the public by selling commercial paper.*

The firms without links to economic groups that did not go bankrupt during this period can be divided into two groups according to their liability structure.

Firms 5 and 7 used mainly their own funds (retained earnings and depreciation allowances).

Firms 6 and 8 used mostly bank credit financing.

*Firm 6's liability structure was composed of 70% foreign-currency loans intermediated by domestic banks. These were medium (2-3 years) and long-term (5-6 years) loans; the interest rate charged on these loans fluctuated between libor plus 5% and libor plus 6%. The remaining 30% were short-term peso loans. In 1981-82 the credit composition changed to 40% foreign-currency loans and 60% short-term peso loans, because it became difficult for the firm to secure foreign loans. During the 1975-81 period the firm made profits, and part of the profits were retained although they were not an important source of financing.*

*Firm 8's credit composition was 50% short-term peso denominated loans and 50% commercial credit from suppliers. The firm only took out one foreign-currency loan intermediated by the Chilean branch of a foreign bank.*

Bankrupt firms, except firm 11, did not use their own funds, but had mostly short-term peso loans; only after 1979 did they take out foreign-currency loans intermediated by domestic banks. The only exception was firm 12 which had easier access to external credit intermediated by the domestic financial system. According to the firm's manager the explanation for this situation rests in the fact that 70% of firm 12 was owned by a multinational corporation.

*Firm 11's liability composition during the 1975-80 period was short-term peso loans and to a lesser degree its own funds. Only in 1980 did the firm obtain a foreign-currency loan intermediated by a domestic bank; the interest rate was libor plus 12%.*

*During the 1975-80 period firm 9 had chiefly short-term peso loans. Afterwards the firm turned some of the peso loans into medium-term (2 year) foreign loans intermediated by domestic banks. In 1981 the firm had to sell some of its assets to reduce liabilities. The firm's manager argued that the sale of assets was a good solution, because it was not possible to ask the stockholders for new capital contributions. There was a high opportunity cost to investing in the firm given the existence of more profitable investment elsewhere.*

*During the 1975-79 period liabilities of firm 10 were in short-term peso loans and one long-term (5 year) foreign-currency denominated fostering loan. The interest rate charged for the foreign loan was libor plus 13%. In 1979-80 the firm turned all its loans into foreign-currency denominated loans.*

*Firm 12's liability composition was 80% foreign-currency loans and 20% short-term peso loans. 90% of the foreign-currency loans were intermediated by domestic banks, and the remaining 10% was obtained directly from foreign banks through article 14 of the Foreign Exchange Law. These direct foreign loans were guaranteed, however, by domestic banks.*

In summary, the firms interviewed had different liability structures during the 1975-82 period. Firms with connections to groups had mainly direct external loans and paid interest rates around libor plus 1-2%. Firms without connections did not have access to direct foreign loans. They took out foreign-currency loans intermediated by domestic banks and paid interest rates around libor plus 6%. Bankrupt firms concentrated on short-term peso loans until 1979-80, after which they were able to procure foreign loans intermediated by domestic banks, though at much higher interest rates. Few firms used their own funds for financing or stockholders' equity capital contributions.

b) Why did firms take out loans during the 1975-82 period?

All the firms interviewed contracted important amounts of credit during this period. Different reasons made firms increase their borrowing. Table 2 summarizes these reasons.

Table 2 shows that various elements induced firms to contract loans. Nevertheless, some reasons are more common than others and are often found in a specific group of firms.

For instance, firms associated with economic groups borrowed to invest in existing enterprises in other sectors not related to the firm's main business. Only firm 4 mentioned investment in new installations and modernization as an important reason for taking out loans.

Table 2. WHY DID FIRMS TAKE OUT LOANS DURING THE 1975-82 PERIOD?

| Reasons | 1 | 2 | 3 | 4 | 5 | 6 | 7 | 8 | 9 | 10 | 11 | 12 |
|---|---|---|---|---|---|---|---|---|---|---|---|---|
| New installations and modernization | 2 | 0 | 0 | 4 | 0 | 4 | 0 | 2 | 0 | 4 | 0 | 0 |
| Acquisition of existing firms in other sectors | 4 | 0 | 0 | 2 | 0 | 0 | 0 | 0 | 0 | 0 | 0 | 0 |
| Acquisition of existing firms in same sector | 0 | 4 | 0 | 0 | 0 | 0 | 0 | 0 | 0 | 0 | 0 | 0 |
| Creation of new industrial units | 0 | 0 | 0 | 0 | 0 | 0 | 0 | 0 | 0 | 0 | 0 | 0 |
| To obtain (or maintain) working capital | 0 | 0 | 4 | 0 | 0 | 3 | 0 | 4 | 4 | 4 | 4 | 3 |
| To finance imports of raw materials | 0 | 0 | 4 | 0 | 0 | 3 | 0 | 1 | 4 | 0 | 0 | 3 |
| To finance imports of equipment | 0 | 0 | 0 | 0 | 4 | 3 | 0 | 1 | 1 | 0 | 0 | 0 |
| To finance exports | 0 | 0 | 4 | 0 | 0 | 0 | 0 | 0 | 0 | 0 | 0 | 0 |
| To offset the effects of tariff reductions and 1975 recession | 0 | 4 | 0 | 3 | 3 | 0 | 0 | 3 | 0 | 4 | 2 | 2 |
| To finance interest payments | 0 | 0 | 0 | 0 | 0 | 0 | 0 | 1 | 2 | 4 | 4 | 4 |
| To offset effects of inflation | 0 | 0 | 0 | 0 | 0 | 0 | 0 | 0 | 0 | 0 | 0 | 0 |
| Others: To finance firm's initial acquisition | 0 | 0 | 0 | 0 | 0 | 0 | 0 | 0 | 0 | 0 | 4 | 0 |

Note: The importance of each element was rated between 0 and 4. 0 means the element did not play a role in the decision to take out loans; 4 means it played an important role.

*Firm 1 obtained important amounts of foreign-currency loans directly from foreign banks. These loans were utilized to finance investments in other sectors. For instance, firm 1 bought 43% of the shares of a bank, which became the group's main bank. The firm also bought an industrial food corporation and an airline which was the only private airline in the country. The firm further invested, though to a much lesser degree, in new installations and modernization of its plant.*

*Firm 2 was a holding company of one of the two most important economic groups in the country. Half of the firm's functions lay in its holding activities. The firm had access to important amounts of direct external financing. It borrowed to buy other corporations in the same industrial sector (non-transport machinery). At the beginning of the period it contracted loans to offset the negative effects the 1975 internal recession had had on sales. The internal recession hit the firm severely. According to the firm's manager it was very important at that moment to belong to a group to obtain the necessary credits to overcome the recession. The firm did not undertake any important net investment in fixed assets during the 1975-82 period.*

*Firm 3 also belonged to an important conglomerate, though it did not act as a holding company for the group. The firm did not invest during the period in either financial or real assets. Firm 3 borrowed mainly to obtain working capital and to export. In order to penetrate new markets the firm had to offer credit lines up to nine months, to clients.*

*Firm 4 had access to direct external loans as well. They used these credits to invest in other sector's companies. Specifically, in 1979 when a construction and real estate boom developed in the Chilean economy, the firm invested in the construction sector. The investment was a complete failure, and in 1982 the firm had to absorb the loss of this investment. The firm also bought up other existing firms. Firm 4 financed its working capital with its own funds. In 1979 the firm enlarged and modernized its plant. It borrowed to finance this investment, although it had enough internal funds to foot it. The reason was that the firm was able to obtain a direct loan at libor plus $1\frac{1}{2}\%$ at a time when the domestic inflation rate was around 39% i.e., it paid a negative real interest rate. Therefore, it was more convenient to finance the investment with a loan rather than with its own funds.*

Different behavior is found among the group of firms unrelated to economic conglomerates. Here we have to differentiate between firms which survived and firms which went bankrupt during this period.

Among the firms that survived the period only two were forced into debt. These firms contracted loans to offset the negative effects of the 1975 internal recession and the decrease in import tariffs, to invest in new equipment, to obtain working capital, and thus finance imports of raw materials and machinery.

*Firm 6 experienced no difficulty in borrowing during the 1975-81 period, although this changed dramatically later in 1982. The main reason in asking for loans was to modernize the firm, as one of the plants was completely rebuilt in 1979-80 because it was obsolete. They also had to increase borrowing at the beginning of the period to offset the fall in sales resulting from the 1975 internal recession. The firm's sales dropped to 1/3 its normal level during those years. Finally, the firm increased its indebtedness to obtain working capital and finance imports of raw materials and machinery.*

*Until 1974 firm 8 was very liquid as it sold 100% of its production for cash and therefore did not need to ask for bank loans. Its working capital rotated very fast. From 1975 on, partly as a result of the fall in demand due to the government's shock policy, the firm began to offer commercial credit to clients as a way of maintaining sales. The working capital needed to operate this way was much greater than the existing resources, so the firm had to resort to borrowing expensive short-term peso loans in the domestic financial market. The firm also started buying raw material on credit (commercial credit from suppliers). The only medium-term foreign-currency loan obtained during the period was used to replace obsolete equipment.*

Firms that went bankrupt during the period fell deeply into debt. The usual answer to the question of why firms borrowed was, initially, that it was done to offset the negative effects of the 1975 internal recession and the decrease in import tariffs and to obtain working capital. Afterwards it became a question of financing interest payments.

*Firm 9 was a producer of men's clothing. During the sixties and seventies an important part of its production was oriented toward institutional uniforms, including the armed forces. Around the mid-seventies the firm realized that a change in sales orientation toward the mass consumer market was badly needed, because the institutional demand for uniforms was very depressed. Therefore, the firm decided to take out loans in order to contract U.S. licenses and foreign experts to implement new designs and marketing style. The firm also borrowed to finance imports of raw materials, mainly fabrics. Due to the low level of import tariffs and later due to the fixed exchange rate it was cheaper to import almost all raw materials than to buy them in the domestic market. Moreover, the firm took out some loans to finance imports of new machinery although they were very insignificant. At the end of the period the firm had to borrow to service its debt.*

*Firm 10 also produced men's clothes. The firm was adversely affected by the 1975 internal recession and the import tariff reduction. Therefore, the owners decided to adjust to the new economic conditions. Following the market signals of the moment they opted for a reorientation of the firm's sales toward external markets, specifically Canada and the U.S. In pursuing this goal the firm took out a major foreign-currency loan in 1976 which was invested in new installations and plant modernization. They also borrowed in the short-term peso loan market to obtain working capital. At the beginning of 1978 the firm realized that it could not compete in international markets, as the government had begun to use the exchange rate as a tool for controlling domestic inflation. The grace period for the foreign loan was over, and from then on the firm began to have dramatic problems in servicing the debt. It then had to take out new loans to fulfill its obligations.*

*Firm 11 was a producer of pipes. During the Allende administration 75% of its shares were in state hands, and 25% privately owned. In 1975 this 75% was liquidated; 50% of the shares were bought back by former stockholders and the remaining 25% by workers. However, the firms was not bought for cash; the state granted five years credit (with one year of grace) to be paid with future profits. Nevertheless, the 1975 drastic fall in demand plus import tariff reductions and the Chilean withdrawal from the Andean Pact sharply reduced the firm's sales. The firm took out short-term peso loans to finance its working capital and survive. Later in the period the company was forced to borrow fresh money just to service its debt.*

*Firm 12 produced rubber products. As mentioned earlier, this firm is an affiliate of a multinational corporation. The policy of the parent company was that each affiliate should obtain financing sources in local markets. The firm borrowed mainly to obtain working capital, to offset the effects of the lowering of import tariffs and to finance imports of raw materials. Later on, a further decline in the firm's competitiveness due to the fixed exchange rate policy prevented it from fulfilling its financial obligations. Therefore, the firm had to take out loans to finance interest payments.*

Table 3. SOURCES OF FINANCING FIRMS WOULD CHOOSE TODAY.

| Sources | 1 | 2 | 3 | 4 | 5 | 6 | 7 | 8 | 9 | 10 | 11 | 12 |
|---|---|---|---|---|---|---|---|---|---|---|---|---|
| Internal funds of the firm | 0 | 1 | 0 | 1 | 1 | 1 | 3 | 1 | 0 | a/ | a/ | 1 |
| New stockholders, increase in equity | 1 | 0 | 0 | 5 | 0 | 0 | 0 | 0 | 0 | a/ | a/ | 0 |
| Domestic banks peso loans | 0 | 0 | 1 | 2 | 3 | 0 | 2 | 3 | 2 | 0 | 0 | 0 |
| Loans from other firms | 0 | 0 | 0 | 6 | 0 | 0 | 0 | 0 | 0 | 0 | 0 | 0 |
| Financial association with foreign firms | 0 | 0 | 0 | 3 | 0 | 0 | 0 | 0 | 0 | 0 | 0 | 0 |
| Financial association with national firms | 0 | 0 | 0 | 4 | 0 | 0 | 0 | 2 | 0 | 0 | 0 | 0 |
| Sources of official credit | 0 | 0 | 0 | 7 | 2 | 0 | 1 | 0 | 1 | 1 | 1 | 2 |
| Foreign credit | 0 | 0 | 0 | 8 | 0 | 0 | 0 | 0 | 0 | 0 | 0 | 0 |

Note: Firms did not rate all the different sources. They only considered the alternatives most relevant to them.

1 indicates the most preferred source of financing.

a/ These firms did not rate all the alternatives, although they explicitly pointed out that they would not use their own funds or increase the firm's capital.

It is also very interesting to comment on the two firms which hardly borrowed at all during the period. Both are independent of economic groups. They constitute an exception to what happened to many firms during those years.

*Firm 5 produced dairy products. The firms was not affected by the re-duction in import duties because it produced nontradable goods. Moreover, since it was a producer of basic goods the internal recession did not affect it as severely as others. Furthermore, given the evolution of the domestic financial market (extremely high interest rates and very short-term loans) the firm opted for developing a big, efficient distribution network. The orga-nization of this network was very important, because it allowed the firm to keep 80% of its sales in cash, and thus avoid the need for short-term loans to finance working capital. In addition, many competing firms could not adjust to new market conditions and went bankrupt during the period. Therefore, firm 5 captured a higher share of the market and made important profits during those years. · The firm undertook important investments during the period, but they were self-financed. It only asked for bank credit to renew machinery.*

*Firm 7 was an affiliate of a multinational corporation. It produced equip-ment to explore for minerals. The internal recession produced a decline in sales, but it was not pronounced as one of its main clients was the copper industry which provides very stable demand. The firm did not borrow during the period; its financial resources were either internal funds (retained earn-ings and depreciation allowances) or financing from the parent company, used mainly to finance imports. Although the firm paid dividends during all those years, internal funds were sufficient for the normal operation of the firm. It did not have any investment plans and did not make any net investments during the 1975-82 period.*

c) What kind of financial sources would firms prefer after experiencing the 1981-82 financial crisis?

Table 3 summarizes the answer given by the firms to the above question. Most firms chose their own funds as the preferred source of financing; the exception was two of the bankrupt firms (firms 10 and 11), which considered their own funds and equity capital increase as the worst alternatives. As a rule, firms were not willing to risk their capital because of the economic and political instability reigning in 1983. All firms agreed they would not choose foreign loans, arguing that their experience with foreign credit was bad. Firm 4 also stated that foreign banks do not differentiate between the firm's condition and the country's situation. Thus, even if the firm is in good financial health, foreign banks will not extend loans because they are not willing to put more money into the country.

Most firms belonging to economic groups declared they would not be willing to take out any kind of loans in 1983 due to their current financial situation, i.e., extremely high debt-capital ratio. Therefore, the best thing to do seems to be to substantially decrease the firm's financial leverage.[3]

The next preferred option was credit from official institutions, specifically long-term state agency credit with subsidized interest rates. The other source chosen was domestic currency denominated bank loans.[4]

### 7.3.3. Changes in Firms' Cost and Asset Structure

a) Cost structure.

There were important changes in firm's cost structure during the 1975-82 period. This was especially true for firms which had significant peso-debts with the domestic banking sector. This phenomenon, though, is more common among the bankrupt firms.

*Firm 10 affirmed that its financial expenses reached 50% of sales in one of the years studied. A similar increase in financial expenses was faced by firm 11; its financial expenses increased three times their participation in total costs. Firm 12 and 9 could, up to a point, offset the increase in financial costs with the decline in operational costs brought about by the fall in the cost of imported materials, mainly during the period of the fixed exchange rate.*

Firms not related to economic groups which took out loans during the period also faced changes in cost structure.

*Firm's 6 financial expenses were zero before 1975; after that year they reached around 10% of the firm's sales.*

*Firm 8 faced financial costs equivalent to 12% of sales during the 1975-81 period. This percentage increased to 26% of sales in 1982 because of the exchange rate devaluation and the rise in international interest rates.*

*Firm 5 and 7, which refrained from loans, did not face an increase in financial expenses, which were close to zero. However, their cost structure did change; operational costs decreased because both firms used imported raw materials whose prices declined as a result of import tariff reductions and the fixed exchange rate policy pursued by the government.*

Among firms related to economic groups, financial costs barely increased, because they did not resort to peso loans. Only firm 1 experienced important financial expenses, not because of high interest rates, but because of high financial leverage. However, the increase in foreign interest rates in 1981 together with the exchange rate devaluation of 1982 had a significant impact on these firms' financial expenses.

b) Asset structure.

The twelve firms interviewed can be clearly divided into two groups with respect to change in asset structure. On one hand, there are firms belonging to economic conglomerates that show a clear tendency to invest in shares of other companies - to invest in financial assets which had no relationship to the main business of the firms.

On the other hand, there are firms without connections which did not invest in other companies' shares. Some of these show no change in asset composition, while others attempted to reduce inventories and invest money in short-term paper in the domestic financial market.

*Firm 1 suffered a major change in asset composition. During the period under study the firm invested in companies in other sectors. Specifically, it bought 43% of the shares of an important bank, and it took over control of an industrial food company and an airline. The type of investments and the amount invested were decided by the firms stockholders. The conglomerate's objectives prevailed over the firm's own objectives.*

*Firm 2 had 50% of its assets in other companies' shares. The firm invested mainly in its own industrial sector. To carry out these investments the group's banks were used. The banks lent money to the firm, and the firm invested this money in other companies.*

*Firm 4 also reported a strong tendency to invest in other areas due to the high profitability associated with them. The firm invested in construction, among other sectors.*

As we pointed out before, the rest of the firms did not alter their asset composition. Firms 6, 7, 8, 11 and 12 reported no change in asset structure.

Firms 9 and 10 at some point opted for selling some of their fixed assets to reduce their debts.

*Firm 9, actually sold some assets it could do without in 1981. According to the manager they did not have resources to invest in financial assets, i.e., it did not boil down to a real choice for the firm to invest or not in ventures outside the firm.*

*Firm 10 attempted to sell some of its fixed assets in 1980-81; this firm held important investment in fixed assets. However, many firms were doing the same thing at that time, and prices had become very depressed so that finally the firm had to renounce the sale of its assets.*

*Firm 5 made important investment during the 1975-82 period, all of them oriented toward enlarging the plant and renewing equipment. All disposable funds were channelled into investment in the firm itself. Also firm 5 enjoys considerable liquidity and operates with a large amount of cash - so much so that during the period it deposited its cash in the short-term domestic capital market.*

Some firms decreased inventories during the years in question and used the money to buy short-term securities in the domestic capital market. However, the interest rate was not the only variable considered to define the level of inventories. The exchange rate and the level of the firm's foreign-currency debt were relevant to those firms with an important volume of imported raw materials and to those firms which after trade liberalization began to import some goods they had formerly produced themselves.

*For example, firm 3 asserted that the 1982 exchange rate devaluations did not affect them, because the firm had a similar proportion of liabilities and assets denominated in foreign currency, mainly imported raw materials, imported final goods, and commercial loans in foreign currency.*

### 7.3.4. The Role of Expectations

Expectations usually play an important role in an economy, especially in a recently liberalized one. Economic agents' expectations can alter the results of any economic policy. Management expectations about three fundamental variables are investigated below: the domestic interest rate on peso loans, the exchange rate and general business prospects.

a) Domestic interest rate on peso-denominated loans.

Most firms answered that they were expecting a decrease in the domestic interest rate in the near future.

*Firm 1 did not have to take out peso-denominated loans. However, they expected arbitrage of domestic and international interest rates, given the degree of financial openness of the economy.*

*Firm 3 said the interest rates charged on peso-loans were absurd. They expected something to happen, because otherwise the whole economy would go bankrupt.*

The only different answers were those of firms 8, 10 and 12.

*Firm 8 affirmed that they did not necessarily believe interest rates would decline, but that they did not have any choice except to pay them. The only alternative was to close the firm, because they did not have other sources of financing.*

*Firm 10 said everybody was expecting a "perdonazo" (a kind of general pardon). Therefore, people kept taking out expensive loans despite their belief about the evolution of the interest rate.*

*Firm 12 expected the interest rate to remain high. This was the main reason why the firm did not take out peso-loans until 1981-82 when access to foreign currency loans was restricted.*

b) Exchange rate.

This question is tied to the 1979-82 period when the exchange rate was fixed at 39 pesos per dollar.
Most firms answered that they did not expect a devaluation of the peso.

*According to firm 5 the 1982 devaluation was a real surprise. Its manager argued that there was a lack of information about external conditions and the macroeconomic behavior of the economy. The available information made everyone believe there was an excess of dollars in the economy.*

*The management of firm 3 argued that neither they nor the top executives in the group expected a devaluation. This fact was really important to the firm, because there was close contact between high executives of the conglomerate and government authorities.*

*Firm 7 said the government position was very clear regarding maintenance of the fixed exchange rate. Furthermore, everybody expected the inflow of foreign capital would last forever.*

Other firms declared that they did not expect a devaluation of the peso, at least until the end of 1981. Those who said they were expecting something to happen by the end of 1981 did not expect, in any case, a maxi-devaluation.

*Firm 2 argued that they had been expecting a devaluation since the end of 1981, but something mild; for instance, the announcement of a "tablita", i.e., an active crawling peg.*

*Firm 4 said they believed in the economic authorities and therefore in the dollar fixed at 39 pesos. However, in 1981 they realized a devaluation was necessary.*

*Firm 1 also began to expect a devaluation by the end of 1981, yet they did not expect a maxi-devaluation.*

Regarding the subject of foreign-currency borrowing and expectations of devaluation, two of the firms argued that even in the event of a devaluation they thought it was still cheaper to take out loans in foreign currency.

*Firm 10 converted all its debts to foreign currency in 1979-80. They argued that no one could work with the levels of peso-loans interest rates. Therefore, as soon as they had the opportunity they opted for taking out dollar loans and running the exchange risk.*

*Firm 6, which had important amounts of foreign-currency loans, declared that they expected the fixed exchange rate policy would never be changed. Moreover, they thought that even in the event of a devaluation it would be cheaper to take out foreign-currency denominated loans than peso-denominated loans.*

*Firms 1 and 4 commented that they could not change the currency denomination of their debts when they realized a devaluation was coming. On the one hand, it was too late to do anything; on the other, domestic banks had maximum limits on their lending capacities.*

c) Business prospects.

Firms' expectations about business conditions changed throughout the period. However, there were important coincidences in the perceptions of all firms. Specifically, most firms characterized the period from 1975 to the first half of 1981 as moderately optimistic or very optimistic, and the period from the second half of 1981 until 1983 as presenting a moderately pessimistic or very pessimistic outlook.

*Only firm 6 describes the years 1975-76 as very pessimistic. The firm faced a drastic contraction in demand due to the internal recession and the reduction in import duties. The expectations during the 1977-78 period were considered to be moderately pessimistic while expectations for the 1979-81 period were considered to be moderately optimistic. The reason for considering this last period to be moderately optimistic was the relatively easy availability of credit and, therefore, the favorable prospects for new investments.*

Firm 1 and 7 declared they entertained very optimistic expectations during the entire period until the first half of 1981.

*Firm 1's sales grew at an average annual rate of 15% during the period; its sales doubled in physical terms while its gross margin increased accordingly. Firm 1 produces nontradable goods.*

*Firm 7 produces for export, and its sales also expanded during the 1975-81 period. There was increasing activity in the copper industry, and there were many foreign companies interested in mining surveys and drilling. Some oil companies were planning to invest their petrodollars in the Chilean mining industry.*

*Firm 4 differentiates two sub-periods. During the years 1975-79 the firm's expectations about business prospects were moderately optimistic, because they were beginning to launch a new business venture. During those years they adjusted the firm to the new economic model introduced in the country. In the 1979-81 interim the apparent results of the economic policy led the firm to assume "the country was being incorporated into the elite of developed countries". Firms were introducing new products, and sales were constantly growing.*

Among bankruptcy victims firm 10 declared their expectations were very optimistic during this period.

*Firm 10 explained that its optimistic expectations were based on its belief in the recognition of human effort, and because they were convinced the country badly needed to increase its exports.*

*Firm 12 differentiates two sub-periods: During the years 1975-79 the firm's expectations were very optimistic. Later, during the 1979-82 period they were moderately pessimistic due to the loss of competitiveness suffered by the firm.*

The rest of the bankrupt firms characterized their expectations during the period as moderately optimistic.

*Firm 11 argued that they were moderately optimistic, because they were convinced the government would not let them go bankrupt. This belief was based on the fact that the firm represented an important technological improvement for the country and provided a possibility of economic independence. Firm 11 produced goods the country formerly imported. In addition, the firm was equipped with modern machinery capable of producing pipes of big diameter.*

Most firms harbored very pessimistic expectations about the future right after the crisis of 1981-82. This was mainly due to their weak financial position caused by high debt level and to the depressed demand for products due to the general economic recession. Economic recovery was slower than had been expected and its effects were not felt until the mid-1980's.

## 7.3.5. Bankruptcies

a) Why did firms go bankrupt during the 1975-82 period?

If we were to summarize the reasons given by the group of bankrupt firms interviewed (see table 4), we could conclude that increased indebtedness was the last cause of failure. However, the story begins in 1975 with the internal recession and the decrease in import tariffs. Then, firms took out expensive loans to survive and adjust themselves to the new outward looking development strategy followed by the government. However, the continuous decrease in import tariffs and peso appreciation due to the fixed exchange rate policy brought about additional difficulties for the firms. They could not pay back the loans and had to take out new ones, but this situation could not be maintained indefinitely. Firms simply went bankrupt. Let us see each of the cases in greater detail.

Table 4. WHY DID FIRMS GO BANKRUPT DURING THE 1975-82 PERIOD?

| R e a s o n s | 9 | 10 | 11 | 12 |
|---|---|---|---|---|
| 1975 internal recession | 0 | 4 | 4 | 0 |
| Decrease in import tariffs | 0 | 0 | 2 | 4 |
| Fixed exchange rate policy | 0 | 4 | 4 | 2 |
| Excessive indebtedness | 4 | 4 | 4 | 4 |
| Cost of credit | 4 | 4 | 4 | 0 |
| 1982 peso devaluation | 0 | 0 | 0 | 0 |
| 1982 internal recession | 0 | 0 | 0 | 0 |
| Others: | | | | |
|    Group bankruptcy | 4 | 0 | 0 | 0 |
|    Loss of monopoly power | 0 | 0 | 4 | 0 |

Note: Firms had to rate every reason from 0 to 4. 0 means the reason did not play any role in the firm's bankruptcy; 4 means the reason played a fundamental role in the firm's bankruptcy.

*Firm 9 went bankrupt in 1981. The reasons given by the manager to explain the firm's failure are excessive indebtedness and the cost of credit. However, according to him, the ultimate reason was the impossibility o accomplishing a program of asset sales to reduce debts. At the beginning of 1981 the owners of firm 9 sold it to an economic conglomerate in an attempt to reduce the debts they had with the conglomerate's bank.*

*As the firm was deeply in debt, the group decided to sell the assets the firm could live without (e.g., land, buildings, etc.) in order to decrease its liabilities. It was the time of the real estate and construction boom, and the firm had a big piece of land which could be sold at an incredibly high price. Nevertheless, they did not have time to pull this off, because in December 1981 the group's bank was intervened by the government, and the conglomerate went bankrupt as did the firm.*

*Firm 10 went bankrupt in March 1983. The 1975 recession and the decrease in import tariffs forced the firm to turn to exports. The firm took out and important loan to carry out this project. However, the fixed exchange rate implied a great loss of competitiveness in external markets for the firm. Thus, its sales decreased and it had to take out new loans to service its debt. The firm attempted to reorient its sales again toward the domestic market, but then the 1982 internal recession hit. The final cause of failure was excessive indebtedness.*

*Firm 11 went bankrupt in 1982. The reasons for failure were the 1975 internal recession, the decrease in import duties, peso appreciation, excessive indebtedness, the cost of credit, and the loss of the firm's monopolistic power in the market for one of its products. Firm 11 was strongly hit by the 1975 fall in aggregate demand, the reduction of import tariffs and the Chilean withdrawal from the Andean Pact. To survive it took out expensive peso-denominated loans. High financial expenses plus the loss of competitiveness brought about by peso appreciation together with the low level of tariffs led the firm to and extremely weak position. When it was in a very delicate financial situation, the "coup de grace" was delivered by a competitive state-owned enterprise which broke the firm's monopoly in the production and sale of big diameter pipes in 1981.*

*The main reasons for firm 12's failure were the decrease in import tariffs, the fixed exchange rate policy and excessive indebtedness. The firm, hard-hit by the decline in import duties, borrowed to remain in operation. The further openness of the economy caused by the fixed exchange rate policy implied an important loss of competitiveness for the firm. According to its manager, the domestic market was invaded with imports from Japan, Korea and Brazil. As a result, the firm was not able to service its debt and had to take out new loans. It went bankrupt in 1982. However, after some time its creditors (the banks) decided to rescue the firm, becoming its owners.*

It is noticeable that excessive indebtedness is the main cause of the bankruptcies. When asking the firms why they kept increasing their debts up to levels they could not possibly manage, the unanimous answer was that they believed in their firms' future and were waiting for a miracle to happen. Moreover, the managers believed in their ability as entrepreneurs, and the cost of closing down the firm was too high for them.

*The manager of firm 9 commented that when an establishment closes it is reduced to half its value.*

*Firm 11 argued they had to look after their workers whom they could not put out in the street given the high unemployment rate existent during the entire period.*

## 7.4. Final Remarks

In the following we will briefly summarize the main findings of this case-study.

During the 1975-82 period firms did not perceive important differences in their relationship with different banks, but they did discern important differences in credit access and conditions depending on the firms' relationship with economic groups.

Indeed, only firms connected with economic groups had access to the cheapest kind of credit, mainly credit obtained directly from foreign banks in the international financial market. Thus, they did not have to resort to expensive peso-loans. The only firm connected with an economic group that did not borrow abroad directly was firm 3, possibly because it is only medium-sized and did not play an important role within the conglomerate.

Domestic banks rationed credit through the interest rate. The interest rate charged on foreign-currency loans intermediated by the domestic banking sector fluctuated between libor plus 3% and libor plus 13%, depending on the firm and its connections with economic groups. However, not only interest rates were used as a rationing device. Banks also asked for different types of collateral (mortgage, securities, etc.) depending on the kind of firm applying for credit.

One of the results of domestic financial liberalization was the increase in the number of banks with which firms operated. During the period before financial reform firms used to work with one or two banks, whereas after the reform the number of banks at least tripled. The explanation for this phenomenon relies on the "indebtedness vicious circle", i.e., businesses continuously needed new loans from new banks to service previous loans.

The reasons for contracting loans differed widely among would-be debtors. Firms connected with economic groups fell into debt to invest in existing companies with the objective of building up the conglomerate and amplifying its scope. The conglomerate's objectives prevailed over the firms' own objectives. This was especially true for firms which acted as holding companies for groups.

The rest of the firms took out loans mainly to survive and be able to adjust to the new economic environment. Most firms started the period with very low levels of working capital due to the limited degree of monetization existent during the 1970-73 period. The fall in sales brought about by the 1975 internal recession and structural changes in the external and financial sectors forced them to borrow heavily.

The cost structure of companies which borrowed peso-loans changed dramatically during the 1975-82 period. Some firms had zero financial expenses in 1974 whereas a couple of years later these expenses reached around 12-15% of sales.

Establishments related to economic groups did not suffer important changes in cost structure, but they presented a fundamental alteration in asset composition. Basically, these firms invested large amounts of resources in financial assets including shares of existing corporations in other sectors, not related to the firms' main business.

In terms of expectations, all firms considered the level of domestic interest rate irrationally high, and most of them were expecting a decline in the rate on peso-loans more in line with the level of the external interest rate.

The fixed exchange rate policy followed by the government between 1979 and 1982 was unanimously believed in among entrepreneurial circles. They had the impression that the external flow of loans would never end, and that the economy was replete with dollars. Only at the end of 1981 did the firms realize that a devaluation might be necessary; nevertheless, they were not expecting a maxi-devaluation.

Expectations of business prospects were in general optimistic (very or moderately so) up to the first half of 1981. Specifically, firms headed for bankruptcy always thought they could make it, and this belief induced them to borrow up to a point of no return. Immediately after the 1981-82 crisis expectations were pessimistic (very or moderately so), and none of the firms had any investment plans. They were simply waiting for the announced economic recovery to knock on their door.

Bankrupt firms failed because of excessive indebtedness; however, there are many reasons which explain why they found themselves in this plight. The evidence obtained in this case-study reveals that some of the companies, in order to overcome what they foresaw as transitory difficulties, borrowed at the beginning of the period (1975-76) to obtain working capital and remain in operation. At that time, though, businesses were facing a significant decline in sales as a result of the 1975 internal recession and the lowering of import tariffs. Many of them began to offer credit to their clients in an effort to maintain sales levels. However, this implied an important increase in working capital, due to the fact that the previous period did not make inordinate demands in this respect. Working capital, in those days, rotated very fast because most Firms' operations were on a cash basis. There is finally evidence that some firms borrowed to reorient their sales to external markets.

The fixed exchange rate policy implemented by the government, together with a uniform import tariff of 10% operated as a further foreign trade liberalization that firms could not withstand. The negative impact of loss of competitiveness on performance forced firms to take out new loans just to service their current debts and survive. The 1982 internal recession found these firms in an extremely weak financial position - so much so that they could not weather the new shock. Moreover, the financial crisis which developed in 1982 was both the cause and the result of the bankruptcies.

# APPENDIX

## Questionnaire

I General Information

1. What is the share of your total sales of the national market?

2. What is the number of workers employed in your firm?

3. What percentage of your sales goes to the national market? In other words, would you define your firm as export-oriented, import-competing or producing nontradables?

4. Does (or did) the firm belong to an economic conglomerate? Which one?

5. (If the firm belonged to a conglomerate) which banks is it related to?

6. Does your firm have state ownership?

7. Does your firm have foreign ownership?

II Firm-Bank Relationship

8. In general, do you think banks, as they were organized during the 1975-82 period, satisfactorily performed all the services companies expected of them

   -yes

   -no

9. In what areas do you consider banks least prepared?

10 Do you think that during the 1975-82 period, large, small or no difference existed among banks in the credit facilities they offered

11 More concretely, were these differences related to:

 - credit facilities

 - terms of loans

 - delays in the negotiation of loans

- minimum deposit required

- guarantees required

- other aspects (please specify).

12. With which three banks did the firm most often carry out commercial transactions?

13. Were the three banks chosen because of the credit differences previously mentioned and/or contacts through the conglomerate?

III Financial Decisions

14. In financing activities, what financial sources did the firm predominantly use during the 1975-82 period? Please, give percentages for each source of financing. If sources changed throughout the period, specify subperiods.

  - domestic-currency denominated bank loans

  - foreign-currency denominated bank loans

  - the firm's own funds

  - increase in equity capital

  - other sources (specify).

15. If bank credit was used, for which of the reasons indicated below was it done? Give a qualifying number from 0 to 4 for each alternative: 0 if the alternative did not play any role, 4 if it played a fundamental role in the firm's decision to take out loans.

  - new installations and modernization

  - acquisition of existing companies in other sectors

  - to obtain (or maintain) working capital

  - to finance imports of equipment

  - to finance exports

- to offset the effects of the decrease in tariffs and the 1975 internal recession

- to refinance short-term credit (to pay interest)

- acquisition of existing companies in the same sector

- creation of new industrial units

- to offset the effects of inflation

- others (specify)

16. If non-bank credit was used, who did you ask for loans?

- friends

- relatives

- cooperatives

- others (specify)

17. When asking for a loan at the bank, what did you stress?

- stability of the firm

- necessity

- value of the project

- others (specify)

18. What kinds of obligations did the banks require of the firm?

- guarantees, securities

- personal signature

- balance-sheet information

- deeds

- mortgage

- others (specify)

19. If you were planning to expand your firm today, which of the following sources of capital would you prefer?

   - internal funds of the firm

   - new stockholders, increase in equity capital

   - domestic bank loans (domestic currency)

   - loans from other companies

   - financial association with foreign firms

   - mortgages

   - sources of official credit (state credit)

   - foreign credit

IV Cost and Asset Structure

20. Did your firm face a change in cost structure after the liberalization of the domestic interest rate in 1975? Particularly, did the firm experience a change in the relative importance of operational expenses vis-a-vis financial expenses?

21. Did the firm experience a change in asset composition between fixed and financial assets during the 1975-82 period? Did the firm tend to invest more in financial assets than in the pre-1975 period?

V Expectations

22. What were your expectations regarding the future behavior of the domestic interest rate?

23. What were your expectations about the evolution of the exchange rate during the 1979-82 period (when it was fixed with respect to the dollar)?

24 How would you characterize your attitude in relation to your firm during the 1975-82 period? Specify sub-periods if your attitude changed throughout those years.

- very optimistic

- moderately optimistic

- moderately pessimistic

- very pessimistic

25. (For the pessimistic answers). What were the main obstacles your firm faced?

26. (For the optimistic answers). What were the main elements which made you perceive an optimistic future?

VI Bankrupt Firms

27. If your firm went bankrupt (specify year of bankruptcy), what was the main reason for failure? Rate each alternative from 0 to 4: 0 means the reason did not have any relevance to the bankruptcy, 4 means the reason was extremely relevant.

  - 1975 internal recession

  - peso appreciation with respect to the dollar (fixed exchange rate policy)

  - decrease in import tariffs

  - excessive indebtedness

  - exchange rate devaluation in 1982

  - 1982 internal recession

  - cost of credit

28. If excessive indebtedness was an important element in explaining the firm's failure, why did the firm borrow beyond its capacity to pay back?

## Notes

1. The questionnaire which was used to interview executives in 1984, is included in the appendix.

2. The Banco de Chile is one of the largest banks in the country. It belonged to the BHC group during the period studied here.

3. Most of the firms belonging to economic conglomerates had problems servicing their debts when the government intervened the groups' banks in January 1983. Firms 1 and 2 actually defaulted a few days after the banking sector intervention and had to negotiate with their creditors.

4. In 1983 the annual short-term real lending rate was 15.9%; the annual inflation rate 23.1%.

# 8. FIRMS' FINANCIAL BEHAVIOR IN A LIBERALIZED CAPITAL MARKET: A FORMAL APPROACH

## 8.1. Introduction

The objective of this chapter is to examine from a formal point of view the firms' financial behavior during the 1975-82 period, in particular their debt and investment policies.

The behavior formalized in this chapter is based on analysis of the corporations' balance sheets and the case studies presented in previous chapters.

Since the data recorded by the firms is registered in the balance sheets at book value, the book value of the variables is used throughout the chapter.[1]

The analysis is made for three different types of corporations: Those belonging to economic groups or conglomerates, those unrelated to groups, and those that went bankrupt during the period.

The chapter is organized in the following way: The second section analyzes the financial behavior of the three groups of firms, and the third section presents some concluding remarks.

## 8.2. Firms' Financial Behavior: A Formal Approach

### 8.2.1. The Model

As mentioned above, the model used to analyze the firms' financial behavior during the 1975-82 period is based on the corporations' balance sheets.

Let us define the corporations' profits in period $t$ as:

$$\pi_t = \delta A_t + \mu F_t - i L_t \tag{1}$$

where:
$\pi$      = net profits[2]
$A$      = non-financial assets
$F$      = financial assets
$L$      = debt
$\delta, \mu$   = rates of return on non-financial and financial assets respectively
$i$      = annual real interest rate
$E$      = equity worth

Using the identity $A_t + F_t = L_t + E_t$; i.e., assets are financed with debt or capital.

$$\pi_t = \delta(L_t + E_t - F_t) \mid \mu F_t - iL_t$$
$$\pi_t = (\mu - \delta)F_t + \delta E_t + (\delta - i)L_t \tag{2}$$

To obtain the rate of return on equity, equation (2) is divided by $E_t$.

$$\phi = \pi_t/E_t = (\mu - \delta)F_t/E_t + \delta + (\delta - i)L_t/E_t \tag{3}$$

where
$L_t/E_t = l$ is the financial leverage of the firm.

There being a direct relationship between financial leverage and the risk evaluation of the firm, financial leverage is intended to be a measure of financial risk (see footnote 6). Moreover, risk-prone firms find it costlier to borrow funds. That is, $i = i(L/E)$, $i' > 0$, $i'' > 0$, and $i(0) = i_0$ which is the riskless interest rate. A firm's financial leverage can not increase beyond a certain limit without implying a rise in the interest rate ($i' > 0$). Moreover, the interest rate augments at an increasing rate with the rise in leverage ($i'' > 0$). That is, the rise in the interest rate experienced by a firm which increments its leverage from 0.3 to 0.4 is smaller than the rise in interest rate experienced by a firm which increments its leverage from 1.3 to 1.35.
Therefore,

$$\phi = (\mu - \delta)F_t/E_t + \delta + [\delta - i(L_t/E_t)]L_t/E_t \tag{4}$$

and,

$$\partial\phi/\partial(L_t/E_t) = \delta - [i + i'(L_t/E_t)]$$

Ceteris paribus, it will be profitable for firms to take out loans if the marginal rate of return on their assets ($\delta$) is higher than the marginal borrowing cost they face ($i + i'L_t/E_t$). As long as the return on firms' assets exceeds borrowing costs, the higher the level of financial leverage the greater the profitability of net worth. However, the profitability of net worth increases at a decreasing rate with the rise in leverage. Furthermore, there is a limit for increasing leverage arising from the fact that financial risk will increase and, hence, it will be costlier for the firm to borrow funds. If the firm continues increasing its leverage, it will get to the point where the marginal cost of financing will be higher than the marginal return on assets. Hence, its profitability will decrease.

The relationship between financial leverage and the rate of return on equity can be seen graphically in figure 1. Assuming, for simplicity's sake, that there is only one type of assets with rate of return $\delta$, the same conclusion can be obtained differentiating between financial and non-financial assets.

Equation (4) can be written as:[3]

$$\phi = \delta + [\delta - i(L_t/E_t)]L_t/E_t \tag{5}$$

where,

$$\partial^2 \phi / \partial (L_t/E_t)^2 = -(2i' + i''L_t/E_t).$$

The relationship between firms' profitability and financial leverage is a concave function.

If the return on assets is lower than the borrowing costs, the firm should reduce its debt-equity ratio to the minimum. On the other hand, if $\delta > i + i'L/E$ indebtedness is convenient for the firm up to a degree where the increase in leverage causes an increase in the marginal cost of borrowing up to a point where the latter exceeds the marginal rate of return on assets; from then on, a rise in the level of firms' indebtedness will decrease its profitability.

Furthermore, there is another element that should be taken into account when defining a firm's indebtedness policy. This element is the risk associated with unexpected devaluation in the case of firms with liabilities denominated in foreign currency. This is especially important for firms producing nontradables without assets denominated in foreign currency.[4]

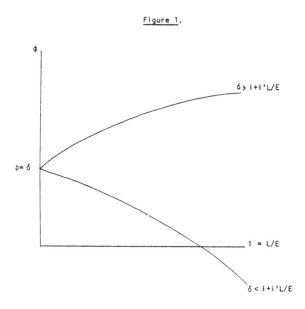

Figure 1.

It is also interesting to examine the relationship between a firm's profitability and the interest rate for a given rate of return on assets and financial leverage. It can be shown that while the rate of return ($\delta$) is higher than the marginal cost of borrowing (the interest rate in this case), indebtedness reinforces profitability and vice versa (Vickers, 1968 and Carbajal, 1980). In other words, in those instances in which the rate of return is greater (lower) than the interest rate on the debt, the rate of return on equity will be greater (lower) where the degree of financial leverage is more pronounced, or where the debt-equity ratio is higher. This is shown graphically in figure 2.

Let us write equation (5) in the following form, assuming the rate of return on assets and the financial leverage are constant.

$$\phi = \delta(1 + l) - il, \text{ where } l = L/E \qquad (6)$$

Notice that when the firm is free of debt ($l = 0$) the rate of return on assets ($\delta$) equals the rate of return on equity (firm profitability, $\phi$).

It can be shown that the lines $l = 0$, $l_1$ and $l_2$ intersect at $A$ where $\phi = \delta = i^5$.

Figure 2.

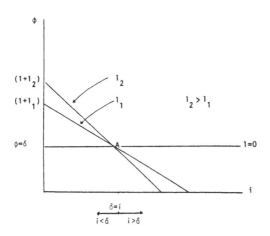

At $A$ $\delta = \phi$, thus, replacing in equation (6) it reduces to

$$\delta = (1 + l)\delta - il$$
$$-l\delta = -il$$
$$\delta = i$$

To the right of $A$ $i > \delta$, the higher the leverage $(l)$ the lower the return on equity $(\phi)$. On the contrary, to the left of point $A$ $i < \delta$; therefore, the higher the leverage the higher the positive differential between the rate of return $(\delta)$ and the firm's profitability $(\phi)$. There is a magnification effect of the rate of return on the profitability rate. For any given proportionate change in the rate of return the existence of the leverage effect will give rise to a magnified change in the rate of return on equity capital. Moreover, the degree of magnification increases as the financial leverage ratio increases. But of course the same magnification effect works in reverse if the income-generating ability of the firm falls. Leverage makes the return on equity higher during good times and lower during bad times. This potential instability introduced into the firm's income expectations by the debt-equity ratio is an important argument to be considered when defining a firm's debt policy.

Table 1 presents some empirical evidence which supports this analysis. The evidence had been obtained from the balance sheets and income statements of the same sample of publicly held corporations studied in previous chapters.

Table 1.   RATES OF RETURN ON ASSETS, INTEREST RATES, FINANCIAL LEVERAGE
AND FIRM PROFITABILITY

| | Net operating profits — Total assets ($\delta$) | Domestic real int. rate ($i_d$) | External real interest rate ($i*$) | Financial leverage (L/E) | Net profits — Net worth ($\phi$) |
|---|---|---|---|---|---|
| | (1) | (2) | (3) | (4) | (5) |
| **Firms with connections** | | | | | |
| 1977 | 8.4 | 39.4 | - 0.8 | 0.9 [a/] | 10.3 |
| 1978 | 10.1 | 35.1 | 2.7 | 0.9 | 10.8 |
| 1979 | 9.3 | 16.9 | - 0.1 | 0.9 | 13.0 |
| 1980 | 6.4 | 12.2 | - 8.6 | 0.9 | 10.1 |
| 1981 | 3.0 | 38.8 | 11.6 | 1.3 | -11.3 |
| **Small firms without connections** | | | | | |
| 1977 | 5.8 | 39.4 | - 0.8 | 0.4 | 4.7 |
| 1978 | 12.3 | 35.1 | 2.7 | 0.6 | 4.2 |
| 1979 | 2.1 | 16.9 | - 0.1 | 0.6 | - 5.9 |
| 1980 | - 0.8 | 12.2 | - 8.6 | 0.7 | -12.8 |
| 1981 | - 0.8 | 38.8 | 11.6 | 1.2 | -25.6 |
| **Bankrupt firms** | | | | | |
| 1977 | 4.6 | 39.4 | - 0.8 | 1.6 | -10.5 |
| 1978 | 5.8 | 35.1 | 2.7 | 2.3 | - 6.8 |
| 1979 | 5.1 | 16.9 | - 0.1 | 1.4 | - 8.0 |
| 1980 | 5.0 | 12.2 | - 8.6 | 1.5 | -15.9 |

Sources:   Col. (1), (4) and (5):   Data base World Bank project on liberalization
and stabilization policies in the Southern Cone
countries.

Col. (2) and (3):      Arellano (1983).

Note:
[a/]      It is likely that the total leverage of firms belonging to economic
conglomerates reported here underestimates their actual leverage because
buying shares with debts was a common practice of these firms during the
period.

In what follows the above formal framework will be utilized to examine the financial decisions made by different groups of firms when facing important structural reforms during the 1975-82 period.

## 8.2.2. Firms Belonging to Economic Groups

As was shown in chapters 5 and 7 firms belonging to economic conglomerates had privileged access to cheaper foreign credit during the 1975-82 period. On the one hand they contracted loans directly in the international financial market under article 14 of the Foreign Exchange Law; on the other, they had access to foreign currency loans intermediated by domestic banks belonging to the same groups.

Due to this favored access to cheaper external credit firms with "connections" faced lower interest rates than the rest of the establishments. It is very likely that the borrowing costs they faced were lower than the rate of return on their assets (financial and non-financial) (see table 1).

Therefore, coming back to equation (3) it can be argued that it was very profitable for "connected" firms to increase their leverage during the period.

$$\frac{\partial \phi}{\partial (Lt/Et)} = \delta - [i + i'(L_t/E_t)] > 0$$

Moreover, the magnification effect of the rate of return on assets on the rate of return on equity capital worked in the positive direction encouraging firms to maintain high financial leverage (see figure 2).

Existing evidence shows that there were no expectations of devaluations beyond the effective evolution of the official exchange rate during the 1977-81 period. Only at the end of 1981 firms began to expect a change in the fixed exchange rate policy. Thus, firms belonging to economic conglomerates, facing financing costs lower than the return on assets, and not expecting exchange rate devaluations until 1981 found it very profitable to borrow in foreign currency.

Furthermore, from equation (3) we have that

$$\frac{\partial \phi}{\partial (Ft/Et)} = \mu - \delta > 0$$

Given the fact that during the period the rate of return on financial assets was higher than the rate of return on real assets ($\mu - \delta > 0$), firms were incentivated to alter their asset composition between financial and non-financial assets. The higher the proportion of a firm's net worth invested in financial assets, the greater its return on equity.

Hence, it was rational behavior for firms belonging to economic groups to maintain a high debt-equity ratio and to invest the external resources they obtained in financial assets.

However, the economic situation of firms with connections changed by the end of the period (1981-82). During those final years they had to face an important increase in the external interest rate and a real devaluation of the peso with respect to the dollar. In order to illustrate the impact these changes had on "connected" firms let us consider:

$$i(l)L_t = i_d(l)L_t^d + i^*(l)eL_t^*$$

where:

| | |
|---|---|
| $e$ | = exchange rate (pesos per dollar) |
| $i_d$ | = domestic real interest rate[7] |
| $i^*$ | = external real interest rate |
| $L^d, L^*$ | = debt in domestic and foreign currency respectively |
| $l$ | = $L_t/E_t$ |

Therefore

$$\phi = (\mu - \delta)F_t/E_t + \delta + [\delta - i_d(l)]L_t^d/E_t + [\delta - i^*(l)]eL_t^*/E_t$$

where,

$$\partial\phi/\partial(L_t^d/E_t) = \delta - [i_d + i_d'(L/E)]$$

and

$$\partial\phi/\partial(eL_t^*/E_t) = \delta - [i^* + i'^*(L/E)]$$

Given the level of domestic interest rates which averaged more than 30% annual during the 1975-82 period, the rate of return on real assets (non-financial) was lower than the marginal borrowing cost. Thus, $[\delta - i_d + i_d'(L/E)] < 0$, and firms with connections would avoid taking out peso-denominated loans during the period.

Moreover, until 1980 it was profitable to take out foreign loans, because the external marginal cost of financing was lower than the return on assets $[\delta > i^* + i'^*(L/E)]$. However, when the external interest rate increased in 1981-82 became disadvantageous to have debts denominated in foreign currency $[\delta < i^* + i^{*\prime}(L/E)]$.

Not only the increase in the external interest rate, but also the fall in aggregate demand due to the internal recession which began in the second half of 1981 decreased the profitability of firms connected to economic conglomerates. Moreover, firms without foreign currency denominated assets which did not produce tradable goods were substantially affected by the real devaluation of the peso in relation to the dollar during 1982. The firms had to adjust to the new economic conditions by decreasing their leverage, but these shocks implied simultaneously a rise in their level of foreign debt in terms of pesos, and a decline in their net worth. Most firms could not manage to reduce their debt-equity ratio. The high financial leverage magnified the effect the decrease in the rate of return exerted on profitability, so that some firms defaulted and had to negotiate with their creditors.

### 8.2.3. Firms Unrelated to Economic Groups

Firms without connections to economic groups had relatively less access to international financial markets. They also had restricted access to loans denominated in foreign currency intermediated by domestic banks. In general, the spread charged to firms without connections was higher than the spread charged to firms with connections (see chapters 5 and 7). The interest rate faced by the former was relatively high and hence their marginal borrowing cost was higher than the rate of return on their assets. Thus, indebtedness was not appropriate for these firms (see figure 1). Moreover, a sensible policy would have considered a reduction in the firm's leverage. Let us recall that,

$$\partial \phi / \partial (L_t/E_t) = \delta - [i + i'(L/E) < 0$$

However, these firms increased their leverage during the period (see table 1); there are at least two reasons for this behavior:

(i) Firms regarded the high interest rates as a transitory phenomenon and expected interest rates to decline in short order.

(ii) Corporations did not have incentives to allocate their profits (in the eventuality they obtained profits) in order to reduce their debts. An explanation of this can be found in the tax reform of 1975 which implied different tax treatment for dividends and retained earnings. For every 100 pesos of before-tax profits the corporate tax on retained earnings was 46, while the corporate tax on dividends was 24.4[8].

Furthermore, in 1980 a law was passed that compelled corporations to pay at least 30% of their profits in dividends.

Hence, if the objective function is to maximize the firm's market value, the corporation will pay dividends and will not retain profits to reduce liabilities.

The market value of the firm is given by the present value of future dividends.

$$E_t = \frac{Dt + \dot{E}}{\sigma}$$

where
$\sigma = $ is the discount rate which is the long-run profitability of the firm.[9]
$D = $ dividends
$\dot{E} = \dot{A} + \dot{F} - \dot{L}$ [10]

The corporation's profits can be allocated to increase assets (financial and non-financial), to decrease liabilities, or to pay dividends. From the above expression it can be seen that the market value of the firm is maximized when dividends are paid. The maximum dividend obtained is equivalent to 75.6% of before-tax profits (before shareholders pay their individual income tax).

Furthermore, firms not related to economic groups did not make net investments in real assets (see chapter 5). This behavior can be explained by the fact that the rate of return on non-financial assets was lower than the rate of return on financial assets, and by the fact that firms rationally postponed their net real investments waiting for a decline in the real interest rate.

This analysis implies that a firm's debt increased with the accumulation of interest,[11] and that net investment in non-financial assets did not take place.

$$L_t = L_{t-1}[1 + i(l)], \; l = L/E$$
$$A_t = A_{t-1}$$

Using the accounting equality,

$$E_t = A_t - F_t - L_t \text{ and replacing } A_t \text{ and } L_t$$

$$\begin{aligned}
E_t &= A_{t-1} + F_t - L_{t-1} - i(l)L_{t-1} \\
E_t &= E_{t-1} + F_t - F_{t-1} - i(l)L_{t-1} \\
\dot{E} &= \dot{F} - i(l)L_{t-1}
\end{aligned}$$

Faced with this situation a firm had three options: The first was to invest in financial assets which offered high profitability, given the prevailing conditions in the domestic financial market. However, in this respect the portfolio of financial investments was more restricted for firms without connections to economic groups. Most firms chose to invest their money in the short-term capital market which was very attractive due to the high level of passive interest rates.[12] A second alternative for these firms was to sell the firm at price $E_t$ (its market value at that moment) to companies with connections to economic groups which had access to cheaper foreign credit. It must be borne in mind, though, that the market value of firms without connections was depressed because of their deteriorated financial situation, which made them excellent investments for the economic groups. This phenomenon helps account for the increase in concentration of wealth during the 1974-82 period. Nevertheless, some firms without connections chose not to sell, because they were expecting a decline in the interest rate and an improvement in their economic situation. In practice this third alternative implied continuing to take out loans at increasing borrowing costs due to the firm's higher financial risk, which in some cases led to bankruptcy, that is, to the loss of the entire equity worth ($E_t \leq 0$).

### 8.2.4. Firms that went Bankrupt During the Period

Chapters 4 and 7 show that firms that went bankrupt during the period already faced serious difficulties in 1975-76. The causes of these difficulties were a severe internal recession and a rapid reduction of import tariffs. These firms, without access to foreign credit, decided to take out expensive short-term loans in the domestic financial market, instead of going out of business (see chapter 6). They borrowed despite the fact that the rate of return on their assets was lower than the marginal cost of borrowing they faced [$\delta < i + i'(L/E)$].

The rationality of this decision focuses on three elements:

(i) Firms were expecting an early recovery of aggregate demand, which had been very much publicized by the government.

(ii) Firms perceived the high level of domestic interest rates as only a transitory phenomenon. They were also expecting a scaling down of the rates.

(iii) Firms envisioned that trade liberalization reform would be abandoned by the government. However, economic recovery was delayed and tariff reductions proceeded until a uniform tariff of 10% was reached. Firms then had to renew their bank loans at the market interest rate which remained high throughout the whole period.

Moreover, since 1979 the fixed exchange rate policy had been strongly affecting firms' profitability. They did not have the option of reducing their liabilities and continued to resort to loans in order to survive. Thus, they kept accumulating interest on their debts.[13]

Furthermore, in view of their worsened financial situation these firms did not have the option of increasing their investment in financial assets ($\dot{F} = 0$). Using the expression derived for the firms without connections to economic groups we have

$$\dot{E} = -i(l)L_{t-1}$$

In this situation, management had two alternatives. Either they could sell the firm at market value or they could continue taking out loans which were increasingly expensive.

It is interesting to underscore here that the extremely high interest rates which lasted for a long time, nonetheless encouraged firms to borrow heavily, even though such efforts were doomed to failure. By the end of the period a moral-hazard-type behavior took over; many firms continued borrowing because they had very little to lose, as they were almost worthless as a result of paying the excessive interest rates in force in the domestic financial market. The contractual interest on their debt absorbed what would otherwise be their shareholders' residual income, and the rate of return on equity fell to a very low level (see table 1).

The high debt of these firms had a perverse effect on their possibilities of survival. At the end of 1981 the economy entered into the second worst recession of the century, and there was important liquidity restriction which made it impossible to maintain the high internal debt. Firms were not able to hold on any more, and they went into bankruptcy.

## 8.3. Concluding Remarks

Conditions prevailing in the domestic financial market during the 1975-82 period did not allow for the normal performance of domestic firms.

Firms without privileged access to cheaper foreign credit faced marginal borrowing costs which continuously exceeded the marginal rate of return on their assets, and when confronted with this non-equilibrium situation, had few alternatives. One was to change their asset composition and increase their investment in financial assets which were more profitable than real assets. A second choice was to sell the firm to the economic groups which had favored access to external credits. The final alternative was to get deeper into debt, while awaiting the expected decline in the interest rate. Since the interest rate did not descend to "normal" levels, firms continued borrowing because they had very little to lose. The persistently high interest rates had already absorbed what would otherwise be the residual income of their owners, and their equity worth was close to zero. At the beginning of the eighties, when new economic shocks hit the Chilean economy, many of these firms went bankrupt.

Firms belonging to economic groups faced marginal borrowing costs lower than the marginal rate of return of their assets. Indebtedness was very advantageous for these firms, and they enjoyed a privileged position during those years. The economic groups found it profitable to buy up the almost-bankrupt firms which did not have access to foreign credit. Thus, an important concentration of wealth took place during the 1975-82 period. Nevertheless, economic conditions changed around 1981-82, when the external interest rate increased, the economy suffered a deep internal recession, and there was a real devaluation of the peso with respect to the dollar. Firms belonging to economic conglomerates had large foreign currency denominated debts, which has a negative impact on their possibilities of survival. In fact, many of these firms faced huge problems in servicing their debts; some of them defaulted and had to negotiate with their creditors.

Given the development of the financial market during the period, it could be affirmed that not only inefficient firms went bankrupt, but also many efficient ones were swept along. They simply could not cope with the anomalous conditions imposed on them.

Notes

1. On the balance sheet assets are shown at book value, and the liability accounts record the actual amount of money capital or funds made available to the firm from the various sources indicated. The book value is equivalent to the historic cost value subject to some adjustments. Alternatively, there is the market value of the variables which is their liquidation or realization value, indicating their economic value in alternative uses. See footnote 6 for further arguments in favor of using book value rather than market value of variables in the context of the present model.

2. As the tax rate is the same for all corporations it will not be considered in the analysis. However, it is important to point out that group-firms may enjoy tax advantages in the sense that they can transfer profits from one firm to another in order to minimize tax payments.

3. In a Modigliani and Miller world each individual or firm is able to borrow as much as they like at a fixed riskless rate of interest; therefore, equation (5) can be written as

$$\phi = \delta + (\delta - i)L/E$$

That is to say, the rate of return or yield on equity of any corporation is a linear function of its leverage [proposition II of Modigliani and Miller (1958)]. Under this condition, if the rate of return on assets is higher than the interest rate it will always be profitable for the firm to increase its leverage.

4. A change in the interest rate does not affect the book value of assets, equity or debt. Moreover, if the change in the interest rate is perceived as transitory the market value of the variables will fluctuate around their book value.

An unexpected devaluation, however, will increase the book value of the debt if the firm has liabilities denominated in foreign currency. If the firm does not have assets denominated in foreign currency and produces nontradable goods, a devaluation will diminish profits or increase losses implying a decline in net worth. Thus, the total leverage of the firm will rise in circumstances when it should decrease in order to avoid an important decline in profitability.

A different result is obtained if the firm has assets denominated in foreign currency and/or it produces tradable goods. In this case an unexpected devaluation will increase the book value of assets and liabilities simultaneously. Moreover, the rate of return of a producer of tradables can increase as a result of a rise in its net operating profits brought about by devaluation. Therefore, the net effect of an unexpected devaluation on a firm's financial leverage and profitability is uncertain.

5. If we were working with the market value of the variables and if a change in the interest rate were seen as permanent by the economic agents, then $E = E(i)$, $E' < 0$ and $l = l(i)$, $l' > 0$, therefore, $l_1$ and $l_2$ would be concave instead of straight lines.

Here, following Vickers (1968), leverage is defined in terms of book values rather than market values. This is done for two reasons: First, leverage is intended to be a measure of financial risk and defining leverage in terms of market values results in a biased measure of financial risk. This bias arises because market values reflect business risk as well as financial risk. Business risk is the risk in the firm's income stream and is independent from the method of finance. Financial risk is the additional risk to stockholders which arises through the use of borrowed funds for the financing of a project and is usually measured by leverage. Thus, financial risk can only exist if there is business risk. If leverage is defined in terms of market values and if business risk increases, then the interest rate will increase causing net worth to decrease, independent of financial risk.

Second, the market value of net worth is determined ex-post, after the firm's decisions have been made, and is in part a consequential effect of the firm's decisions. In this case the interest rate would become a function of the market value of equity and would also be determined ex-post. This is an operational difficulty when working with static models. A measure of financial risk and cost of financing which are only known after all decisions have been made can not be used to determine these decisions.

6. The normal case is $\delta > i$ and therefore $\phi > i$. The difference between $\phi$ and $i$ is a risk premium obtained by the shareholders since their investment is riskier than the lenders' investments. Interest payments have a higher degree of certainty than a firm's profitability.

7. The domestic interest rate refers to the predominant segment of the financial market, i.e., short-run credit (30-89 days). The external interest rate is the rate paid for external credits contracted through article 14 of the Foreign Exchange Law (plus the cost associated with the obligatory deposit and the intermediation cost).

8. The situation for every 100 additional pesos of before-tax corporate profits was (see Marfán, 1984):

a) Retained earnings case

| | |
|---|---:|
| (1) Before-tax profits | 100 |
| (2) Tax on profits (primera categoría [10% of (1)] | 10 |
| (3) After-tax profits | 90 |
| (4) Additional tax [40% of (3)] | 36 |
| (5) Retained earnings after tax (3)-(4) | 54 |
| (6) Corporate tax on retained earnings (1)-(5) | 46 |

b) Dividend payment case

| | |
|---|---:|
| (1) Before-tax profits | 100 |
| (2) Tax on profits (primera categoría) [10% of (1)] | 10 |
| (3) After-tax profits | 90 |
| (4) Additional tax [40% of (3)] | 36 |
| (5) Dividends | 54 |
| (6) Tax credit for shareholders [40% of (5)] | 21.6 |
| (7) Dividends before the overall income tax (5) + (6) | 75.6 |
| (8) Corporate tax on dividends (1) - (7) | 24.4 |

Furthermore, if dividends after the overall income tax (75.6 -54$r$, where $r$ is the marginal tax rate) are considered, only with a marginal tax rate higher than 40%, both retained earnings and dividends were equally taxed. There were only two income brackets with marginal tax rates higher than 40%. These corresponded to taxable annual income over 37,330 dollars of January, 1984.

9. The long-run profitability of the firm is an ex-ante concept and is always positive by definition. On the contrary, the rate of return on equity ($\phi$) or short-run profitability of the firm is an ex-post accounting concept that can be negative.

10. $\dot{X} = X_t - X_{t-1}$

11. To the extent firms borrow to cover financial costs the demand for credit could behave perversely with respect to the interest rate because the "financial cost" effect could exceed the pure price effect, i.e.,

$$\left| \frac{\partial C^d}{\partial (iL)} > 0 \right| > \left| \frac{\partial C^d}{\partial i} < 0 \right|$$

where $C^d$ = demand for credit.

12. The real interest rates paid for short-run deposits were:

| 1977 | 1978 | 1979 | 1980 | 1981 | 1982 |
|------|------|------|------|------|------|
| 5.2  | 18.7 | 4.4  | 5.0  | 28.7 | 22.4 |

13. As mentioned in chapter 4, the information about the total number of bankruptcies during the 1975-82 period shows that in the first years of the period a relatively small number of enterprises went bankrupt. The largest number of bankruptcies took place in 1982 when the Chilean economy went through a deep recession. An important part of the number of bankruptcies occurring in 1982 can be explained by the presence of firms that would have gone out of business at the beginning of the period had they not had access to borrowing in the recently liberalized financial market. The fact that these firms borrowed so heavily to survive during this period left them in such a weak financial position that they could not resist the 1982 internal recession.

## 9. FINANCIAL LIBERALIZATION IN CHILE: WHAT CAN WE LEARN?

The Chilean experience during the 1970's offers an example of complete financial market deregulation, implemented simultaneously with the liberalization of foreign trade and domestic commodity markets. The aim of this research has been to study the main effects financial liberalization had on the Chilean economy, specifically in the industrial manufacturing sector.

Liberalization and modernization of the financial sector was a major policy objective of the Chilean military regime. The economic authorities expected that domestic financial market liberalization, together with the opening up of the capital account of the balance of payments would produce the optimal results of increasing domestic savings, maximizing investment and raising investment's average efficiency (see chapter 2).

However, the actual outcome was totally different from what was expected. Chilean financial reform, which relied completely on the ability of the market to allocate funds efficiently, brought about a perverse financial deepening and perverse resource allocation in the domestic economy.

The results of liberalization reform contradicted the results predicted by the economic model on which it was based. The economic growth which did occur involved a financial deepening which was not associated with growth in the real sector of the economy. In particular, it was not associated with growth in the tradable goods sector, which theoretically should have been the dynamic engine of the new economic model (see chapter 6).

The unbalanced economic growth between the real and financial sectors was encouraged by enormous differences between the return on real capital and short-run interest rates in the financial market. The disequilibrium between these two rates was an important obstacle in promoting the real investment necessary to face growing foreign competition. Productive firms opted to invest their resources in financial assets, which offered very high profitability in a very short period of time (see chapter 4).

This disequilibrium was emphasized by the existence of economic conglomerates in a context of complete deregulation of the financial sector. The contradiction between the financial and real sectors was reproduced within the groups. One of the most important lessons to be learned from the Chilean financial liberalization is the enormous danger involved in the opportunity for financial intermediaries to abandon their specific role and transform themselves into instruments which favor the conglomerates' objectives. In Chile the financial intermediaries became, themselves, consumers of credit.

Therefore, there is a delicate balance between encouraging the development of financial intermediation and pushing it in undesirable directions. Complete deregulation of a financial market with unequal distribution of power can be a formula for reinforcing the wealth and power of the already rich and powerful. Those with political or financial influence seek loans from commercial banks to buy shares, a process that has very little to do with the improved allocation of resources which efficient financial intermediation should achieve (see chapters 5 and 7).

Moreover, free market policies can not solve the problem of fragmented financial markets in LDC's. Segmentation persists after liberalization, implying strong inequality in credit access (see chapter 5).

The objective of financial development is to facilitate the saving-investment process, to provide working capital for those who need it, and to offer the means to carry out transactions and payments in national and international trade.

The function of the financial system is to accommodate borrowers at lower costs and easier terms than they could get by direct loans from ultimate lenders. For instance, one role of the financial system is to transform the term structure of the flow of funds in order to adjust it to the borrowers' needs. This generally implies an extension of the maturity of the loans to finance investment projects with delayed returns.

It is important to recognize that financial intermediation is a powerful ally in the development process, but although the functions of the financial system are crucial, they can not be considered an objective in themselves. Moreover, as the Chilean experience shows, not every form of capital market development will contribute to economic growth and development.

Due to the specific nature of financial markets they can not operate efficiently without regulations. One reason for this need is the fact that goods and labor move in response to price signals much more sluggishly than fluid funds. Specifically, prices in goods and labor markets move much more sluggishly in response to excess supply or demand than the prices of financial assets. Real sector adjustments are mainly manifested in periods of recession and inflation. These conditions can lead to important instability in the financial sector, since the latter reacts very rapidly to disequilibrium in the real sector. Therefore, following Tobin's recommendation for the case of international financial markets, it is necessary to throw some sand in the wheels of the financial markets (Tobin, 1978).

A lack of regulations in the financial market tends to result in periods of acute financial instability. This was the case in the British financial market before 1866 and the U.S. market before 1929. Domestic crises, or at least panics, declined substantially in frequency and intensity after regulations were applied (Kindleberger, 1978).

Therefore, the development of a financial market needs some regulation in order to prevent perverse results such as those obtained in the Chilean case.

On the basis of past experience there are two fundamental requirements for a financial development strategy in the Chilean case: efficiency and equitable access to credit. In the following four aspects of such a financial policy are considered: (i) interest rate management, (ii) definition of equitable credit policies, (iii) regulation of financial institutions, and (iv) policy on foreign borrowing.

The history of financial development in Chile shows that the monetary authority can not play a passive role with respect to the interest rate. Two illustrations of a passive role are the fixing of nominal interest rates without considering the inflation rate, and the laissez-faire of the 1975-82 period. In both cases the results are extremely negative: In the first case, the fixing of nominal interest rates implemented during the pre-liberalization period, with the exception of the years 1965-70, resulted in negative real rates. These negative real interest rates, lower than the real return on capital, meant large implicit subsidies for debtors and inefficient resource allocation. In the second case the laissez-faire policy led to extremely high real interest rates which were only sustainable in a speculative economy. As shown in chapter 4, high interest rates led productive firms to decrease investment in physical capital and increase financial intermediation and speculation. This policy also resulted in large spreads between active and passive domestic interest rates, indicating the absence of perfect competition in the banking industry (see chapter 3 and 5).

Therefore, it is necessary for the financial authority to monitor the interest rate in an attempt to reach a positive real cost of credit in line with the return on capital. The aim of this policy should be to encourage capital accumulation and discourage short-run speculation. Moreover, positive real interest rates would contribute to a more efficient allocation of investment.[1]

The past experience also indicates that a long-run capital market does not emerge by itself. Furthermore, the paying of interest on 30-day deposits during the financial liberalization period encouraged the intermediation of very short-term maturities (see chapter 3). The supply of long-term finance is an important requirement in increasing real investment. Active financial policies are needed to create this market, especially in economies with high price and institutional instability. Financial institutions tend to restrict long-term loans, because interest rate and liquidity risks are implied in the imbalance between the spans of deposits and loans. Therefore, it is necessary to lengther the maturity of the deposits which earn interest, encouraging medium and long-term deposits through positive real returns.

Another issue that needs to be considered in a financial development strategy is equitable access to credit. The financial liberalization implemented during the 1975-82 period shows that it is not a good strategy to rely completely on the market's ability to allocate funds efficiently. As shown in chapter 5, there was an important difference in the access to cheap foreign credit during the 1975-82 period. Small firms without connections to financial institutions were rationed in the foreign currency loan market and had to pay the extremely high real domestic interest rate to obtain funds.

In order to ensure equitable access to credit selective credit policies are needed. These policies should be directed toward sectors or projects which meet two conditions: first, the use of resources should be easily controlled and the risk of credit transfer to other projects should be minimum. Second, selective credit should be directed to activities where the main bottleneck is financial.

Selective credit policies are not necessarily related to subsidized interest rates (mechanism widely used during the pre-liberalization period) but rather to a system of credit security - for instance - the creation of a credit insurance mechanism which could substantially reduce the risk faced by banks when lending to small firms, or alternatively the creation of a guaranty fund. This is a very important point for small firms which normally do not have collateral to offer to obtain loans and are therefore, discriminated against in credit markets. Also, selective credit policies can be related to access to long-term financing; this is important for investment projects with slow maturities.

Regulation of financial intermediaries is an extremely important aspect of financial development strategy. This is evident in view of the recent Chilean experience. Chapters 5 and 7 have shown that complete deregulation of the financial market during the 1975-82 period led to excessively risky banking practices, resulted in an unacceptable concentration of market power, and led to self-dealing and conflict-of-interest abuses by banks and non-banking firms belonging to economic conglomerates. Chapter 4 has also shown that the reform attempt resulted in a domestic productive sector characterized by widespread bankruptcies.

A failure of public policy with respect to financial markets is extremely serious, because it can create damage that extends far beyond the financial sector. Financial market failure can mean economy-wide failure, recession, widespread unemployment, and bankruptcies. The essential functions of financial regulation are to ensure the safety and soundness of the financial system, and to foster efficient allocation of capital by promoting competition and limiting opportunities for fraud and self-dealing.

In a laissez-faire system depositors have incentives to evaluate the riskiness of a financial intermediary's balance sheet and policies, because their deposits are at stake. In a system with deposit insurance these incentives are eliminated.[2] Therefore, there must be a regulatory agency which either provides the correct incentives for intermediaries, or imposes restrictions on them that limit possibilities for excessive risk-taking. [3]

There are diverse alternatives to implement control of financial intermediaries. There is a broad range of choices between the extremes of detailed legislation on the one hand and persuasive control on the other.

The disadvantage of detailed legislation is the impossibility of considering all potential situations. Hence, someone can always find a loophole in the law.

Persuasive control on the other hand, should consider some key regulatory issues.[4] First, there must be total separation between banks and non-banking firms in order to prevent unsound practices such as those experienced by economic conglomerates during the financial liberalization reform. This restriction attempts to ensure the professional management of private financial institutions. Banks can not be affiliated with private corporations and can not engage in non-financial business unrelated to banking, either directly or through subsidiaries. Moreover, restrictions of a bank's ability to lend to members of its board of directors, bank officers, or other employees are necessary to insure safe, sound practices on the part of financial intermediaries.[5]

In second place, financial regulation should consider minimum ratios of deposits to bank capital for the banking industry. Strengthening capital requirements would be advantageous because by placing more of an intermediary's own capital at risk, incentives to control risk-taking would be reinforced. Moreover, the additional capital would directly provide an extra margin of safety, both for the agency which insures the bank's deposits and the uninsured depositors. However, it is not desirable to rely solely on strengthening the capital requirements. The question of the appropriate level of capital of a financial institution should not be addressed independently from the riskiness of the rest of an institution's portfolio: Two institutions with identical ratios of deposits to capital can represent very different risks. Hence, information that allows the regulatory agency to assess the riskiness of financial institutions is necessary.

Therefore, in third place, it is also important to strengthen public disclosure requirements in order to be able to control and evaluate the risk to which an institution is exposed. The regulatory agency should require financial intermediaries to report information and follow specific accounting standards that would permit an assessment of the interest rate risk and the credit risk to which they are exposed.[6]

In the fourth place, regulations of credit concentration should be explicitly established. Also, it is necessary to establish minimum liquidity standards to assure that financial intermediaries are not taking undue risks or engaging in other practices that endanger their depositors' money.

The recent Chilean experience also shows that complete liberalization of the financial system to inflows of foreign capital is not sufficient to integrate domestic and foreign financial markets (see chapter 5 and 7). The access to external credit is not homogeneous, not only due to domestic regulations and market failure, but also due to the characteristics of international financial markets. Moreover, external financial openness is not neutral with respect to the resource allocation process, especially during the transition period from a closed to an open economy (see chapter 6). International capital inflows affect the domestic money supply and the level of the exchange rate, hence the degree of protection of domestic activities.

Therefore, external financial openness should also be regulated. It should be part of an overall development strategy, in which the resources obtained should be channelled toward the investment-savings process. A foreign borrowing strategy should be evaluated according to two basic criteria: How much it contributes to increase investment and how efficiently the resources it generates are allocated. The experience of Chile and the rest of the Latin American countries during the seventies indicates that the way external resources are regulated and channelled into the domestic economy directly affects their final allocation in consumption or investment (see Ffrench-Davis, 1983a; especially, papers by Bacha and Fishlow).

The allocation of resources and the level of investment will be different depending on whether the intermediation of foreign resources is carried out by private firms, commercial banks, the Central Bank or a public development agency.

The centralization of foreign borrowing in a public agency can be recommended on several grounds when an external credit restriction exists, because in this case the social price of the exchange rate exceeds its market price.[7]. In the first place, it can be argued that the nation will have to make foreign exchange available for foreign debt service payments regardless of whether the borrower is the public or the private sector. The absence of international bankruptcy courts, due to political sovereignty, is one important reason why governments are ultimately responsible for the country's foreign debt (Díaz-Alejandro, 1984b). Therefore, foreign borrowing should at least be monitored by the government.[8]

A second argument deals with the risks inherent in foreign borrowing. Most individual private firms or banks are unlikely to be borrowing on a large enough scale to diversify their foreign debt by currency of denomination. This is not the case with any larger institution which can centralize the risk of appreciation of foreign currencies. The same argument is valid for the management of interest rate risk. The agency can change the incoming foreign resources into domestic currency before they are transferred to the internal market. This way domestic borrowers do not have to face the exchange risk. Moreover, these resources can be transferred at interest rates compatible with those in force in the domestic market. In the process of transferring these resources, the public development agency should avoid subsidies which could lead to an inferior allocation of resources.[9] This policy contributes to the integration of the external and internal segments of the financial market.

Furthermore, in the absence of new, more flexible forms of finance the public agency can borrow abroad at the prevailing terms. It can then lend to domestic borrowers at longer terms which are compatible with the financing needs of productive investment.

Although international external finance normally plays a pivotal role in the development process, filling in the gap between gross domestic savings and gross domestic capital formation, the fact remains that the largest part of finance for development financing must be, and is, domestically mobilized, transformed and allocated. This was especially true after the international debt crisis. From 1982 on many countries have faced credit rationing imposed in international capital markets.

Therefore, the conclusion may be reached that adequate organization of the domestic financial system and the creation of a beneficial environment for productive investment and savings are essential preconditions for a lasting development process.

Notes

1. As discussed in chapter 2, the main effect of positive real interest rates is an improvement in the investment allocation process. The effect of positive real interest rates on savings is not clear, because there are substitution and income effects working in opposite directions.

2. The purpose of deposit insurance is to eliminate financial panics and bank runs. Measured by this criterion, deposit insurance has been very successful.

3. This regulatory agency should have an excellent technical level.

4. The regulations discussed here refer principally to commercial banks, because they are the main financial intermediaries in the Chilean financial sector.

5. Since the period of financial instability that occurred in the thirties, U.S. financial regulations consider these issues. In 1933 a banking act known as the Glass-Steagall Act was passed requiring the separation of banking and securities activities. Provisions of the act attempted to divorce the banking and securities industries by barring banks from underwriting or dealing in non-bank securities, debt or equity. Moreover, in 1966 Congress passed the Bank Holding Company Act which, among other restrictions, prohibits bank holding companies from owning companies that are not engaged in bank related activities.

   However, nowadays technological changes, limited deregulation, and the introduction of bank-like services by securities firms and others have eroded the strength of these legal prohibitions and encouraged some expansion and diversification by banking firms. These changes have intensified the debate over further loosening of restraints. At issue is the question of whether further deregulation will lead to more efficient, competitive financial service markets or whether it will promote concentration, instability and undesirable trade practices.

6. Only in 1980, the Superintendencia de Bancos e Instituciones Financieras (Superintendency of Banks and Financial Institutions) began to apply a system of risk assessment experimentally. However, it was already too late to prevent the oncoming financial crisis.

7. The argument favoring centralization of foreign borrowing does not include commercial foreign credit.

8. The Chilean experience in relation to private sector foreign borrowing during the 1975-82 period illustrates the importance of this issue. It was thought by the economic authorities that since most of the foreign debt was contracted by the private sector, without any government guarantee, the increase in foreign indebtedness did not represent a threat to the country as a whole. As events later showed, this distinction between private and public debt was highly artificial, and the Chilean government ended up taking over all the private-sector foreign debt, independent of the fact that there were no previous government guarantees for these loans.

9. The agency would assume the positive or negative difference between foreign and domestic interest rates.

# REFERENCES

1. Aghevli, B.B. and M.S. Khan, "Government Deficits and the Inflationary Process in Developing Countries". *IMF Staff Papers* vol. 25 No.3, September, 1978.

2. Arellano, J.P., and R. Cortazar, "Del Milagro a la Crisis: Algunas Reflexiones Sobre el Momento Económico," *Colección Estudios CIEPLAN*, No. 8, July, 1982.

3. Arellano, J.P. "De la Liberalización a la Intervención: El Mercado de Capitales en Chile". *Colección Estudios CIEPLAN*, No. 11, December, 1983.

4. Balassa, B. "Policy Experiments in Chile, 1973-83" in G.M. Walton (ed) *The National Economic Policies of Chile*, Greenwich CT Jai Press, 1985.

5. Bernanke, B. "Bankruptcy, Liquidity and Recession". *American Economic Review*, May, 1981.

6. Boskin, M.J. "Taxation, Saving and the Rate of Interest." *Journal of Political Economy*, vol. 86 No. 2, April, 1978.

7. Bruno, M. "Stabilization and Stagflation in a Semi-Industrialized Economy", in Dornbusch, R. and J. Frenkel (eds.), *International Economic Policy Theory and Evidence*. Johns Hopkins Press, 1979.

8. Carbajal, C. "Rentabilidad, Tasas de Interés y Supervivencia de la Firma". *Desarrollo Económico* vol. 20 No. 19, October-December, 1980.

9. Cavallo, D. "Stagflationary Effects of Monetarist Stabilization Policies", unpublished Ph.D. dissertation. Harvard University, 1977.

10. Chandavarkar, A. "Some Aspects of Interest Rate Policies in Less Developed Economies: The Experience of Selected Asian Countries". *IMF Staff Papers*, March, 1971.

11. Corbo, V. "Inflación en una Economía Abierta: El Caso de Chile". *Cuadernos de Economía*, Universidad Católica de Chile, April, 1982.

12. Corbo, V. "Chile: Economic Policy and International Relations since 1970" *Documento de Trabajo* No. 86, Instituto de Economía, Universidad Católica de Chile, 1983.

13. Corbo, V. "Reforms and Macroeconomic Adjustment in Chile during 1974-84", *World Development* vol. 13 No. 8, August, 1985.

14. Corbo, V. and J. De Melo, "Lessons from the Southern Cone Policy Reforms" *Research Observer* vol. 2 No. 2, The World Bank, July, 1987.

15. Cortázar, R. and J. Marshall, "Indice de Precios al Consumidor en Chile: 1970-78". *Colección Estudios CIEPLAN* No. 4, November, 1980.

16. Cortázar, R., A. Foxley and V. Tokman, *Legados del Monetarismo. Argentina y Chile.* Buenos Aires, Ediciones Solar, 1984.

17. Dahse, F. *El Mapa de la Extrema Riqueza.* Ed. Aconcagua, 1979.

18. Díaz-Alejandro, C. "Good-bye Financial Repression, Hello Financial Crash". *The Hellen Kellogg Institute for International Studies Working Paper* No. 24, University of Notre Dame, Indiana, 1984a.

19. Díaz-Alejandro, C. "Latin American Debt: I Don't Think we are in Kansas Anymore". *Brookings Papers of Economic Activity*, No. 2, 1984b.

20. Dornbusch, R. "Stabilization Policies in Developing Countries: What Have we Learned?". *World Development* vol. 10 No. 9, September, 1982.

21. Dornbusch, R. "Comentarios Sobre R. Ffrench-Davis and J.P. Arellano, Apertura Financiera Externa: La Experiencia Chilena en 1973-80", in Ffrench-Davis, R. (ed.), *Las Relaciones Financieras Externas y su Efecto en la Economía Latinoamericana.* FCE-CIEPLAN, México, 1983a.

22. Dornbusch, R. "Remarks on the Southern Cone". *IMF Staff Papers*, 30, March, 1983b.

23. Edwards, S. "Economic Policy and the Record of Economic Growth in Chile: 1972-83", in Walton, B. (ed.), *op cit.*, 1985a.

24. Edwards, S. "Stabilization with Liberalization: An Evaluation of Ten Years in Chile's Experiment with Free-Market Policies, 1973-1983", *Economic Development and Cultural Change* vol. 33 No. 2, January, 1985b.

25. Edwards, S. and A. Cox-Edwards, *Monetarism and Liberalization: The Chilean Experiment.* Ballinger Publishing Co. Mass, 1987.

26. Espinosa, N., I. González and M. Morales, "La Quiebra de Empresas en Chile. Período 1975-82". Memoria programa de Graduados Magister en Administración. Universidad de Chile, 1982.

27. Eyzaguirre, N. and O. Larrañaga, "Macroeconomía de las Operaciones Cuasi-Fiscales en Chile". ILADES/Georgetown University, *Serie de Investigación* No. 31/90, November, 1990.

28. Ffrench-Davis, R. *Políticas Económicas en Chile 1952-70.* CEPLAN Ediciones Nueva Universidad. Universidad Católica de Chile, 1973.

29. Ffrench-Davis, R. "Las Experiencias Cambiarias en Chile: 1965-79". *Colección Estudios CIEPLAN* No. 2, December, 1979.

30. Ffrench-Davis, R. "Liberalización de Importaciones: La Experiencia Chilena en 1973-79". *Colección Estudios CIEPLAN* No. 4, November, 1980.

31. Ffrench-Davis, R. and J.P. Arellano, "Apertura Financiera Externa: La Experiencia Chilena en 1973-80", in Ffrench-Davis, R. (ed.), *Las Relaciones Financieras Externas y su Efecto en la Economía Latinoamericana.* FCE-CIEPLAN, México, 1983a.

32. Ffrench-Davis, R. "El Problema de la Deuda Externa y la Apertura Financiera en Chile". *Colección Estudios CIEPLAN* No. 11, December, 1983b.

33. Ffrench-Davis, R. "Indice de Precios Externos: Un Indicador Para Chile de la Inflación Internacional, 1950-83" *Colección Estudios CIEPLAN* No. 13, June, 1984.

34. Flaño, N. "La Recesión y el Ajuste Automático: Una Visión Crítica". *Apuntes CIEPLAN* No. 32, May, 1982.

35. Foxley, A. "Inflación con Recesión: Las Experiencias de Brasil y Chile". *Colección Estudios CIEPLAN* No. 1, July, 1979.

36. Foxley, A. "Stabilization Policies and Their Effects on Employment and Income Distribution. A Latin American Perspective", in Cline and Weintraub (eds.), *Economic Stabilization in Developing Countries*. Brookings, Washington D.C., 1981.

37. Foxley, A. *Latin American Experiments in Neo-Conservative Economics*. University of California Press, 1982.

38. Frenkel, J. "The Order of Economic Liberalization: Discussion" in K. Brunner and A.H. Meltzer (eds), *Economic Policy in a World of Changes*. Amsterdam, North-Holland, 1982.

39. Fry, M.J. "Money and Capital or Financial Deepening in Economic Development?". *Journal of Money Credit and Banking* vol. 10 No. 4, November, 1978.

40. Fry, M.J. "Savings, Investment Growth and the Cost of Financial Repression". *World Development* vol. 8 No. 4, April, 1980.

41. Fry, M.J. "Models of Financially Repressed Developing Economies". *World Development* vol. 10 No. 9, September, 1982.

42. Gava, E. "La Reforma Financiera Argentina". *Ensayos Económicos*. September, 1981.

43. Galvez, J. and J. Tybout, "Microeconomic Adjustment in Chile During 1977-81: The Importance of being a grupo" *World Development* vol. 13 No. 8, August, 1985.

44. Galvis, V. "Financial Intermediation and Economic Growth in Less Developed Countries: A Theoretical Approach". *The Journal of Development Studies* vol. 13 No.2, January, 1977.

45. Gatica, J. *Deindustrialization in Chile*. Westview Special Studies on Latin America and the Caribbean, Boulder, Colorado, 1989.

46. Giovanini, A. "The Interest Elasticity of Savings in Developing Countries: The Existing Evidence". *World Development*, July, 1983.

47. Harberger, A.C. "Observations on the Chilean Economy, 1973-1983" *Economic Development and Cultural Change* No. 33, April, 1985.

48. Held, G. "Regulación y Supervisión de la Banca en la Experiencia de Liberalización Financiera en Chile (1974-1988)" In Massad, C. and G. Held (eds.) *Sistema Financiero y Asignación de Recursos. Experiencias Latinoamericanas y del Caribe.* Grupo Editor Latinoamericano, 1990.

49. Hodgman, D. "Credit Risk and Credit Rationing". *Quarterly Journal of Economics*, May, 1960.

50. Hodgman, D. "The Deposit Relationship and Commercial Bank Investment Behavior". *Review of Economics and Statistics*, August, 1961.

51. Hoffmann, R. "Organización Institucional para el Control y Manejo de la Deuda Externa: El Caso Chileno". *Cuadernos de la CEPAL* No. 28, June, 1979.

52. Howrey, E.P. and S.H. Hymans, "The Measurement and Determination of Loanable-Funds Savings", *Brookings Papers of Economic Activity*, 3, 1978.

53. INSORA, *El Financiamiento de la Industria en Chile: Análisis de Fuentes y Usos de Fondos*, 1962.

54. Jaffee, D. and F. Modigliani, "A Theory and Test of Credit Rationing". *American Economic Review*, December, 1969.

55. Jaffee, D. *Credit Rationing and the Commercial Loan Market.* John Wiley and Sons. Inc. New York, 1971.

56. Kane, E.J. and B.G. Malkiel, "Bank Portfolio Allocation, Deposit Variability, and the Availability Doctrine" *Quarterly Journal of Economics*, February, 1965.

57. Kapur, B.K. "Alternative Stabilization Policies for Less Developed Economies". *Journal of Political Economy* vol. 84 No. 4, August, 1976.

58. Keeton, W. *Equilibrium Credit Rationing.* Garland Publishing Inc. New York and London, 1979.

59. Kindleberger, Ch. *Manias, Panics and Crashes: A History of Financial Crisis.* New York: Basic Books, 1978.

60. Krumm, K. "Investment During an Attempted Liberalization: Argentina 1976-81", unpublished doctoral dissertation. Stanford University, July, 1983.

61. Leff, N.H. and K. Sato, "Macroeconomic Adjustment in Developing Countries: Instability, Short-Run Growth, and External Dependency". *Review of Economics and Statistics* vol. 62 No. 2, May, 1980.

62. Marfán, M. "Una Evaluación de la Nueva Reforma Tributaria". *Colección Estudios CIEPLAN* No. 13, June, 1984.

63. Mathieson, D. "Financial Reforms and Capital Flows in a Developing Economy". *IMF Staff Papers*, September, 1979.

64. Mathieson, D. "Financial Reform and Stabilization Policy in a Developing Economy". *Journal of Economic Development* vol. 7 No. 3, 1980.

65. McKinnon, R. *Money and Capital in Economic Development* Brookings Institution, Washington D.C., 1973.

66. McKinnon, R. "Savings Propensities and the Korean Monetary Reform in Retrospect", in McKinnon, R. (ed), *Money and Finance in Economic Growth and Development*, Marcel Dekker Inc. New York, 1976.

67. McKinnon, R. "Financial Repression and the Liberalization Problem Within Less Developed Countries", in Grassman and Lundberg (eds), *The Past and Prospects for the World Economic Order*. Mac Millan Press, 1981.

68. McKinnon, R. "The Order of Economic Liberalization: Lessons From Chile and Argentina", in K. Brunner and A. Meltzer (eds), *Economic Policy in a World of Changes*. Amsterdam, North-Holland, 1982.

69. Meller, P. "Chile" In Williamson (ed.) *Latin American Adjustment: How much has Happened?* Institute for International Economics, Washington D.C., 1990.

70. Meller, P., E. Livacic and P. Arrau, "Una Revisión del Milagro Económico Chileno (1976-1981)". *Colección Estudios CIEPLAN* No. 15, December, 1984.

71. Modigliani, F. and M. Miller, "The Cost of Capital, Corporation Finance and the Theory of Investment". *American Economic Review* vol. 48, June, 1958.

72. Morán, C. "Economic Stabilization and Structural Transformation: Lessons from the Chilean Experience, 1973-87", *World Development* vol. 17 No. 4, April, 1989.

73. Morandé, F. and K. Schmidt-Hebbel (eds.), *Del Auge a la Crisis de 1982*, Instituto Interamericano de Mercados de Capital, ILADES, Santiago, 1988.

74. Muñoz, O. "Crecimiento y Desequilibrios en una Economía Abierta: El Caso Chileno 1976-81". *Colección Estudios CIEPLAN* No. 8, July, 1982.

75. PREALC, "Monetarismo Global y Respuesta Industrial: El Caso de Chile". *Serie Documentos de Trabajo* No. 232, 1984.

76. Ramos, J. "Segmentación del Mercado de Capital y Empleo". *El Trimestre Económico* vol. 21(2) No. 202, April-June, 1984.

77. Ramos, J. *Neoconservative Economics in the Southern Cone of Latin America 1973-83*, Johns Hopkins University Press, Baltimore, 1986.

78. Revell, J. *Cost and Margins in Banking. An International Survey.* OECD, Paris, 1980.

79. Roe, A. "High Interest Rates: A new Conventional Wisdom for Development Policy?. Some Conclusions from the Sri Lankan Experience". *World Development* vol. 10 No. 3, March, 1982.

80. Rojas, F. "Transnational Banks and Local Entrepreneurs, Reflections on the Rise and Fall of an Alliance: Chile 1973-82", mimeo Duke University, 1983.

81. Shaw, E. *Financial Deepening in Economic Development.* New York Oxford University Press, 1973.

82. Sheahan, J. "Market-Oriented Economic Policies and Political Repression in Latin America". *Economic Development and Cultural Change* vol. 28 No. 2, January, 1980.

83. Sherman, J. "La Industria Textil y de Prendas de Vestir y la Apertura al Exterior: Chile 1974-78". mimeo CIEPLAN, October, 1980.

84. Sjaastad, L. and M. Cortés, "El Enfoque Monetario de la Balanza de Pagos y las Tasas Reales de Interés en Chile". *Estudios de Economía* No. 11, Universidad de Chile, 1978.

85. Sociedad de Fomento Fabril (SOFOFA), "Encuestas Industriales Trimestrales" No. 1, 2, 4 and 5.

86. Stiglitz, J. and A. Weiss, "Credit Rationing in Markets with Imperfect Information". *American Economic Review*, June, 1981.

87. Taylor, L. Book Reviews. *Journal of Development Economics*, 1974.

88. Taylor, L. *Macro Models for Developing Countries.* McGraw-Hill Book Company, 1979.

89. Taylor, L. *Structuralist Macroeconomics.* Basic Books Inc. New York, 1983.

90. Tobin, J. "A Proposal for International Monetary Reform". *The Eastern Economic Journal* 4(3.4), July-October, 1978.

91. Torche, A. "Distribuir el ingreso para satisfacer las necesidades básicas" in F. Larrain (ed.), *Desarrollo Económico en Democracia.* Edic. U. Católica de Chile, 1988.

92. Trivelli, M. "Análisis Financiero de las Empresas Manufactureras de Chile en el Período 1974-76". Memoria para optar al título de Ingeniero Civil Industrial Universidad de Chile, 1978.

93. Van Wijnbergen, S. "Interest Rate Management in LDC's". *Journal of Monetary Economics*, September, 1983a.

94. Van Wijnbergen, S. "Interest Rate Management in Developing Countries: Theory and Simulations Results for Korea". *World Bank Staff Working Papers* No. 593, 1983b.

95. Vergara, P. "Apertura Externa y Desarrollo Industrial en Chile: 1974-78". *Colección Estudios CIEPLAN* No. 4, November, 1980.

96. Whitman, M. "Global Monetarism and the Monetary Approach to the Balance of Payments". *Brookings Papers on Economic Activity*, 3, 1975.

97. Zahler, R. "Repercusiones Monetarias y Reales de la Apertura Financiera al Exterior: El Caso Chileno 1975-78". *Revista de la CEPAL* No. 10, April, 1980.

98. Zahler, R. "Recent Southern Cone Liberalization Reforms and Stabilization Policies: The Chilean Case". *Journal of International Studies and World Affairs*, 1983.

For Product Safety Concerns and Information please contact our EU
representative GPSR@taylorandfrancis.com Taylor & Francis Verlag GmbH,
Kaufingerstraße 24, 80331 München, Germany

Printed and bound by CPI Group (UK) Ltd, Croydon, CR0 4YY
08/05/2025
01864379-0003